D1824708

Sinfree Makoni

LANGUAGE IN AFRICA

Selected Papers
Volume One
Edited by David Bade

www.integrationists.com

International Association for the Integrational Study of
Language and Communication

This collection ©2020 by Sinfree Makoni.
Acknowledgements:
'An integrationist perspective on colonial linguistics' was originally published in *Language Sciences* 35 (2013) 87–96.
'Sociolinguistics, colonial and postcolonial: an integrationist perspec-tive' was originally published in *Language Sciences* 33 (2011) 680–688.
'A critique of language, languaging and supervernacular' was originally published in *Muitas Vozes*, Ponta Grossa, v.1, n.2 (2012), p. 189-199.
'From human linguistics to system 'D' and spontaneous orders: an approach to the emergence of indigenous African languages' was originally published in *Linguapax Review* 5 (2017) 39-79.
'Multilingualism: spontaneous orders and System D: a concluding note' was originally published in published in *International Journal of Bilingual Education and Bilingualism*, 2014 Vol. 17, No. 6, 714–717
'Plural formations of literacy and Occam's Razor principle: a commentary' was originally published in Kasper Juffermans, Yonas Mesfun Asfaha and Ashraf Abdelhay (eds.), *African Literacies: Ideologies, Scripts, Education*, pp.355-368, Newcastle upon Tyne: Cambridge Scholars Publishing, 2014.
'African languages as European scripts: the shaping of communal memory' was originally published in SarahNuttall and Carli Coetzee (eds.), *Negotiating the past: the making of memory in South Africa*, pp. 242-248. Oxford: Oxford University Press, 1998.
'Romanticizing differences and managing diversities: a perspective on harmonization, language policy, and planning' was originally published in *Language Policy* 15 (2016) 223–234.
'Disinventing and (Re)Constituting Languages' (with Alastair Pennycook) was originally published in *Critical Inquiry in Language Studies: an international journal*, 2(3) (2005), 137–156
'Disinventing multilingualism: from monological multilingualism to multi-lingua francas' (with Alastair Pennycook) was originally published in Marlyn Martin-Jones, Adrian Blackledge and Angela Creese (eds.), *The Routledge Handbook of Multilingualism*, pp. 439-453. London: Routledge, 2012.
'From misinvention to disinvention of language: multilingualism and the South African Constitution' was originally published in Sinfree Makoni, Geneva Smitherman, Arnetha F. Ball and Arthur K.Spears (eds.), *Black Linguistics: Language, Society, and Politics in Africa and the Americas*, pp.132-151, Routledge, 2003.
'The Lord Is My Shock Absorber': A Sociohistorical Integrationist Approach to Mid-Twentieth-Century Literacy Practices in Ghana' was originally published in Adrian Bleckledge and Angela Creese (eds.), *Heterogossia as Practice and Pedagogy*, pp. 75-97, Springer, 2014. (*Educational Linguistics* 20)

**International Association for the Integrational Study of
Language and Communication**

2015
David Bade, Rita Harris, Charlotte Conrad. *Roy Harris and
Integrational Semiology 1956-2015: A bibliography.*

2020
Sinfree Makoni. *Language in Africa.* (Selected papers vol. 1)
David Bade. *Efficiencies and Deficiencies: Essays on
Cataloging and Communication in Libraries.*

Forthcoming in 2020
Sinfree Makoni. *Selected Papers*, volumes 2-4
David Bade. *Integrational Linguistics for Library & Information
Science: Linguistics, Philosophy, Rhetoric and Technology*

.

The International Association for the Integrational Study of Language and Communication

The IAISLC was founded in 1998. It is managed by an international Executive Committee, whose members are:

Adrian Pablé (University of Hong Kong), Secretary
David Bade (University of Chicago, retired)
Charlotte Conrad (Dubai)
Stephen J. Cowley (University of Southern Denmark)
Daniel R. Davis (University of Michigan)
Dorthe Duncker (University of Copenhagen)
Jesper Hermann (University of Copenhagen)
Christopher Hutton (University of Hong Kong)
Peter Jones (Sheffield Hallam University)
Nigel Love (University of Cape Town)
Sinfree Makoni (Penn State University)
Rukmini Bhaya Nair (Indian Institute of Technology)
Jon Orman (Brighton)
Talbot J. Taylor (College of William & Mary)
Michael Toolan (University of Birmingham)

Anyone wishing to join the Association can do so by email apable@hku.hk or by sending their name and address to the Secretary:

Dr Adrian Pablé
School of English
Run Run Shaw Tower
Centennial Campus
The University of Hong Kong
Hong Kong S.A.R

Contents

The Birth of Decolonial Integrational Linguistics

"Literacy and language education are as much tools
of social control as forms of social emancipation."

This quotation from Sinfree Makoni's paper "From Misinvention to Disinvention of Language: Multilingualism and
the South African Constitution" is perhaps the most concise
and exact summary of his lifelong message as a scholar,
teacher and engaged intellectual as anyone could possibly
write. So why am I writing an introduction? Because what
follows from that recognition depends entirely upon how
language, literacy and education are understood.

The papers selected and collected in these volumes
represent the development of Sinfree's critiques of linguistic
theorizing about language, literacy, and language education
from his early works "The futility of being held captive by
language policy" (1993), "African languages as European
scripts: the shaping of communal memory" (1998) and
"From Misinvention to Disinvention of Language: Multilingualism and the South African Constitution" (2003) through
the papers written after his liberating encounter with the writings of Roy Harris during the 2004-2005 period. It is clear
in the early papers that he had already made his own way
towards a critique that had remarkable similarities with
Harris's critique of the "Language Myth", as can be seen
from yet another passage from the 2003 paper:

Consider the case of code-switching. Most sociolinguistic research on codeswitching is premised on the
assumption that speakers code-switch naturally from
the different languages which they control. So, for
example, a speaker who mixes English, Afrikaans,
and African languages is assumed to have the ability

to use English, Afrikaans, and African languages in their "unmixed" forms as separate codes. It is a logical inference, but unfortunately it is inaccurate and cannot be supported by the evidence from the sociolinguistic situation of urban African settings. In these urban centers the "mixed" forms are themselves the linguistic norm, the starting point in the process of language socialization for most people, and at times the only version of language for every-day encounters. Most people only encounter the "unmixed" speech as part of the formal process of education. The uneducated speakers may never have encountered the languages in their "unmixed" state. Thus the speakers cannot be said to have the capacity to speak languages which they do not control, may never have controlled, and are unlikely to get exposed to unless they get formally educated!

Having paid attention to the linguistic situation in the world around him, many of the assumptions underwriting linguistic theory had to be jettisoned, beginning with "the language", in a move that exactly paralleled Harris's path towards his critique of the "Language Myth." Harris in fact embarked upon his own critique in response to a comparable linguistic situation that he found when studying medieval manuscripts:

> The first time I began to have doubts about the concept 'a language' was on one occasion years ago during my period as a research student when I had to plough through at some speed a great number of medieval texts, manuscripts and anthologies of various provenances, looking for 'examples'. One evening I found myself reading a poem and realized, to my surprise, that although I could understand it well enough, I had no idea where it originated, what date it was, or what language it was written in, except that – I presumed – it must be some variety of

Romance. At the time I explained this experience to myself as being due to the fact that my (imperfect) acquaintance with Old French, Old Provençal, Old Spanish, Catalan and various Italian dialects was sufficient to enable me unconsciously to construct a kind of hypothetical protolingua that approximated to whatever language the poet had been using. But later I came to realize that this 'explanation' was even more difficult to understand than the facts it was supposed to 'explain'. (Roy Harris, letter to David Bade, 18 February 2006)

In the case of Harris, the linguistic situation was a diversity of written language produced in a world without linguistic standardization; in Sinfree's case, he was confronted with spoken language that was not considered 'a language' until 'reduced to writing', and written languages that were created and codified by people who could neither speak nor understand in the manner of those whom they desired to govern and 'educate'. The mix of literacy, language education and social control were all there, as was this young language teacher's recognization that literacy and language education can also be socially liberating.

Although there is an international interest, and membership in the IAISLC is not aligned to any race or gender, Integrational Linguistics could easily be considered to be primarily the expression of a few white male British intellectuals in ivory towers, Oxford above all, a point which Sinfree delicately made in his paper "Sociolinguistics, colonial and postcolonial: an integrationist perspective":

Integrationist linguistics addresses epistemological linguistic issues in western contexts; and its examples, *by and large*, are also drawn from the same contexts.

Upon his introduction to the writings of Roy Harris and Integrational Linguistics, Sinfree set out to "explore its putative relevance to non-western colonial and postcolonial contexts" and since then he has become one of the leading interpreters and developers of Integrational Linguistics. The otherness of his perspective has made his voice a welcomed presence at IAISLC conferences, and indeed, Sinfree has himself taken a leading role in bringing integrationally oriented linguists together and into conversation with a large group of scholars from worlds very different from Oxford and the University of Chicago (the latter being my own milieu for nearly 20 years).

These four volumes, planned as the first IAISLC publication since 2015, are intended to celebrate this unique voice that we have come to appreciate more and more as Sinfree keeps writing and bringing us all together with his rainbow coalition of decolonial and southern theorists. As is to be expected in any collection of an author's works covering nearly 30 years, there are overturns and overlaps: what seemed the proper way to approach, examine and critique a particular linguistic situation in 1993 does not always seem so proper in 2003 or 2019, and may be revisited from a different perspective. Papers written on the same topic for different audiences or readerships draw upon the same sources to make the same or similar points, sometimes in the same language, but any attempt to eliminate that overlap would render one or more of the papers incomprehensible. That is simply to acknowledge that in a collection such as this, between one paper and another the author changes, theories change, the reader changes and the world changes, but since we necessarily carry our pasts along with us, Sinfree's past with all its twists and turns is here for all to read. Those who do read will be richly rewarded, as was this editor.

David Bade
Rachel's Farm
27 June 2020

I

An Integrationist Perspective On Colonial Linguistics

Abstract

In this article, I explore the relevance of integrationism as a prism through which one can examine the construction of languages within colonial linguistics (CL). I examine the complex legacy that CL has left and that is still apparent in language labels, practices, and ideologies. In addressing the construction of languages within CL, I argue that terms such as indigenous languages misrepresent the time-and locale-specific nature of linguistic communication. In a real sense, indigenous languages are a product of prolonged interaction between colonialists and colonized Africans. The emergence of languages as products of colonial encounters radically changes pre-existing language practices and beliefs about the nature of language and communication. However, I also note that some strands of CL are in consonant with integrational positions. Yet the relationship between integrationism and CL is complicated: On the one hand, CL analyzes the making and remaking of languages within specific political and historical politics, unlike integrationism wherein the historical specificity and locale of the contexts where creativity is constructed are insignificant. On the other hand, the centrality of the role of lay person-oriented linguistics in integrationism, as an alternative to professional linguists, can be aligned with colonial and postcolonial linguistics, which seeks to replace colonialism and African elites with more lay-oriented participation in civil society.

1. Prolegomena

Notwithstanding the growing body of literature on the study of various aspects of language using integrationist perspectives, there is as yet no integrationist investigation that has focused on colonial linguistics (CL from henceforth) in an African context. Although past studies have explored political dimensions of integrational scholarship, none has developed a CL in Africa from an integrationist perspective. The aim of this article is to contribute to the growing literature on integrationist linguistics by looking critically at colonial perspectives in African linguistics and to a historical and integrationist perspective of the study of African languages. The article starts from the premise that the language myth is one of the central concepts within Harris' (1987, 1989, 2006, 2009) work on integrationism. Drawing insight from the concept of 'language myth' as used in integrationism, it appears that the dominant modes of framing languages as structures and indigenous African languages as natural are products of Western philosophy that subscribe to the idea of 'language myth.'

CL, which is defined as the study of the construction of languages within a universalizing/totalizing colonial framework, has left a very complex legacy in language scholarship in Africa. Part of the complexity lies in its culture-centrism, which Grace (2002) neatly captured. According to Grace, *culture-centrism* is

> the assumption (whether conscious or not) that characteristics of one's own culture are in fact characteristics of human nature. It is the assumption that what is done within this culture is natural, whereas what others do differently requires a cultural explanation... Linguistic theory has become culture-centric to a disturbing degree. It has come to view human language as a whole from the perspective of a particular cate-

gory of speaker—those who are most adept in composing and analyzing autonomous texts. And this of course, is a category of which linguists are representatives.

While a relatively large body of colonial studies literature exists in disciplines closely related to linguistics (e.g., literary theory, history, and cultural studies), writing about CL is relatively new, perhaps because of a philosophical orientation towards language scholarship that idealizes language and conceptualizes it as 'discrete, rule-governed systems ... with an emphasis on ... classification and the resolution of categorical ambiguity' (Bolton and Hutton, 2000, p. 1). Thus, my primary objective is to analyze CL through the prism of integrationism in order to contribute to the development of a political approach to integrationism. Together with other critical approaches to language, a political orientation that underpins CL challenges the 'language myth' (Harris, 2006; Makoni, 2011). At face value, a juxtaposition of CL and integrationism may appear counter-intuitive because integrationism is apolitical as a project, while CL is a highly political enterprise. In order to analyze CL through an integrationistic prism and thereby develop a politicized perspective, I investigate a very specific orientation toward colonialism. A local, bottom-up perspective best captures the ambivalent, ambiguous impact of colonialism on African cultural formations, with language and ethnicity being the most salient. A local perspective also enables me to capture the 'idiosyncrasies' in the workings of colonial agents, the complexity of agency, the 'linguistic responsibility' and distinctions between languages (Harris, 1987:171), especially indigenous and colonial languages.

3

2. Introduction

Interest in 19th century African linguistics is based on an attempt to understand the nature of contemporary epistemology and the genealogy of African languages. Although interest in the nature of CL and epistemologies of African languages has increased over the years (Errington 2008; Gilmour 2006; Makoni 2011) none (that I am aware of) has examined such epistemologies or the nature of CL of African languages from an integrationist perspective. As a result, this paper begins an academic conversation and argues that an integrationist study of CL is needed. The article explores the relevance of integrationism to CL in an attempt to contribute to the development of a political dimension to integrationism which includes investigating the impact of colonial categories on contemporary sociolinguistics. In an attempt to explore the applicability of integrationism to CL, I analyze the epistemology of African languages (and, indeed, the construct of language itself and the notion of a linguistic speaker) by investigating the constraints and space colonialism created for reflection on languages through a critique of the micro-genesis of African languages and the manner in which these languages have been conceptualized. Through the lens of integrationism, I address the following specific questions:

(i) What are the politics and epistemologies of African languages, and what is their relevance to integrationism?
(ii) What different genres are used in the representation of African languages in colonialism, and what is the potential significance of integrationism?

3. Summary of key principles of integrationism relevant to European colonial linguistics

Integrationism was introduced by Harris (1987, 1989, 2006), who identified its three parameters: (i) biomechanical, (ii) macrosocial, and (iii) circumstantial. Biomechanical relates to both mental as well as physical abilities of individual participants. Macrosocial refers to well-established practices in the community or some group within the community. Circumstantial relates to the conditions that arise in specific communication situations. In general terms, integrationism is critical of (i) 'orthodox linguistics' which Harris (2006) refers to as segregationist, (ii) the autonomy of language, (iii) homogeneous communities, (iv) a sender-receiver model, and (vi) professional linguists' exclusive monopoly of knowledge about language. Harris advocates a lay person's expertise instead of that of professional linguists.

As already mentioned, the central tenet of integrationism, as articulated by Harris in his long career, is a critique of 'orthodox linguistics,' which is founded on the 'language myth.' In Harris' view, the concept of 'language myth' is one of the defining features of segregationist approaches to language scholarship, which is influenced by Western philosophy. According to Harris (2009), Western philosophy is founded on a 'myth' that he defines as a 'convenient fiction. . . an illusion'. In explaining the basis of segregationism, Harris (2010) states that segregationism as an epistemology is founded on the mythical status of language in the sense that languages do not correspond to anything in social reality but, rather are a consequence of viewing language through the semantics of 'reocentricism' and psychocentrism (Pablé, 2010). Segregationism treats languages as discrete entities that can be distinguished from each other and postulates the existence of distinctions between internal and external aspects of language. A series of distinctions are also made between phonology and phonetics, semantics and syntax, etc. Language is a separate domain from context, history, and geography. In a segregationism framework, language use can be separated from language learning. Geography and history are treated as separate domains of

5

analysis from language. From a psychocentric perspective, *language* can be described as a finite set of structures constructed as having external validity.

Another closely related construct Harris criticizes is telementation, which is characterized as the encoding and decoding of propositions of texts assumed to 'stand alone' or to exist as 'autonomous texts' that require little or any contexts and exist in unilingual contexts. George Grace (2002) enumerated some features that might be attributed to telementation, even though Grace was not writing with integrationism in mind over and above the encoding and decoding framework identified by Harris:

(i) The prototypical function of language is to communicate factual information.
(ii) The prototypical manifestation of human language is a form of such distinct systems 'languages.' A competent speaker is able to decode all or most of the texts produced by the system.
(iii) Each language consists of whatever is necessary to know in order to construct, and to specify the meanings of, the linguistic expressions permitted in the language

Harris has argued in a number of his publications that comprehension is much more complex than telementation suggests and that (contrary to the claims in telementation) meanings are, to a large extent, unstable and, therefore, 'created' and recreated in each interaction. In colonial and postcolonial Africa, contexts are largely plurilingual and complicated by incongruent frames of reference and contradictory episteme. If telementation is premised upon unilingual contexts, its validity in a colonial and postcolonial context is highly questionable. In fact, if integrationism is used as a prism through which one analyzes colonial and postcolonial African linguistics, two additional layers must be added to avoid a situation whereby African CL inadvertently reinforces the very segregationism from which it seeks to depart: (i) Knowledge of language should be integrated from knowledge about the world, and (ii) the formal characteristics of narratives are indistinguishable from what is being narrated. I add the last two layers because of the context embedded nature of African rhetorical and cultural practices.

4. Integrationism and the making and unmaking of language in colonial contexts

African languages were socially constructed as part of the 'invention' of Africa (Mudimbe, 1988). If African languages are 'inventions', then indigenous African languages are historical products and, therefore, a result of prolonged interaction between colonialists and Africans. In fact, if indigenous languages are a by-product of continuous and prolonged interaction, then, ironically, powerful advocacy of indigenous languages is a re-inscription of the colonial mentality they are seeking to challenge and undermine.

The prolonged exchange between Europeans and colonial 'natives' may be a powerful site of political conflict in which, because of creativity, language is *made* and *unmade* in both speech and writing. The political dimension of power struggle and its dialogic character are situated in historical and political contexts when integrationism is extended to colonial contexts.

Nonetheless, the term 'invention' is used in African Studies in a technical sense to 'historicize [the] development' of some of the constructs 'and explore how they were exploited, manipulated and transformed by colonial, and local authorities' (Spear, 2003, p. 4). The other most powerful account of invention was Ranger's 'Invention of Tradition in Colonial Africa'.[1] Ranger argued that, to a large degree, notions about language and ethnicity were a result of colonialism and did not even exist in their current form in pre-colonial Africa. In other words, the existence of ethnicities preceded their appropriation by members ascribed to them, in some cases. For example, Ranger cited the ethnic consciousness among the Makoni as Manyikas in Zimbabwe, which only began to take place in the late 1930s. For a considerable amount of time in colonial Africa, the Manyikas and the Nubas in southern Sudan were ethnicities in search of members and languages in search of speakers. Although Ranger (1987) was one of the key architects of the notion of 'invention,' he had subsequent reservations about the conceptual validity of the term in that it downplayed the agency and 'responsibility' of local Africans in the construction of African ethnicities and language. It can be argued from an Integrationist perspective that the notion of invention underestimates the creativity of individual Africans in colonial encounters by implying a sense of homogeneous, uniform practices.

In some contexts, it is not feasible to either determine who belongs to which ethnic group or whether the notions of ethnicity and language as organizing principles are viable. The problematic nature of determining ethnicity is important because of the relationship between ethnicity and African languages (*ethnolects*). The assignment of people to ethnicities parallels the arbitrariness with which people are assigned to languages: Both reflect the enormous power of notions such as mother tongue, native language, etc., which are critical components of segregationist linguistics. In Africa, the project of assigning individuals to ethnicities and attributing native languages to them is misleading because if language is a myth, constructs such as mother tongue are irrelevant.

---

[1] A much more sophisticted account of invention is by Briggs (1996).

Secondly, such constructs are misleading because they conjure a sense of uniform experience. In other words, they suggest that everyone who allegedly shares the same language has identical experiences of the language. Integrationism is critical of the implied uniformity in terms such as *native languages* and *mother tongue* because communities are extremely diverse and rarely do any two or more individuals have identical social and linguistic experiences. The overall argument is that ethnicity and African languages are both social constructs. In fact, Makoni et al. (2007) extended the argument by illustrating the degree to which notions about language (indigenous African languages, in particular) mask their politically and socially constructed nature by evoking the complex discourses of authenticity.

The idea of languages as constructed was aptly captured by Joseph (2006), who described languages as not only structural but also political in non-African contexts. What is striking about Joseph's proposition is not the role of language in politics or the language of politics but, rather, that language itself is political and, by extension, analysis of language is as well. Dealing with issues in Southern Africa, the idea of language as political was echoed by Jeater (2007), who, considering Zimbabwe, argued that the emergence of manufactured, indigenous languages used as a principal mode of engagement may, contrary to initial assumptions, alienate the educated elite from the rest of the population. This alienation renders it harder, rather than easier, for ruling elites in African states to meaningfully communicate with their own citizens, suggesting that the wrongs of the past cannot be easily rectified through the use of constructed, indigenous languages. This also shows the limitations of language policies for making society more egalitarian.

It is against the above background that the notion of invention has been proposed. *Invention* is a postcolonial construct that challenges calcified notions of identity and

9

linguistically structuralistic and positivistic assumptions that languages are 'fixed things' out there, static, and monolithic, a position aligned with Harris' ideas of myth and segregationalism. From an invention perspective, languages and identities are neither code-based nor rule-based but, rather, constantly evolving and dynamic. As such, they are a product of an ethnographic and, at times, asymmetrical engagement in social contexts. In short, what constitutes African languages is conditional, and consistent with lay orientation to integrationism, people may shift into and out of the languages and identities they construct (Makoni and Pennycook, 2007).

The complexity, fluidity, and density of colonial contexts are aptly captured by the famous missionary/adventurer David Livingstone, whose 19th century observations can be said to precede observations which were subsequently inform the critical concepts of integrationism as an analytic and interpretive framework:

> There is, however, quite a redundancy of words for expressing ideas in which an European mind feels little interest; there are for instance, at least a score of words each designating a different variety of walking - the slow walk of sickness, of laziness, of pride holding the head. . . (David Livingstone, 1858, p. 4)

From an integrationist perspective, the continuously increasing number of words used to describe 'varieties of walking, sickness,' etc., does not mean the languages are redundant, as Livingstone argued. The continuously changing meaning of the same words used to describe a 'fool' and what Livingstone termed 'redundant' might mean, at least from an Integrationist perspective, that words like 'fool' were not fixed and the multiplicity of their meanings was, as would be expected in an integrational enterprise, negotiated in the interactional encounter. The idea of 'useless redundancy' is a well-established feature of how 'primitive' languages from the late eighteenth century were viewed. Take for instance, the Nuer language in south Sudan, which is characterized by European colonialism as having an *ad infinitum* vocabulary:

> The Nuer language as I have found it has an extensive vocabulary. I have listed over 3.1000 words in the above mentioned dictionary, many of them root-forms only. I constantly find how limited my knowledge of the language is. One finds new words each day. It seems like an endless mine. (Miner, 2003)

From a segregationist perspective, which echoes European colonial language formation, the Nuer language in south Sudan has an extensive, redundant vocabulary. Miner goes further and describes it as a language in which one finds new words every day. Yet integrationism challenges this long-held view about redundancy in language by providing a more plausible explication of what is considered redundancy. From an integrationist standpoint, each word has a number of meanings, and nothing is either given in advance or predetermined, a perspective that challenges the ideological principles of dictionaries. If the meanings of words are variable and cannot be given in advance, then the idea of the countability of words is difficult to sustain. Put differently, inasmuch as languages are not countable, neither are words because as in integrationism, any object can potentially be labeled in an unlimited number of ways. Communicational practices shape the contexts in which they occur. Furthermore, what counts as background or relevant objects is situation dependent. There are no two individuals who contextualize in an identical way, and what constitutes words in such contexts may vary depending upon the ways in which the entextualization takes place. This means what counts as

11

word may vary considerably depending upon the contexts in which it occurs (www.royharrisonline.com/integrational-linguistics/integrationism-introduction.html. Accessed 1.6.12).

Nonetheless, the argument that any object can be labeled and described in an 'unlimited number of ways' must be treated circumspectly. If any object can be described in completely unlimited ways, then communication becomes much messier than it is already is, and ironically, this article is a futile exercise. To this end, contrary to the claims of integrationism, which dismisses telementation, I must, on the one hand, accept a degree of telementation while, on the other, concede that differences will exist in how meanings are interpreted. Some meanings will remain enigmatic, even if factual and fictitious biographical details of the participants are recognized.

Yet in integrationism, 'fact' and 'fiction' are similar because both are predicated on imagination. In this regard, even though objects can be described in many ways, the range of potential descriptors and plausible interpretations attributable to an object must be at least somewhat constrained. The limited nature of the descriptors is apparent in the tendency to describe different objects using the same label, as opposed to the describing the same object in many ways (Pablé, 2010). In fact, in language scholarship, the standard language ideology (Milroy, 2002), 'meta-discursive regimes' (Bauman and Briggs, 2003: 15), and semiotic processes such as erasure and fractal recursivity (Irvine and Gal, 2000) create uniformity, which has the effect of constraining linguistic 'idiosyncrasy.' By imposing a semblance of uniformity in a sea of diversity, the different semiotic practices and 'meta-discursive regimes' (Makoni, 2012; Bauman and Briggs, 2003) introduce uniformity into language practices and contribute to a specific idea of language reinforced by the nature of writing. Writing creates an illusion of visual stability that is subsequently projected into language.

In sharp contrast, European colonialism and invention as strategies sought to contain diversity as a political enterprise. The linguistic equivalent in Harris' terminology is segregationism in which the messy, heteroglossic, fluid, and fuzzy language practices consistent with Harris' Integrationism (Bakhtin, 1986; Heller, 2007) are the exception rather than the norm. The diversity is partially created by transidiomatic expressions (Jacquemet, 2005) and individual styles and orientations to speech. On the other hand, the nature of these transidiomatic expressions and individual orientations to speech depend largely on the communicative activities in which the individual is engaged; thus, the degree of diversity is somewhat constrained due to a large number of factors, including individual history.

The concept of African languages as ideas 'emerged' through the application of a number of distinct but related strategies that ultimately 'fixed' African languages in specific ways. Analysts may construe 'fixing' to refer to the 'extraction' of form from fluid language practices and assignment of meaning to them. This process is based on the assumption that a stable relationship exists between meaning and form. Another strategy was the attribution of form and uniform linguistic structures to fluid semiotic practices (Irvine, 2008). Using these strategies made it possible to 'fix' languages by situating them in space and time, which generate all practices regarded as instantiations of a particular language. After African languages were 'fixed,' they were represented in linguistic form through a number of genres. These genres were not objective statements about the languages but, rather, powerful discourse procedures through which languages were represented. The 'fixing' of African languages was described in a discourse analogous to one from the 19th century that echoed positivist discourses in which phonemes (i.e., meanings of words) were 'uncovered' and not necessarily 'made' in some communicative contexts. For example, Ray Huffman (1929, p. 3), working in the Sudan in the early 20th century, reported three new phonemes for Nuer, which Miner (2003) later noted made it appear that "Nuer had a nearly complete set of corresponding close and open vowels!"—complete when analyzed from a European/Indo-European view of language 'system'.

'Fixed' languages were described or created in texts and genres that played critical roles in shaping how African languages were to be imagined. Part of the process of imagining African languages was the use of orthography. Although orthography is technical, it is intimately related to issues about identity (Bird, 2001). In fact, Bird emphasized that orthography is both technical and social. The degree to which orthography shapes how languages are imagined is clearly evident in the Sudan where, prior to 1956, some African languages were written in Roman script, but after Sudanese independence, there was pressure to write them in Arabic script (Sharkey, 2008), drawing attention to the political significance of orthographies. Both scripts were motivated by a belief that the scripts were a reflection of speech. In integrationism, writing and speech are different systems, even though they mutually influence one another.

I now turn to an analysis of prefaces and forewords of grammars and dictionaries in order to illustrate how linguistic labels, language practices, and ideologies of African languages were created through colonial intervention. I use a number of cases to illustrate the various ways in which Segregated linguistic codes were created and the context within which they occurred by focusing on micro-dynamics of the activists, the ways they related to each other, their sense of their responsibilities, and their orientation towards the 'natives' whose 'language' they were inventing.

14

The positions of missionaries toward their linguistic enterprises were more complicated than might be assumed, as reflected in the preface to Livingstone's book *Language of the Bechuanas*, where, referring to his comments on grammar, he wrote the following:

> [This was] printed for private circulation among members of the Livingstone's Expedition, with a view of imparting a general idea of the structure of South African Languages. It was written in 1852, and no opportunity has since been enjoyed for amplification. This may possibly be done by someone engaged in the study, making such alterations and additions as may be necessary.
> David Livingstone (D.L.)
> January, 20th February, 1858

Livingstone was quite aware of the incomplete nature of his text. However, he also expressed no perturbation that it might form a basis for some 'amplification' without any full attribution of the sources and the degree to which he himself built upon previous research, as he pointed out:

> About to leave New England for Natal, in 1846. I tried in various ways and places to find something on the language of the people-Amazulu-among whom I was hoping soon to labor. [I came across] a few Kaffir words in defective orthography.[2]
> LEWIS GROUT.
> Umsunduzi Mission Station
> September, 1859

---

[2] "I came across" is my addition to render the sentence meaningful.

In addition, African languages were conceived in contradictory ways (Irvine, 2008), as 'primitive' but also advanced: 'They form the chief peculiarities in the structure of the language and there exists the closest relationship between the primitive and almost perfect.' Regardless of whether African languages were conceived as 'primitive' or 'perfect,' the philosophical beliefs reflected the culture-centric nature of CL. African languages are 'primitive' or 'perfect' from the perspective of 'a particular category of speaker ... those who are most adept in composing and analyzing autonomous texts' (Grace, 2002). Unlike Integrationism, this 'culture-centric' nature of CL does not seriously take into account an individual lay person's experiences.

5. Textualization/representation of African languages
In this section, I situate critical constructs of integrationism within discourses of CL. *Discourses of Integrationism* refers to genres in which CL are situated, such as prefaces of grammars and dictionaries. In this article, *textualization/representation* (Blommaert, 2008) refers to the different genres typically used in writing African language grammars as part of the 'vernacular regimes' (Dube, 2002, p. 814) of the colonial era, with missionaries making substantial contributions. However, one must bear in mind that great variation existed among missionaries, not only among different congregations but also different individuals; thus, the idea of a uniform myth should not be taken for granted in African colonial scholarship. The same missionary might also vary his or her approach at different stages of his or her career. Most missionaries tended to move from one place to another, so the statements made below are generalizations. In spite of these differences, the following is a taxonomy of some of the genres used when languages (which were hitherto unwritten) were framed and committed to Roman script:

6. Extract one

(i) A Manual of the Chikaranga Language with Grammar, Useful Conversational Sentences and a Vocabulary.
(ii) Esquissegrammaticale (grammatical sketch).
(iii) A Shona Dictionary with an Outline Shona Grammar.
(iv) An Outline of Xhosa-Kaffir Grammar.
(v) First book in Zulu-Kaffir: An Introduction to the Study of Zulu-Kaffir Language and Kaffir Grammar.
(vi) Bud-m'bele's (Kaffir Scholar's Companion.)
(vii) Kuverenga (reading in Shona). An Introductory Shona Reader with Grammatical Sketch.
(viii) A Handbook of Chikaranga or The Language of Mashonaland.
(ix) Notes on Nambya
(x) First Elementary Grammar.

The texts listed above are important because they mark the 'birth' of African languages (Blommaert, 2008). Before the 'textualization' of African languages, Africans obviously communicated but not through language as the concept is now understood. This is partly because African languages as we currently understand them are a direct construction of colonial thinking. The crystallization of African languages as ideas brought with it attitudes toward these languages, language-based identities, and attribution of rights to language, consequently creating a bizarre situation in which languages have rights but speakers of those languages are still in search of rights (Wee, 2011).

The different types of texts cited in Extract One are important examples of the genres or discourse forms used to describe African languages. The myth in African languages has to be understood with the discourses/styles in which it is situated. The list is, however, neither exhaustive nor mutually exclusive. For example, the *Reader* existed separately at times but was combined with the genre *Grammatical Sketch* (see [vii]) at other times. In some cases, the texts were produced with monolingual speakers in mind; in other cases, they were explicitly designed to aid in the development of proficiency in African languages among colonialists. For example, Louw's (1915) *Manual of the Chikaranga Language* contains a concluding section that deals with direct translations from English to *Chikaranga* and conversely.

In spite of the diversity and complexity of the genres, they share one common feature: substantial prefaces. Prefaces provide autobiographical, linguistic, historical, and, at times, geographical information about speakers of the languages in question. In some cases, they also delve into controversies on names, as indicated by Springer (1905):

> It is in fact well-known to those who have extensive knowledge of the people in Mashonaland, that there is no one term which applies to the language of the whole country. Various terms have been invented by the white men, most commonly being *Chiswina*, the meaning being the language of the filthy people. As white people, whether missionaries or not, we are here to try and lift the native from his filth, so it is not fitting that we should fix on him a name of opprobrium which shall stamp him throughout the generations. Let us remember that our own forefathers were not always as fastidious as we are. . . (p. 3)

As the above quotation illustrates, the naming of the languages was a source of controversy among different White communities; whether naming constituted a problem worth addressing is a moot point. Nonetheless, labeling or naming these 'objects' that are now called 'languages' had sociolinguistic implications because of their ethno-linguistic significance (Irvine, 2008). The naming of languages not only created a new category of identity but also created

18

complexities in African identities, leading to the formation of the 'first glossy Lingala' (Meeuwis, 2009, p. 240). The naming of languages created puzzling questions such as, 'What languages do you speak?' 'Speaking' language X implies that a person is in control of all the varieties of that language. However, it is hard to demonstrate that an individual is in control of all the varieties falling under the rubric of language X since it is difficult to determine, from a sociolinguistic point of view, where the boundaries of each language are situated (Blommaert, 2008).

On the other hand, the act of naming was critically important because it made it possible to manage language as an object of study. Lexicographers were now able to produce dictionaries, translate Bibles, develop teaching materials, etc. In essence, naming languages led to an ideology that produced grammars-as-text. Since languages were now named and the geographical areas in which these objects were situated were identified, these objects could now be managed more effectively. Their boundaries could be relatively 'policed' and could serve the bureaucratic interests of colonial and contemporary Africa, even though language boundaries were determined with considerable arbitrariness. For example, after the Rejaf conference in the Sudan in 1932, the British found it difficult to determine the boundaries of some of the languages (Abdelhay et al., 2011).

The ideology of one name-one referent is a product of monoglot ethnocentrisms, which is founded on 'referential stability' (Harris and Hutton, 2007, p. 208) and which, to some extent reflects 'culture-centrism.' Referential stability may account for the efforts of European missionaries to determine 'accurate' or appropriate names for African languages. A monoglot perspective runs contrary to the many names the 'same' language may have. For example, English in Zimbabwe may be referred to as *Chingezi*,

Chrungu. Shona is also referred to using a generic term *Chivanhu*. The idea of Shona as a people's language implies that those who do not speak Shona are not people!

Language names (e.g., English, French, German, etc.) also consolidate the view that individuals' experiences are identical; hence, the labels refer to something that really exists. In colonial and postcolonial Africa, the idea of the same language experience renders it possible to have language planning, to count languages, and to carry out census. A language planning project would be radically different if integrationism constituted the basis on which it (integrationism) is predicated.

The policed objects are, at times, framed in terms of national or official languages. For example, in Louw's (1915) *A Handbook of Chikaranga: The Language of Mashonaland,* the place where Chikaranga could be found is identified as a region called Mashonaland. Similarly, McGregor (1905) wrote the following about the location of Kikuyu in East Africa:

> The country of Kikuyu is one of the most fertile and healthy districts of British East Africa. It is situated in the northwestern position of the Protectorate, and is practically on the Equator. The Uganda Railway, from about mile 326 to mile 360, runs through the south-western position of the country, and forms almost the boundary of the same. The district over which is spoken, with few modification, stretches away in a north-easterly direction from the railway until it embraces in the folds that great landmark, Mount Kenya (McGregor, 1902, p. iv).

More importantly, missionary efforts produced a 'rewriting' of grammars, solidifying what was fluid into calcified entities (Errington, 2008; Makoni and Pennycook,

20

2007; Meeuwis, 2009) and 'sponsoring distinctions between linguistic objects and discourse episodes' (Harris, 1989, p. 104).

The contact between African language practices, European colonial variants, and European languages produced a complex amalgam that was to form the basis of the so-called 'urban vernaculars' (McLaughlin, 2008) and led to the formation of what came to be referred to as 'missionary languages' (chibaba). The chibaba and similar entities came to be referred to as 'indigenous languages' when, in an ironic sense, the very suppression of local speech forms led to their enhanced status, particularly in educational contexts. African elites played a key role in resisting the emergence of some of these missionary varieties, which contributed to the creation of a diglossic situation (Meeuwis, 2009).

7. Manuals and Esquisse Grammaticale

The *Manual* and *Esquisse Grammaticale* professionally developed genres that produced 'grammars-as-text' (Blommaert 2008) and 'grammars-in-text.' 'Grammars-as-text' meant that grammars could be read as discourse and, thus, are amenable to a textual analysis, while 'grammars-in-text' meant that structures can be inferred from the text. Two different traditions exist in African linguistic scholarship: the British tradition (which is manifest in Southern Africa) and the Belgian African tradition in Central Africa. In terms of the British tradition, one of the most widely used formats in the representation of African languages is the *Manual*. For instance, Louw's (1915) grammar is referred to as *The Manual of the Chikaranga Language with Grammar, Exercises, Useful Conversational Sentences and Vocabulary (English-Chikaranga, Chikaranga-English)*. It appears as if the *Manual of the Nyanja Language* by Reverend Alexander Hetherwick of the Church of Scotland (Louw, 1915, p. vii) provided a template for Louw's manual.

21

Interestingly enough, in the introduction of the *Chi-karanga Manual*, Louw (1915) drew attention to the issue of naming languages and their geographical locale when he wrote the following:

> *Chikaranga* is the language spoken by the natives of Mashonaland, Southern Rhodesia. It is known by different names in different parts of the country. In the Salisbury (now Harare) district it is called *Chiswina*; in the Umtali (Mutare, both in Zimbabwe) district it is known as *Chimanyika*, while it bears the name of *Chindau* in Gazaland. In the district of Victoria the natives call it *Chigovera, Chimali*, etc. ... (p. v)

The section on grammar is made up of a single section on the alphabet, phonetics, and phonology, consistent with the principles of segregationism. The section on grammar is composed of 38 sections, whose prominent elements are nouns, genitive particle, verbs, adverbs, compound tenses, and the construction of sentences. The inclusion of constructs such as nouns, verbs, and adverbs, whose origins can be traced back to Latin grammars, reflects the efforts to fit African discourse practices into pre-existing templates. This seems to suggest that African discursive practices were viewed through the lenses of Latin and Indo-European languages and, in turn, yielded 'grammars-as-structure.' The use of the same Indo-European meta-discursive regimes produced notions of African 'languageness' that rendered African languages more comparable to Indo-European languages.

Besides the linguistic nature of the section on grammar, the *Manuals*, unlike the *Esquisse Grammaticale*, were written with the objective of facilitating language teaching and learning, which is also apparent from their organization in terms of lessons and exercises, a format clearly associated more with language teaching and learning materials than with linguistic grammars. In the case of the *Chikaranga Manual*, the approach to the description of *Chikaranga* linguistics involved two interrelated processes: comparing *Chikaranga* with English and reversing that same process by comparing English with *Chikaranga*. Through a strategy of 'contrastive analysis,' potential areas of difficulty were identified, particularly those in which there were major differences between African languages and English as the source language.

Take, for instance, lesson one in the *Chikaranga Manual*, which deals with the alphabet and pronunciation. This lesson compares the ways in which *Chikaranga* was pronounced with English /b, d, f. . ./. According to Louw (1915), these sounds were 'all pronounced as in English except the letters with diacritics' (p. 3). In other cases, the *Manual* was written not to describe how the 'natives spoke' but, rather, to accommodate how Europeans spoke: 'The aspirate is not always distinguished by Europeans, [but] we have decided to disregard it except where its omission might cause confusion' (Louw, 1915, p. 4). Yet Louw was aware of the diversity of the potential users of his *Manual*, as evident from the fact that the exercises in Part II were designed for those living in 'lonely places' while those in Part III were designed for those at an elementary stage or travelers who were in the country temporarily. The following are examples of some of the sentences taken from the *Chikaranga Manual*.

Write in Chikaranga:
1. Go to the house.
2. Look in my house and bring a chair outside.
3. Go among the trees and look for my little kitten.
(Louw, 1915, p. 13).

All of the above sentences are instructions consistent with the format of a *Manual*. However, it is interesting to note that the teaching materials had errors that, within the code-based and rule-based theoretical framework in use at the time, might conceivably be made by non-native speakers, as demonstrated by the example below from Shona, which is spoken in southern Africa:

1. *Ndinesimbanaiwe (I am stronger than you).
2. Ndinesimbakupfuuraiwe (I have a house bigger than yours).
3. *Ndinesimba kupfuura iwe (The boy is stronger than the girl).
4. Mukomana mukuru kupfura musikana (The boy is stronger than the girl).

From a formal, structuralism perspective, sentence 1 is ungrammatical because of the use of *na*, and in sentence 3, the sequencing of the adjective *mukuru* (big) before the noun *musikana* (girl) is grammatical in English but not in African languages. It is, therefore, possible to explain within a 'contrastive analysis' that the sentences perceived as ungrammatical are, in fact, examples of interlingual transfer. It is, however, worth noting that the writers of these grammars were not oblivious to the fact that the examples in the manuals were ungrammatical:

> These notes are not 'a *Nambya* Grammar,' a complete, thoroughly checked, reliable work. A Grade One pupil cannot be a teacher, and in fact I am still in Grade One as far as *Nambya* is concerned. My notes represent only a first stage in the study of the *Nambya* language; they will have ... I am sure ... many mistakes. (Moreno, 1988, p. 3)

24

While acknowledging the non-native forms produced in the *Manuals*, the writers attributed them to the unwillingness and complete ignorance of their native-speaking informants. In fact, Louw (1915) pointed out the following:

> ...many mistakes will no doubt be found as this language is known. Those, however, who know what it is to **reduce a new language** [emphasis mine], and what it is to search for every word, and to get the same often from very unwilling and unintelligent natives, will not be too critical in this issue.

Ironically, in this context, perhaps as in others in which the non-native speakers were more powerful than the native speakers, 'mistakes' made by the non-native speakers were attributed to the native speakers' lack of cooperation. From an Integrationist perspective, the notion of ungrammaticality is of secondary importance. Rules do not form the analytical apparatus paradigm because it is not possible to construct a systematic set of rules for something as fluid as language.

It is conceivable that colonists, therefore, used descriptions of African languages for prescriptive purposes and as a means of social control of the natives. From such a perspective, description and prescription were not separate processes but different sides of the same coin.

Nevertheless, although the *Manual* by Louw (1915) was European in perspective, serious efforts were made to capture how Africans might have perceived and experienced the world around them. Referring to Louw's *Manual*, Gaimersham commented,

> Many are the rules and demands of science. But one claim seems to me be paramount, especially for a European author of an *Ntu* grammar viz, to look

upon the grammar of an *Ntu* language from the *Ntu* point of view, instead of pressing it into the frame of Indo-European languages. I do not know how far I may succeed in dealing with the Zulu grammar from the *Ntu* point of view or to be allowing the Zulu language to be master. (Gaimersham 6th January 1927).

The argument that languages could be written from an *Ntu* perspective means that even if fluid African amalgams were rule-governed, the rules had to be cognizant of individual idiosyncrasies and identities—diversity consistent with integrationism. The idiosyncrasies demonstrate the degree to which languages were closely tied to individual history, wishes, and desires in a manner that, with some exaggeration, is congruent with integrationism.

As already pointed out, the *Esquisse Grammaticale* is a 'mature,' more highly professionalized technical genre of language description (Blommaert, 2008). The *Esquisse Grammaticale*, like the *Manuals*, was important insofar as its construction led to the emergence of language as a construct. These manuals, regardless of what they were called, formed the genesis of language as a construct and served as what Blommaert (2008) called 'a birth certificate' (p. 15) for language. However, if the objective in the design of the *Manual* was to facilitate second language learning, then the major objective of *Esquisse Grammaticale* was to classify African languages into different levels, such as phonology, morphology, syntax, and word lists and texts consistent with 'segregational linguistics.'

The *Esquisse Grammaticale* was not directly meant for pedagogical purposes but was part of large-scale Belgian academic efforts of the 1950s to comprehensively 'describe and classify the languages of the Congo' (Blommaert, 2008, p. 6). The descriptive tradition was fruitful in that it produced large multi-volumes (Blommaert, 2008), and classifica-

26

tions of African languages were produced in this framework. Unlike integrationism within an invention paradigm, the descriptions and multi-volumes facilitated various forms of social control of Africans in the Congo. It is this social and political nature of invention that differs from integrationism, which, with the exception of Hutton (2011), is to a large extent apolitical. I am, therefore, seeking to develop a political perspective of integrationism. As a rule, integrationism does not have any political orientation.

The figure below appears in a preliminary description of Nuer written by Eleanor Vandevort (http://www.dlib.indiana.edu/collections/nuer/scanned_verb/252.jpg viewed 9 June 2020):

Martin Aliric said.

A man cannot "bit" his brother-gat man, he can "lam" him. "Bit" is the stronger word and cannot be anulled, but "lam" can. Their meanings are much the same, but their differences consist in the regulations controlling their use on others.

He also said he has never found a satisfying word for "promise".

Bita gɔɔydɛ. (That's what people do who make excuses as to why they cannot believe.)

It is difficult for African colonial linguistics to be completely segregationist. Although the extracts above do not exhaust the different contexts in which they are used, they reflect some awareness of potential contexts in which the expressions are used, which can be construed as a form of integrationism. For example, the meanings of the words are explained by identifying the potential contexts in which the words might be used. 'A man cannot 'bit' his brother - gat man, he can 'lam' him.'

Even if a philosophical argument is made that each language has an independent 'grammar' designed by the powerful, both colonial and postcolonial linguists must find a way to reconcile linguistic features. The meanings that may vary considerably, depending on the nature of each inter-subjective interaction, suggesting that no linguistic features are independent of the interaction that forms the basis of the data collection. The grammars that are subsequently formalized usually refer to those people who are 'most adept in composing and analyzing 'autonomous text.' (Grace   www.ling.hawaii.edu/faculty/**grace**/elniv23.html   ) Furthermore, 'if grammar is tailored to the needs and properties of language users (to whatever degree), and language users are not what they used to be, then it follows that grammar is probably not what it used to be' (Newmeyer, 2002, as cited in Grace, 2002).

8. Concluding reflections
In the concluding section, I now turn to answer briefly the questions I posed at the beginning of the paper. In this article, I analyzed the contexts in which African languages were constructed and the nature of social and linguistic strategies used therein. I also examined the complex role of native Africans as sources of data and their resistance to the newly created 'linguistic languages,' as Becker (1995) called them. The singular frameworks reinforced by the analytical frameworks and the exclusive grid of conversion had its limitations because it could neither capture nor contain 'the distinctive detail and the divergent dynamic of these processes' (Dube, 2002, p. 811).

Because of the particularity of each speaker's encounters and discursive practices, a separate grammar is necessary for each individual. This high degree of idiosyncrasy is elided in postcolonial African sociolinguistics because of segregationist preoccupation with establishing invariant rules and centrality of syntax. Even though each individual may have a distinct grammar, communication is still possible because, in most cases, pragmatic cues are adequate to render it feasible. However, miscommunication may be much more widespread than neat sociolinguistic projects might lead one to believe, compelling one to be critical of telementation, which is ahistorical and not cross-cultural. Regardless, miscommunication is itself a fruitful exercise as it constitutes the basis on which social advancement may take place. Theoretically, structuralism in African sociolinguistics does not account for such rampant idiosyncrasy.

References
Abdelhay, A., Busi, M., Sinfree M. (2011). "The Naivasha Language Policy: the language politics and the politics of language" *Language Policy* (14): 1-18.
Bakhtin, M. (1986). *Speech genres and other late essays.* Holquist, M. (Ed.), C. Emmerson Trans. University of Texas Press, Austin, TX.
Bauman, R., Briggs, C. (2003). *Voices of Modernity: Language Ideologies and the Politics of Inequality.* Cambridge University Press, Cambridge, UK.
Becker, A.L. (1995). *Beyond Translation: Essays Toward Modern Philology.* University of Michigan Press, Ann Arbor, MI.
Bird, S. (2001). "Orthography and identity in Cameroon" *Notes on Literacy* 26 (1-2), 3-34. http://dx.doi.org/10.1075/wll.4.2.02bir.
Blommaert, J. (2008). "Artefactual ideologies and the textual production of African languages" *Language and Communication* 28 (4), 291-307. http://dx.doi.org/10.1016/j.langcom.2008.02.003.

Bolton, K., Hutton, C. (2000). Special issue. *Interventions* 2 (1), 1-5.

Briggs, C. (1996). "The politics of discursive authority in research on the 'invention of tradition'" *Cultural Anthropology* 11 (4), 435-469. http://dx.doi.org/ 10.1525/can.1996.11.4.02a00020.

Dube, S. (2002). "Conversion and translation: colonial registers of a vernacular Christianity" *The South Atlantic Quarterly* 101 (4), 807-837. http://dx.doi.org/10.1215/00382876-101-4-807.

Errington, J. (2008). *Linguistics in a Colonial World: A story of Language, Meaning, and Power*. Blackwell, Malden, MA.

Gilmour, R. (2006). *Grammars of Colonialism: Representing Languages in Colonial South Africa*. Palgrave Macmillan, Basingstoke, UK.

Grace, G. (2002). "Collateral damage from linguistics? The role of culture-centrism" *Ethnolinguistic Notes* 4 (3) (retrieved 9 June 2020 from http://www.ling.hawaii.edu/faculty/grace/elniv23.html).

Harris, R. (1987). *The Language Machine*. Cornell University Press, Ithaca, NY.

Harris, R. (1989). "How does writing restructure thought?" *Language and Communication* 9 (2), 399-406. http://dx.doi.org/10.1016/0271-5309(89)90012-8.

Harris, R. (2006). *Integrationist Notes and Papers 2003-2005*. Tree Tongue, Crediton, UK.

Harris, R. (2009). "Implicit and explicit language teaching" In: Toolan, M. (Ed.), *Language Teaching: Integrational Approaches*. Routledge, London, pp. 24-47.

Harris, R. (2010). *The Great Debate About Art*. Prickly Paradigm Press, Chicago.

Harris, R., Hutton, C., 2007. *Definition in Theory and Practice, Lexicography and the Law*. Continuum, London, UK.

Hartman, A.M. (1905). *English-Mashona Dictionary with More Phrases*. Juta Press, Cape Town.

Heller, M. (Ed.), 2007. *Bilingualism: A Social Approach*. Palgrave Macmillan, Basingstoke, UK.

Huffman, R. (1929). *Nuer-English Dictionary*. D. Reimer, Berlin.

Hutton, C. (2011). "The politics of the language myth: reflections on the writings of Roy Harris" *Language Sciences* 33, 503-510.

Irvine, J. (2008). "Subjected words: African linguistics and the colonial encounter" *Language and Communication* 28 (4), 323-343. http://dx.doi.org/10.1016/j.langcom.2008.02.001.

Irvine, J., Gal, S. (2000). "Language ideology and linguistic differentiation" In: Kroskity, P.V. (Ed.), *Regimes of Language Ideologies, Politics and Identities*. SAR, Santa Fe, NM, pp. 35-83.

Jacquemet, M. (2005). "Transidiomatic practices, language and power in the age of globalization" *Language and Communication* 25 (3), 257-277. http://dx.doi.org/10.1016/j.langcom.2005.05.001.

Jeater, D. (2007). *Law, Language and Science. The Invention of the 'Native Mind' in Southern Rhodesia*. Heinemann, Portsmouth, NH.

Joseph, J. (2006). *Language and Politics*. Edinburgh University Press, Edinburgh, UK.

Livingstone, D. (1858). *Analysis of the language of the Bechuans*. W.Hawes Press, London.

Louw, C.S. (1915). *A manual of the Chikaranga Language with Grammar, Exercises, Useful Conversational Sentences and Vocabulary*. Philpot & Collins, Bulawayo, Zimbabwe.

Makoni, S. (2011). "Sociolinguistics, colonial and postcolonial: an integrationist perspective. *Language Sciences* 33 (4), 680-688. http://dx.doi.org/10.1016/j.langsci.2011.04.020.

Makoni, S. (2012). "Language rights discourses: African experiences" *Journal of Multicultural Discourses* 1 (1), 1-20. http://dx.doi.org/10.1080/17447143.2011.595493.

Makoni, S., Brut-Griffler, J., Mashiri, P. (2007). "The use of 'indigenous' and urban vernaculars in Zimbabwe" *Language in Society* 36 (1), 25-49. http://dx.doi.org/10.1017/ S0047404507070029.

Makoni, S., Pennycook, A. (Eds.) (2007). *Disinventing and Reconstituting Languages.* Multilingual Matters, Clevedon, UK.

McGregor, A.W. (1905). *A Grammar of the Kikuyu Language.* Clay and Sons, London, UK.

McGregor, M. (1902). *First book in Zulu-Kaffir: An introduction to the study of Zulu-Kaffir.* Mesr Vause Slatter and Company, Pietermaritsburgh and Durban.

McLaughlin, F. (2008). "On the Origins of Urban Wolof: Evidence from Louis Decement's 1864 Phrase Book" *Language in Society* 37, 713-735.

Meeuwis, M. (2009). "Involvement in language: the role of the congregation Immaculati Cordis in the history of Lingala Mariae" *Catholic Historical Review* 95 (2), 240-260.

Milroy, L. (2002). "Investigating change and variation through dialect contact" *Journal of Sociolinguistics* 6 (1), 30-31.

Miner, E. (2003). 'The development of Nuer linguistics. Nuer field notes' <http://www.dlib.indiana.edu/cllections/nuer/edward ss/linguistics.html> (retrieved 9 June 2020).

Moreno, A. (1988). *A Nambya Dictionary.* Mambo Press, Gweru, Zimbabwe.

Mudimbe, M. (1988). *The Invention of Africa: Gnosis, Philosophy, and the Order of Knowledge*. Indiana University Press, Bloomington, IN.

Newmeyer, F. (2002). "Uniformitarian assumptions and language evolution research" In: Wray, Alison. (Ed.), *The Transition to Language*. Oxford University Press, Oxford, UK, pp. 359-375.

Pablé, A. (2010). "Language, knowledge and reality: The integrationist on name variation" *Language and Communication* 30 (2), 109-122.

Ranger, T. (1987). "The invention of tradition in colonial Africa" In: Hobsbawn, E., Ranger, T. (Eds.), *The Invention of Tradition*. Cambridge University Press, Cambridge, UK, pp. 211-262.

Sharkey, H. (2008). *American Evangelicals in Egypt: Missionary encounters in an Age of Empire*. Princetown University Press, Princeton.

Spear, T. (2003). "Neo-traditionalism and the limits of invention in British Colonial Africa" *Journal of African History* 44, 3-27. http://dx.doi.org/10.1017/S0021853702008320.

Springer, H. (1905). *A Hand-book of Chikaranga, or the Language of Mashonaland*. Methodist Episcopal Mission, Rhodesia.

Vandevort, Eleanor (n.d.) Field notes. [Digitized collection of manuscript notes] Viewed 9 June 2020 at: http://www.dlib.indiana.edu/collections/nuer/index.html

Wee, L. (2011). *Language without Rights*. Oxford University Press, Oxford, UK.

II

Sociolinguistics, Colonial And Postcolonial
An Integrationist Perspective

Abstract

In this article we explore and describe the emergence of languageness in order to evaluate the adequacy of an integrationist paradigm in explaining language experiences in colonial and postcolonial contexts. Integrationist linguistics addresses epistemological linguistic issues in western contexts; and its examples, *by and large*, are also drawn from the same contexts. In this article we explore its putative relevance to non-western colonial and postcolonial contexts. Using colonial linguistics as a framework for our description, we argue that pre-colonial communication systems and contemporary non-institutionalized systems (urban youth vernacular use, online language use) conform to a view of a language and communication as theorized within integrational linguistics. To a large extent, in pre-colonial Africa there was no sense of ethnic and language awareness as understood in western contexts. Theoretically, in integrationism, language and action are inextricably intertwined. This is in sharp contrast to the conceptualization of the same relationship in colonial and postcolonial contexts. In these contexts the relationship between language and action is strictly separate because speech is regarded as unreliable; hence the importance of inferring meaning and intentions, although how speech is regarded and how action is regarded are distinct, they mutually influence each other.

1. Prelude

Ironically, we appreciate the opportunity to contribute towards Roy Harris's festschrift, even though most of our work is in colonial and postcolonial Africa, an area which has not been of primary interest to integrationism. The opportunity enables us to reflect on the relevance of integrationism to colonial and postcolonial African sociolinguistics.

2. Introduction and rationale

This paper is an effort to situate integrationism within colonial and postcolonial contexts. It seeks to use an integrationist framework to enhance our understanding of the emergence of notions about language, grammar and lexicography, and electronic exchanges on Facebook. The objective of the analysis is to explore the relevance and descriptive adequacy of integrationism in contexts where either there is no concept of language or, if there is a concept of language, it is incompatible with its conceptualization in western linguistics.

3. Conceptualizing language in integrationism

Integrationism was introduced by Harris (1980, 1981, 1998, 2009). As a theory, it recognizes three parameters namely (i) biomechanical, (ii) macrosocial, and (iii) circumstantial. The first of these parameters relates to the mental as well as physical abilities of each of the individual participants. The macrosocial parameter is related to well established practices in the community or some group within the community. The third relates to the specific conditions that arise 'in a particular communication situation'.

Integrationist theory is critical of what it refers to as 'orthodox linguistics', which it describes as segregationist. In integrationism the notion of language in western linguistics is a 'myth' because it does not correspond to anything in

36

social reality, but is rather a consequence of viewing language through the semantics of 'reocentricism' (Harris, 2010). Integrationism as an approach to language study is anathema to views of language as 'a fixed code', 'a hermetically sealed unit' (Makoni, 1993) or 'things linguistic' (Nicolai, 2007). The proposition that language is a myth is founded on psychocentric and reocentric assumptions (Pablé, 2010). In a psychocentric perspective language can be described from a finite set of structures, which have external validity. Although the claim is that language is a myth, it has social and real consequences or 'collateral damage' (Makoni and Pennycook, 2007). In integrationism, language is inextricably embedded in contexts of use, and meanings are achieved through continuous and dynamic negotiations, a position which echoes views by other scholars whose work might be described in one form or another as reflective of integrationism, for example the work by such theorists as Bazerman (1985), Bakhtin (1986), Latour (1988), and Vygotsky (1978).

From an integrationist standpoint, segregationism makes a series of questionable distinctions. For instance, language is distinguished from context; linguistic knowledge from non-linguistic knowledge; content from language; language from language from users; language from action; learning language from life (Ellis, 2008); language use from language learning; internal from external aspects of language; syntax from semantics; and phonology from phonetics, which are 'convenient fictions of the classroom, intellectual hangovers from centuries during which western education was based on the copying and studying of approved texts' (Harris, 2010).

4. Segregational paradigm and the African experience
In African contexts, the segregationist account may have led to the 'birth' of African languages. In fact, Africa has been

described as a continent with a large number of languages. Yet, in the same breath Africa is viewed as a 'continent without language'; although 'Africans used languages in a linguistic sense to communicate with each other, there were no languages in the socio-linguistic sense' (Samarin, 1998). What Samarin underscores about pre-colonial Africa is indeterminacy in human linguistic behavior and the primacy of communication. Indeterminacy as a phenomenon is arguably central to integrationism. Central to Samarin's claim is that in pre-colonial Africa, the segregationist concept of language did not exist. The idea of language as understood in western scholarship in pre-colonial Africa is therefore a 'myth'. If the claim that 'in the beginning there were no languages' (Makoni, 1993) is correct, then the idea of language in African contexts is part of a process of invention, a process set in motion in colonial Africa.

The construction of African languages transformed the African 'landscape' to fit into European preconceived ideas about language and society (Samarin, 1984). European languages provided the analytical apparatus and the generative grid through which African grammars had to fit. This grid was based on the native languages of the colonizers. Thus, the 'singular frame and the exclusive grid neither capture nor contain the distinctive detail and divergent dynamics' (Dube, 2002, p. 811) of the communicational experiences of Africans. And it is from this process that the fabrication of African languages emanated. The resultant grammars and, ipso facto, African languages, are *'colonial imaginings'* (Dube, 2002, p. 811). It is these imaginings that form the basis of contemporary sociolinguistic theorizing. Their use and formal status in contemporary Africa is a legitimating exercise and becomes a quest to authenticate a fabrication.

The process of invention has been at two different levels. First, the speech forms used for communication acquired a name which, in practice, is an example of segregationist practice. Second, an ethnic identity based on language was then introduced. For example, in Southern Africa, speech forms used for communication in the area currently known as Kwa-Zulu Natal became Zulu; the speakers were assigned an ethnicity and were then referred to as Zulus. Yet prior to this the speech forms used for communication were simply referred to as isintu (human speak) and speakers were referred to as 'usuthu'. In this regard, what constitutes African languages is culturally and historically contingent and not natural, thus the limitations of a language in which biological metaphors are drawn from ecology; and while it is incontrovertible that maintaining ecological diversity is advantageous to humanity, a similar argument cannot uncritically be made in support of language diversity.

The notion of indigeneity in current use in sociolinguistic studies of Africa and other postcolonial contexts such as India masks the historical and socially constructed nature of languages (Makoni and Pennycook, 2007). It creates a pre-existing neatness or uniformity that did not exist. Similarly, constructs such as the standard 'language ideology' (Milroy, 2001), 'meta-discursive regimes' (Bauman and Briggs, 2003) and semiotic processes such as '*erasure*', '*fractal recursivity*' and '*iconicity*' (Irvine and Gal, 2000) create uniformity and constrain linguistic 'idiosyncrasy', engendering a view of languages as singular, specific and bounded.

Invention transformed dialogical and 'heteroglossic' material into monological texts (Blommaert, 2008). The invented texts were produced in a wide range of genres: grammatical outlines, grammatical sketches, word lists, orthographies and dictionaries. In these genres, human linguistic behavior was de-contextualized in order to allow for isolable entities that could be described and explained (Harris, 1998). All these genres create and fix invariant and

39

context-free meanings and therefore distort the nature of human linguistic behavior. The concept of African languages therefore 'emerged' through an application of a number of strategies, which ultimately 'fixed' African languages in specific ways. 'Fixing' refers to the 'extraction' of form from fluid language practices and assigning meaning to them. This process is based on a bifurcation of form and meaning, and the creation of a stable relationship between the two, downplaying the fluidity and indeterminacy of language. Yet in reality multiple meanings of single forms, heteroglossic, fluid, and fuzzy language practices (Bakhtin, 1986; Heller, 2007) constitute the norm. The attribution of form and uniform linguistic structures to fluid semiotic practices (Irvine, 2008) creates a mythical uniformity. Yet, on the other hand, this made it possible to 'fix' languages by situating them in space and time thus generating all practices considered as instantiations of a particular language. In this regard, African languages are a discursive act, a product of complex discursive features reminiscent of Butler's (1993) 'perfomativity' or what Thorne and Lantolf (2007) refer to as Linguistics of Communicative Activity.

The data that formed the basis of the construction of African languages was collected from a diverse range of sources. First, the ideal data was elicited from the 'natives themselves, especially from those who have not yet learned to adapt their speech to European idiom and ways of thought' (Louw, 1915, p. iv). The assumption was that natives who had not been influenced by colonialists were 'authentic, an essentialization of a complex process'. Authenticity meant 'untouched' or 'untainted' by colonialism, and 'true' African languages could be elicited from those untouched by colonialism. The state of being 'untouched' or 'untainted' by social processes even obliquely is unlikely, because the intercultural exchange which formed the basis of the data collection had an impact on both parties, that is the colonialists and the 'natives'. The search for an 'uncorrupted' language user who could act as a source of language may have been motivated by a positivistic philosophy of linguistic facts. The search for an ideal source of speech is complicated because it is not clear which is the language of a native speaker, because in urban contexts, and in online communication, rarely is any speech restricted to a single language. For instance, in a Facebook communication between two sisters, one asks the other what the sister is saying because she uses signs that are unfamiliar to her and seems to be constructing her own idiolect:

> Young sister: algunas personas son las sacudidas..
> sacudidas !!!!!!!!!!!!
> Big sister: keing? wat ol dis meme

Research into urban vernaculars has always been haunted by the problem of determining who were the ideal informants necessary in constructing a language, and conversely whether it was necessary to determine the language in order to determine who could serve as an 'ideal speaker', or be a legitimate speaker of 'the language'. 'Nativeness' is rendered even harder in heteroglossic contexts because "the consensus principle ... begs ... two crucial questions. It begs the question of how to determine the population of 'native speakers', and it also begs the question of how to identify 'the language'." (Harris, 2010, p. 43).

Even when the 'ideal' speakers of African languages were identified, the ontology of African languages was complicated because what may be defined as appropriate linguistic features and their meanings varies depending on the nature of each intersubjective interaction. This suggests that the linguistic features are negotiated anew and thus are not independent of an interaction, because words and meanings are 'spontaneous creations of the mind, which function as tools for the contextualization of those activities in which you are engaged' (Harris, 2010, p. 176).

Second, there was no systematic interpretive matrix used to assign social meaning to language. Throughout the colonial period, Africans played a secondary role in the framing of their languages because all the material written about them, that is, grammars, hymns, sermons and catechisms, were all written by non-users of African languages, with the exception of some few languages. This practice introduced what Mannheim (1991), following Becker (1982), refers to as 'exuberance'. Mannheim distinguishes 'exuberance' from 'deficiency'. In Mannheim's account 'exuberance' involves adding linguistic properties, which are absent from the 'original' speech forms; whereas deficiency, on the other hand, refers to 'omitting features associated with the speech practices of the original language practices' (Mannheim, 1991, p. 128; see also controversies in Arabic linguistics, Alhaawary, 2003; Suleiman, 2004). The 'exuberance' or 'deficiency' can also be accounted for by the fact that the grammarians relied heavily at times if not exclusively on memory to record the data.

To overcome the putative limitations of the 'native' as a reliable source of data, some missionaries opted to collect data by immersing themselves in African communities. Texts were elicited from a wide range of sources. Popular texts consisted of conversations among the 'natives', and songs as well as performances by *izinyanga* (quasi-priests in any one of the Nguni languages), songs in praise of *abathakathi* (witches in Zulu) and other narratives such as *ngano* (folktales in Shona). Meanings in these text types were fluid and constantly negotiated but were presented in the resultant grammar books as 'fixed', with discernible meaning: a bifurcation which has been central to western linguistics from its early days (Harris, 2010, p. 13).

If it is incontrovertible that the analytical template and 'roots' of some indigenous languages rest in western colonial enterprises, the situation is more complicated in Arab-speaking Africa because of the conflicting ideological positions and different orientations of, for example, southern Africa vis-à-vis Arab-speaking Africa. Suleiman (1999), for instance, points out that a linguistic awareness of the role of vowels and consonants which is tied to grammar is a product of a foreign model of analysis (Goldziher, 1994, p. 6). For Suleiman (1999), Arabic grammatical traditions are descriptively weak because they could not successfully account for indeterminacy, the distinction between oral and written and the adequacy of an orthographic system. Yet an integrationist does not view this as a weakness. In fact, from the viewpoint of integrationist theory this is how communication systems operate.

5. Labeling codes and the surrogationalist problem in African languages

One of the major ways in which naming is carried out is reocentricism, which is a form of surrogationalism. In reocentricism the assumption is that the referent has an external existence, and that there is a stable relationship between a name and its referent. An integrationist approach is based on the assumption that the relationship between a name and its referent is unstable or indeterminate. The naming of languages draws upon a surrogational perspective on naming. The counting of languages and the attribution of a number of speakers to a language assumes that the relationship between a name and its referent is stable and consistent. An example of a reocentric approach to language is the *Ethnologue*. Naming of languages masks the possibilities of variation in naming in that people may have different understandings of the referent. For example what one person may understand

and construe as English, Swahili and French may differ between people (Pablé, 2010).

Irrespective of the limitations of reocentricism, naming is part of a discourse of '*othering*'. Naming languages began with foreigners literate in Arabic and European languages; traders, explorers, and colonizers wanted to know the people they were dealing with. Because the names of languages were assigned by outsiders, these names did not necessarily correspond with how the speakers might have referred to the language they spoke, or more importantly, how they experienced themselves socio-communicatively.

Nonetheless, labeling or naming of these 'objects', which are now called 'languages', had sociolinguistic consequences because of their ethno-linguistic significance (Irvine 2008). Yet the act of naming was critically important because it made it possible to manage languages as objects of promotion, planning and maintenance. The naming of languages not only created a new category of identity but also complexities with regard to African identities. For instance 'if you speak Zulu, ergo you are Zulu' (Blommaert, 2008). The naming of languages produced puzzling questions such as 'What languages do you speak?', as opposed to the typical African language question 'do you speak?'[1] which on its own suggests that names of languages are not part of the lexicon of speakers of these languages. This indicates that language among lowly literate Africans is conceptualized without necessarily positing the existence of languages as spatially or ethnically bounded entities, or without cutting lang-

---

[1] In most African languages in Southern Africa, in a communication encounter, if one of the interlocutors determines that the other does not understand what was said, the question 'what language do you speak?' is never asked. Instead, the question asked is: uyakhuluma (Zulu/Ndebele), uyathetha (Xhosa), wabua (Tswana), uyabulala (Shangani), etc. all of which mean 'do you speak?' in what segrationists would describe as different languages.

uage up into different languages (cf. Canut, 2002) or constituent parts such as verbs, nouns, etc. It is for this reason that Rampton (2001) describes this as a conceptualization of language that works without a notion of a community or with relatively low group cohesivness (Brubacker, 2005).

In realizing the limitations of the 'discrete code' conceptualization of language, some researchers have suggested the notion of hybridization in reference to language practices in complex plurilingual contexts. However, the notion of hybridization does not resolve the problematic of a coded, discrete entity, because it is predicated on an assumption that there exist two distinct codes or separate entities which are combined.

6. Pluralization of singularity and singularization of plurality

Expositions about language are further complicated because there is no semantic equivalent of the term language in African languages as in other traditional societies, such as among Australian Aborigines (Goddard, 2011). In Nguni languages, the equivalent of language is human speak (*isintu*) or human language (*chivanhu*) in Shona (one of Zimbabwe's official languages). The term language may be used to refer to ways of speaking, perhaps equivalent to register, style, etc.

The notion of language in African societies is further complicated because the 'concept language' is construed differently depending upon local contexts. For example unlike in segregationist linguistics, in Africa it is difficult to make objective statements about language across historical and social spaces. In integrationism, it is not necessary to identify 'universal' criteria for defining languages, dialects, etc. For example the word 'languages' in Cameroon refers to French and English, i.e. abstract entities which have currency in university language departments and academic papers, not what primary schoolteachers call 'patois' or 'dialect'.

Since Africans cannot be separated from their lineage, naming one's language is not an objective act but a set of communicative resources which are intricately interwoven with individual and social identities. From such a perspective it is not necessary to construe language and identity as separate entities, since they are closely interwoven.

Western-academic discourse conceptualizes local languages in a plural form, as the sum of a number of distinct languages, i.e. it engages in a pluralization of singularity. In a pluralization of singularity languages are enumerable, separable and nameable entities. The *Ethnologue* is an example par excellence of such an approach in which languages can be enumerated. On the other hand, exponents of a local discourse on language in education conceptualize local languages in a generic form to refer to the whole communicative-linguistic practices and manners of 'black people' – a form of singularization of plurality. Traditional approaches to language are more comparable to integrationist approaches to language than western discourses about language in Africa.

The idea of language as a code has also been challenged by anthropological research. Anthropological research frames language in terms of resources, events and behavior (Gumperz and Hymes, 1986; Kroskrity, 2000; Bauman and Briggs, 2003). The idea of language as resources or ensembles in which the individual voices of speakers are articulated partially echoes integrationist approaches to language, particularly the idea of a combination of diverse linguistic features. The idea of linguistic resources has implications on distinctions between monolingualism and bilingualism, or indeed multilingualism. It may not always be necessary to draw such distinctions if a shift is made from a code-based African linguistics to a speaker-oriented integrationist framework.

Similarly, linguistic languaging has been proposed to resolve conceptual problems that are a consequence of viewing language as a code (Mignolo, 1996; Joseph, 2006; García, 2007; Jorgensen and Quist, 2008; Møller, 2008; Creese and Blackledge, 2010; van Camp and Juffermans, 2010; Juffermans 2011). Linguistic languaging or its expanded version, translanguaging, cannot resolve the limitations of the idea of language as a myth, a code, because both linguistic languaging and the idea of a code are caught up in the same paradigm from which they seek to escape. The problems inherent in language as a noun cannot be resolved by conceptualizing it as a verb, because neither question the assumption that language is a valid epistemological unit.

In languaging, (according to Mignolo), language is an object that is a product of converting a complex process into an external object called language that has a grammar and vocabulary, and can be regulated and owned and used as an instrument to control the population. From the sociopolitical perspective of languaging not all societies have a language but they will always be languaging. Languaging precedes language. There cannot be language without languaging. The converse is plausible; there can be languaging without necessarily there being language.

7. Lexicography and integrationism in Africa: In the beginning there were no words

Naming languages made it possible for lexicographers to compile dictionaries, translate Bibles and develop teaching materials, etc. In other words, naming languages led to an ideology that produces 'grammars-as-text'. The dictionaries typically had substantial sections outlining grammatical aspects of African languages; semantic, syntactic, phonological information as part of a definition of the word, etc. The

47

dictionaries are based on an ideology which magnifies the discreteness of the constituent parts such as the lexicon, grammatical and semantic knowledge which is inconsistent with an integrationist framework.

> From an integrationist stance to know what a 'word' means and how it relates to reality is to know what to do with it in very concrete situations, which is why language and action are not two separable domains; doing something with language is not just confined to 'reformative acts' as understood in speech-act theory (Pablé, 2010, p. 111).

The philosophical underpinnings of lexicography are as follows:

(i) There is an entity called language.
(ii) Language is made up of words and words have meanings that are largely fixed.
(iii) Words may have identical semantic equivalents across different languages, hence the validity of bilingual dictionaries

Driven by an ideology that sought to reduce uncertainty and indeterminacy in communication, the writing of grammars and dictionaries was part of a process of determining explicitness, running contrary to indeterminacy in communication and ambiguity and uncertainty, all of which are central to communication. Integrationism, therefore, poses a serious challenge to the lexicographical enterprise because in an integrationist framework, meanings of words are therefore realized through context of use; a point underscored in the integrationist paradigm (see also Vygotsky, 1978; Bakhtin, 1986). Meanings of words are indeterminate and individuals can initiate changes and create their own idiosyncratic meanings. Take for instance a group of South African township youth who were asked about how they understood new words introduced in speech; one of them responded as follows:

X: ...*a language that is always changing, progressing I cannot daai ding. Its daai ding my friend. I can come up with my own perceptions of what daai ding means for me.*
Y: *We create words all the time. There is a term that started me don't know from where but I caught on it, the more people I met the more people I use ... one is contra bouras. When you say contra boras you mean someone has a good backside.*

Because of the flexibility of the meanings of the words, fixing their 'meanings' through dictionaries greatly reduces the variability and complexity of their meanings and does not take into account the indeterminacy evident in everyday communication. Examples from the Aycard (2009) study show spontaneous use and meaning making indicating that '...to know what a word means and how it relates to reality is to know what to do with it in very concrete situations' (Pablé, 2010, p. 111). It is the context that determines meaning, whereas dictionaries give the impression that the meaning of a word is fixed. Accepting that indeterminacy is central to communication also creates an epistemological tension in linguistics, as one of the fundamental objectives of linguistics is to describe languages with the view of establishing systematicity. Harris proposes that a way of resolving the tension between compiling dictionaries while still retaining indeterminacy is to construe the meanings of words in dictionaries as institutionalized, which is in sharp contrast to their fluxity in everyday usage.

This institutionalization of the meanings of words is also evident in bilingual dictionaries. Bilingual dictionaries and indeed monolingual dictionaries are founded on the assumption that different language users perceive the boundaries between languages in an identical way, and the relationship is stable.

Facebook communication also demonstrates variability in the presentation of words, and what we understand by words as the following examples from Facebook communication aptly demonstrates:

AA: i h8 u.i rili h8 u.y do u mek me unhapi?u let t go on 4 a yr n a half so y u concrnd ryt nw.z t coz i..or dat u jus wana get on my nervs?congrats u did t.i wont b tokn 2 u 4 i dnt noe hw long.u r gon deal with t.i dnt nid ur apology evn tho wat said z true.ts nt ur lyf so y e f/// bthr?wer u dat perfct nywae..1 dae am ...gon ask u dat n u gon b spichles n u gon noe wat t filz lyk.

XX: Calm down baby grl ♥ u got remember carry on smile cuz theres always som1 checkin u out =) dnt let them c u down they aint worth it tell erm lynn sed bug of leave ma bestmate alone.

Some of the spellings are extremely variable; for example the same individual spells girl in three different ways: grl, gal, gl. The deviance in spelling and word representation may be interpreted as a marker of social rebellion and assertion of independence. A majority of the individuals who produce the deviant spelling are college educated thus it can be assumed that they have an idea of what constitutes orthodox spelling.

8. Bilingualism and the discrete codes

The idea of a language as a discrete code or what Cummins (2007) refers to as 'solitudes' is central to sociolinguistics theorizing, as evident in concepts such as code-switching, code-mixing, bilingualism and multilingualism, all of which are predicated on distinctions or boundaries (solitudes) between languages. In fact, the idea of bilingualism or multilingualism as a series of sequential entities renders it intellectually feasible to refer to distinctions between first and second, or third languages, and indeed the idea of a native speaker. For instance, the centrality of linguistic solitudes suggests that bilingual language learning is a linear process with monolingual norms as a target (García and Sylvan, 2011). An alternative view to an autonomous based multilingualism is proposed by García, who frames multilingualism as dynamic linguistic practices which are related in complex but interrelated ways; language learning is not linear and cannot be distinguished from language use. The non-linear and dynamic model that García is articulating is effectively captured in metaphors of a bicycle and monocycle. Dynamic bilingualism cannot produce either the balanced wheels of two bicycles (as in additive bilingualism) or in a monocycle (as in subtractive bilingualism), but instead bilingualism as framed by García can be construed as an 'all-terrain vehicle with individuals using it to adapt to both the ridges and craters of communication in uneven terrains'. This view is more akin to integrationist perspectives to communication in which individuals create and develop the necessary resources to serve their linguistic interests.

9. Communication and the integrationist framework
Integrationism has a more complex orientation to communication. In integrationism, for communication to take place speakers draw on and exploit a wide range of linguistic features and semiotic systems. During communication, ungrammaticality is of no consequence because 'breaking rules and making up new ones is what people really do when people are interacting' (Walt Whitman cited in Johnstone, 1999, p. 313). After all, language is integrated and cannot be separat-

ed from other semiotic systems in which verbal and semiotic repertoires and life histories are intimately tied together. Data from Facebook communication shows the integration of language and visuals because each linguistic entry is accompanied by a photograph, ostensibly of the author, as the following examples (see Fig. 1) show.

Fig. 1.

In some cases the visuals may be altered but the linguistic text is not as a rule changed.

The photograph (Fig. 1) above is an excellent example of transmodality integration. In the photograph from Facebook communication the sandals and feet of the young lady are commented upon negatively reinforced by the word 'fail' in capital letters and 'not ayobaness' (meaning not good).

Another characteristic feature of integrationism apparent in Facebook communication is consistent with what Harris (2010) refers to as 'temporal integration' in which the text is dated and the reactions dated.

RM: I h8 hm,I h8,I h8 my maths teachr ..curse u mr. . .who z suprtn.
(I hate him, I hate him, my maths teacher, curse you who is supporting you ?) literal translation.
July 30 at 2:25am via Mobile Web. View feedback (4) Hide Feedback (4).
TC who lyks hm anyways opr evn listns 2 hm.No wonder pple wnt mr. thn hm.
July 30 at 2:47 pm 1.personal loading.

In Facebook communication context is a complicated process that includes not only the technological environment created by technology but minute details such as when the text was produced, how it was transmitted and the nature of the responses, some of which may be hidden and others open to everybody. Facebook communication provides empirical support to Harris's (2010) sophisticated understanding of context.

An integrationist approach based on the tenet of consillience allows us to conceptualize an integrationist speaker, one who is able to use different communicative abilities, different techniques (Pablé, 2010). The notion of an integrationist speaker may rectify some of the problems which limit the validity of constructs such as the ideal speaker or mother tongue, because it draws attention to what an individual does in a holistic way' in a social space. Integrated speakers combine semiotic systems in many ways. Even though no two or more individuals combine semiotic systems in the same way (Johnstone, 1996) this does not necessarily invariably result in miscommunication, if there is a mutual recognition of the

53

participants' diverse linguistic resources, even though incongruent frames of reference (epistemes, intertextuality and evocative potential) are in conflict. Communication is still feasible because 'human communication does not operate on the basis of certainties of this order' (Harris, 2010, p. 52).

The integrationist communication model is suitable to colonial and postcolonial contexts because miscommunication takes place when plurilingual speakers with heterographic and dynamic backgrounds encounter monolingual speakers with normative communication skills with different and conflicting sociolinguistic frames of reference. However, even though each interaction is new it is not produced de novo. The production depends, to a large extent, on previous communicational experiences, drawing on a 'lingua memory' (Becker, 1977) that is unique to each individual. This explains why 'Linguists of all persuasions acknowledge on the basis of their everyday experience of language, that no two individuals talk alike' (Johnstone, 1996, p. 185). Each individual's experience is unique, hence for communication to take place there has to be some overlap between them. The overlap may be broader and more dense between some individuals than others. Individual experience may lead us to situate systematicity more in an individual than in groups, because of the diversity and heterogeneity of groups. This is not to deny the existence of sytematicity of one degree or another within and across a group.

Even though the idea of an individual speaker is a welcome turn to a more speaker-based linguistics, the speaker has to be embedded in a sophisticated context. Facebook processes of forming 'friends' shows how such networks are formed and are always emergent because new Facebook friends may be added and other people 'defriended' (removed from the list of Facebook friends); thus the networks are always evolving and emergent as the following example illustrates:

SM is now friends with Lu Sajo Mwaip and 2 other people AB and WM.

The issue therefore from a Facebook communicational perspective is not only whether one is a native or not but where in the network one is situated relative to other people. Facebook is an excellent example of a tangled web of connections. Within the connections, there are groups who are more tightly connected to each other than they are to other groups.

10. Concluding reflections
In this article we have attempted to view African colonial linguistic projects and Facebook communication in post-colonial Africa from an integrationist perspective. We have argued that integrationism may be relevant to an analysis of pre-colonial African communication systems and some Facebook communication. Within Facebook communication we have demonstrated that there are more than two types of integration, temporal and transmodal.

Integrationism provides us with opportunities to view language planning, language maintenance, and indeed language rights from different perspectives. Indeed integrationism challenges us to reconceptualize such constructs because if language is a myth, then what is being planned, in language planning? If language is a myth, then it is difficult to seriously retain the notion of linguistic rights because this would be ascribing rights to mythical phenomena.

References
Alhawary, M. (2003). "Elicitation techniques and considerations in data collection in early Arabic grammatical tradition" *Journal of Arabic Linguistic Tradition* 1, 1-24.
Aycard, P. (2009). *Speak As You Want: Just Be Free. A*

Linguistic-Anthropological Monograph of
Iscamatho-Speaking Youth. University of Leiden,
Leiden.

Bakhtin, M. (1986). *Speech Genres and Other Late Essays.*
University of Texas Press, Austin, Texas.

Bauman, R., Briggs, C. (2003). *Voices Of Modernity:*
Language Ideologies and the Politics of Inequality.
Cambridge University Press, Cambridge.

Bazerman, C., 1985. "Physicists reading physics: schema-
laden purposes and purpose-laden schema" *Written*
Communication 2, 3-23.

Becker, A.L. (1982). "The poetics and noetics of a Javanese
poem" In: Tannen, D. (Ed.), *Spoken and Written*
Language. Ablex, Norwood, pp. 217-238.

Blommaert, J. (2008). "Artefactual ideologies and the
textual production of African languages" *Language*
and Communication 28 (4), 291-307.

Brubacker, R. (2005). "The 'diaspora' diaspora" *Ethnic and*
Racial Studies 28 (1), 1-19.

Butler, J. (1993). *Bodies that Matter: On the Discursive*
Limits of 'Sex'. Routledge, London.

Canut, C. (2002). "Perceptions of languages in the Mandingo region of Mali: Where does one language begin
and the other end?" In: Long, D., Preston, D. (Eds.),
Handbook of Perceptual Dialectology. John
Benjamins, Philadelphia, pp. 31-41.

Creese, A., Blackledge, A. (2010). "Translanguaging in the
bilingual classroom: pedagogy of learning and
teaching" *Modern Language Journal* 94, 103-115.

Cummins, J. (2007)." Rethinking monolingual instructional
strategies in multilingual classrooms" *Canadian*
Journal of Applied Linguistics 10 (2), 221-238.

Dube, S. (2002). "Conversion and translation: colonial
registers of a vernacular christianity" *South Atlantic*
Quarterly 101 (4), 807-837.

Ellis, N. (2008). "The dynamics of language use, language change, and first and second language acquisition" *Modern Language Journal* 41 (3), 232-248.

García, O. (2007). *Bilingual Education: An introductory Reader.* Routledge, London and New York.

García, O. and Sylvan, C. (2011). "Pedagogies and practices in multilingual classrooms: Singularities in Pluralities" *Modern Language Journal* 95(iii), 385-400.

Goddard, C. (2011). "The lexical semantics of language (with special reference to words)" *Language Sciences* 33 (1), 43-57.

Goldziher, I. (1994). *On the History of Grammar Among the Arabs: An Essay in Literary History.* John Benjamin, Amsterdam.

Harris, R. (1980). *The Language-Makers.* Duckworth, London.

Harris, R. (1981). *The Language Myth.* Duckworth, London.

Harris, R. (1998). *Introduction to Integrationist Linguistics.* Pergamon, Oxford.

Harris, R. (2009). *Rationality and the Literate Mind.* Routledge, New York.

Harris, R. (2010). *After Epistemology.* Bright Pen, Gamlingay.

Heller, M. (Ed.) (2007). *Bilingualism: A Social Approach.* Palgrave Macmillan, Basingstoke.

Irvine, J. (2008). "Subjected words: African linguistics and the colonial encounter" *Language and Communication* 28 (4), 323-343.

Johnstone, B. (1996). *The Linguistic Individual: Self Expression in Language and Linguistics.* Oxford University Press, Oxford.

Johnstone, B. (1999). "Lingual biography and linguistic variation" *Language Sciences* 21, 313-321.

Jorgensen, N., Quist, P. (2008). "Bilingual children in

monolingual schools" In: Auer, P., Wei, L. (Eds.), *Handbook of Multilingualism and Multilingual Communication*. Mouton de Gruyter, Berlin and New York, pp. 155-174.

Joseph, J. (2006). *Language and Politics*. Edinburgh University Press, Edinburgh.

Juffermans, K. (2011). "The old man and the letter: Repertoires of literacy and languaging in a modern multiethnic Gambian village" *Compare: a Journal of Comparative and International Education*. 41(2), pp.165-179.

Kroskrity, P.V. (Ed.) (2000). *Regimes of Language: Ideologies. Politics and Identity*. School of American Research, Santa Fe, NM.

Latour, B. (1988). *The Pasteurization of France*. Harvard University Press, Cambridge, MA.

Louw, C.S. (1915). *A Manual of the Chikaranga Language with Grammar, Exercises, Useful Conversational Sentences and Vocabulary*. Philpot & Collins, Bulawayo.

Makoni, S. (1993). "The futility of being held captive by language policy" *Per Linguam* 9 (1), 1-2.

Makoni, S., Pennycook, A. (Eds.) (2007). *Disinventing and Reconstituting Languages*. Multilingual Matters, Buffalo, NY/Toronto/Clevedon.

Mannheim, B. (1991). *The Language of the Inka since the European Invasion*. University of Texas, Austin, Texas.

Mignolo, W.D. (1996). "Linguistic maps, literary geographies, and cultural landscapes: languages, languaging, and (trans)nationalism" *Modern Language Quarterly* 57, 181-196.

Milroy, J. (2001). "Language ideology and the consequences of standardization" *Journal of Sociolinguistics* 5 (4), 530-555.

Nicolai, R. (2007). "Language contact: a blind spot in 'things linguistic'" *Journal of Language Contact* 1, 1-11.

Pablé, A. (2010). "Language, knowledge and reality; the integrationist and name variation" *Language and Communication* 30, 109-122.

Rampton, B. (2001). "Ethnicity and the crossing of ethnic boundaries" In: Mesthrie, R., Asher, R. (Eds.), *Concise Encyclopedia of Sociolinguistics*. Elsevier Science, Oxford.

Samarin, W.J. (1984). "The linguistic world of field colonialism" *Language in Society* 13, 435-453.

Suleiman, Y. (1999). *The Arabic Grammatical Tradition: A Study in Ta'lil*. Edinburgh University Press, Edinburgh.

Thorne, S., Lantolf, J. (2007). "A linguistics of communicative activity" In: Makoni, S., Pennycook, A. (Eds.), *Disinventing and Reconstituting Languages*. Multilingual Matters, Buffalo, NY/Clevedon, pp. 170-196.

van Camp, K., Juffermans, K. (2010). "Postcolonial ideologies of language in education: voices from below on English and local language(s) in The Gambia" In: du Plessis, T., Webb, V., Cuvelier, P., Meeuwis, M., Vandekerckhove, R. (Eds.), *Multilingualism from Below*. Van Schaik, Pretoria, pp. 1-20.

Vygotsky, L. (1978). *Mind in Society*. Harvard University Press, Cambridge, MA.

Further reading

Anderson, B. (1983). *Imagined Communities: Reflections on the Origin and Spread of Nationalism*. Verso, London.

Brumfit, C. (2001). *Individual Freedom in Language Teaching*. Oxford University Press, Oxford.

Del Valle, J. (2009). "Total Spanish: the politics of a Pan-Hispanic grammar" *PMLA* 124 (3), 880-886.

Errington, J. (2008). *Linguistics in a Colonial World: A Story of Language, Meaning, and Power*. Wiley-Blackwell, Malden, MA.

Fabian, J. (1986). *Language and Colonial Power: The Appropriation of Swahili in the Former Congo 1880-1938*. Cambridge University Press, Cambridge.

Gilmour, R. (2006). *Grammars of Colonialism: Representing Languages in Colonial South Africa*. Palgrave Macmillan, Basingstoke.

Hill, J.H. (2002). "'Expert Rhetorics' in advocacy for endangered languages: who is listening, and what do they hear?" *Journal of Linguistic Anthropology* 12, 119-133.

Hillelson, S. (1935). *Sudan Arabic Texts*. Cambridge University Press, Cambridge.

Hopper, P. (1998). "Emergent grammar" In: Tomasallo, M. (Ed.), *The New Psychology of Language*. Lawrence Erlbaum, Mahwah, NJ.

Hymes, D. (1974). *Foundations of Sociolinguistics: An Ethnographical Approach*. University of Pennsylvania Press, Pennsylvania, PA.

Jacquemet, M. (2005). "Transidiomatic practices, language and power in the age of globalization" *Language and Communication* 25, 257-277.

Jeater, D. (2007). *Law, Language and Science: The Invention of the 'native mind' in Southern Rhodesia*. Heinemann, Portsmouth.

Juffermans, K. (2010). *Local languaging: literacy products and practices in Gambian society*. PhD thesis, Language and Culture Studies, Tilburg University.

Khubchandani, L. (1997). *Revisualizing Boundaries: A Plurilingual Ethos*. Sage Publications, New Delhi/Thousand Oaks, CA/London.

60

Makoni, S. (2003). "From misinvention to disinvention of language: multilingualism and the South African Constitution" In: Makoni, S. et al. (Eds.), *Black Linguistics: Language, Society, and Politics in Africa and the Americas*. Routledge, London and New York.

Makoni, S., Smitherman, G., Ball, A., Spears, A. (Eds.) (2003). *Black Linguistics: Language. society, and politics in Africa and the Americas*. Routledge, London and New York.

Makoni, S., Brut-Griffler, J., Mashiri, P. (2007). "The use of 'indigenous' and urban vernaculars in Zimbabwe" *Language in Society* 36, 25-49.

Maturana, H., Varela, F. (1987). *Tree of Knowledge*. Shambhala, Boston, MA and London.

Moller, J.S. (2008). "Polylingual performance among Turkish-Danes in late-modern Copenhagen" *International Journal of Mulitlingualism* 5 (3), 217-236.

Mudimbe, V.Y. (1988). *The Invention of Africa: Gnosis Philosophy and the Order of Knowledge*. Indiana University Press, Bloomington, IN.

Pennycook, A. (2006). "Postmodernism in language policy" In: Ricento, T. (Ed.), *An Introduction to Language Policy: Theory and method*. Blackwell, Malden, MA, pp. 60-74.

Pennycook, A. (2007). *Global Englishes and Transcultural Flows*. Routledge, London.

Peterson, D. (2004). *Creative Writing: Translation, Book-keeping, and the Work of Imagination in Colonial Kenya*. Heinemann, Portsmouth, NH.

Ranger, T. (1987). "The invention of tradition in colonial Africa" In: Hobsbawn, E., Ranger, T. (Eds.), *The Invention of Tradition*. Cambridge University Press, Cambridge, pp. 211-262.

Reddy, M.J. (1979). "The conduit metaphor: a case of frame conflict in our language about language" In: Ortony, A. (Ed.), *Metaphor and Thought.* Cambridge University Press, Cambridge, pp. 284-297.

Robbins, J. (2010). "God is nothing but talk: modernity, language, and prayer in a Papua New Guinea society" *American Anthropologist* 103 (4), 901-912.

Sharkey, H. (2007). "Arab identity and ideology in Sudan: the politics of language, ethnicity, and race" *African Affairs* 107, 21-43.

Spear, T. (2003). "Neo-traditionalism and the limits of invention in British Colonial Kenya Africa" *Journal of African History* 44, 3-27.

Springer, H. (1905). *A Hand-book of Chikaranga, or, the Language of Mashonaland.* Methodist Episcopal Mission, Rhodesia.

III

A Critique Of Language, Languaging And Supervernacular

Abstract: *In an attempt to overcome the structuralist mind set regarding language, a growing body of literature accepts that language does not break down neatly into autonomous, clearly-defined languages. This observation, which is increasingly becoming a mantra of sociolinguistics, is not new at all, despite claims to the contrary. Chomsky (1986) and Davidson (1986) were quite skeptical of the existence of languages. The mythical status of language is concealed by the fact that we have names for languages.*

In an attempt to overcome the structuralist mindset regarding language, a growing body of literature accepts that language does not break down neatly into autonomous, clearly-defined languages. This observation, which is increasingly becoming a mantra of sociolinguistics, is not new at all, despite claims to the contrary. Noam Chomsky (1986) in *Knowledge of Language* and Donald Davidson (1986) in an aptly titled chapter 'A Nice Derangement of Epitaphs' were quite skeptical of the existence of languages. The mythical status of language is concealed by the fact that we have names for languages. Hausa, Arabic, Wolof, Berber, and Tarjumo are some language names that form the basis of linguistic description in this book.

Two main observations need to be made. First, in the sociolinguistic literature, each language is attributed a single name (e.g., English, Chinese, etc.). Rarely do languages cited in the literature have more than one name. Reviewers and editors often compel authors for the sake of clarity to use a single name. Ethnologue keeps a list of alternative names, but also chooses one name among many other alternatives. (Obviously, the use of a single name overlooks situations in which many different names are used to refer to a single language, and many languages are named using a single name).

In a manner which is consistent with a sociolinguistic reality, many different names are used to refer to the same lang-uage. The idea of one language, one name, is pervasive in Western monolingual oriented linguistic metalanguage and makes it difficult to capture the sharp ideological positions that are possible in the use of multiple names for the 'same' language, as the Berber/Amazigh example shows. These names are not interchangeable. The use of the name Berber is an endorsement of official state ideologies, while Amazigh is part of the political apparatus associated with rebel movements.

Second, the controversy about whether languages have names or not is only significant insofar as it is assumed that there exists something called *language*. Languages are not natural objects. Rather,

> A 'language'... is a metalinguistic extrapolation that has become attached to a particular language name, it does not matter whether the name is *English, French,* or whatever. It does not even matter whether it has an army or navy. But there has to be a name. No name; no language. That is the higher order metamyth ... (Harris 2009: 41-42)

Integrationists such as Harris (2009) drew attention to a philosophical approach to handling the claim that language does not break down into neat bounded units when he suggested that first order categories do not neatly break into second order categories. *First order* refers to here and now activities, ongoing communicational activity, or contextually meaningful behavior; it is situated in real time and real space and unfolds in unplanned ways. *Second order* refers to meta-linguistic categories that include names of languages, societies, communities, etc. Using these terms indicates that first order categories cannot neatly break down into second order categories. Communication does not neatly break into languages.

The idea that language does not break down into neat categories also has radical implications for the nature of analysis because language does not present itself for study as a neatly disengaged range of homogeneous phenomena, patiently awaiting description by an impartial observer, as suggested by the misleading expression 'linguistic data'. On the contrary, language offers a paradigm case of interference by investigation. A relatively large number of scholars have addressed this issue and the notion of *languaging* (Swain 2006, 2009, 2010; García 2007, 2009; Creese and Blackledge 2010; Jaquemet 2005; Maturana and Varela 1998; Becker 1993, 2006; Khubchandani 1997; Ramanathan 2009).

Swain and Lantolf, with their focus on second language acquisition, construed *languaging* as a tool to mediate cognition, an activity, a form of producing a visible and audible product. From this perspective, languaging is everything. Swain and Lantolf adopt a totalistic interpretation of languaging, leaving very little room for ways of framing alternatives. Languaging in Swain and Lantolf's orientation is too powerful, making it weak as an explanatory construct.

Garcia (2007, 2009), Creese and Blackledge (2010), Moller (2008), Jacquemet (2005), and Shohamy (1999) construed languaging as a social semiotic process that is

65

different from code-switching. The critical issue for Creese and Blackledge (2010) and García is that languaging and its other variants, translanguaging and polylanguaging, involve the idea of a code or codes. In such a way of thinking, translanguaging entails movement between different languages (Makoni 2013). The mechanical view of languaging is complemented by a search for meaning that is best captured by the fact that languaging/translanguaging constitutes the utilization of any semiotic resources to convey meaning. From such a framework, meaning exists independently of languaging, and the role of languaging is to articulate the meaning from the sender to the receiver, since any languaging is premised on a theory of communication. In the studies by García, Creese, and others, meaning is articulated through a conduit framework. This framework is founded on a deterministic framework of language and communication and a non-dynamic way of understanding interaction that runs contrary to the idea of language as social action, which I am trying to support in this section of the chapter and is like many other frameworks in that it is speaker-centric.

Maturana and Varela (1998), philosophers from Chile, approached the idea of languaging from a philosophical position. They construed language from a biological perspective in which they construe language in a manner consistent with their perspective on biology. By languaging they are understanding language as a self-organization and self-production system in which human actions occur. The striking aspect of Maturana and Varela's view is that the term *languaging* occurs for the first time in the Spanish translation! Languaging, as used by Maturana and Varela, was preceded by many variations in Western sociolinguistics.

Ramanathan's framing is closely aligned with that of Mignolo (1996, 2000), and both are explicitly political. Ramanathan regards languaging as a form of, and a resistance to, being silenced. From that approach, languaging is a rebellious act, a form of resistance at one point in a historical moment. However, Mignolo adopts a political position and a longer historical perspective. He construes languaging as a product of colonial or elite interruption of communication in pre-colonial or, as I would like to put it, outside elitedom. Languaging is, therefore, a process, a product of communication disruption. Languaging cannot exist outside communication, but the converse applies as well: communication does not require the existence of language because language is a 'variable extra'. Mignolo's framework has a sharp sense of history and can explain the complex relationship between macro, meso, and micro forces. This sense of temporal history and construction of time is clearly appropriate and might serve postcolonial linguistic scholarship, which the authors in this volume are seeking to develop. The weakness of a framework which is founded on languaging is that it does not escape the idea of a code, a language. You can only translanguage, perform a form of languaging, if you assume in the first instance that there are codes called languages.

The politics of the ontology of *supervernaculars*

The notion of *supervernacular* is increasingly popular and may become the pivotal foundational concept for an emerging sociolinguistic framework (Orman 2012:349). Because the term is widely used, at least in African contexts, it merits a close analysis. I see this brief essay as part of my effort to make sense for myself of the meanings of the terms and those allied to them. *Supervernacular* is modeled after Vertovec's (2006, 2007) notion of *superdiversity*, which he defined as 'diversification of diversity' (Vertovec 2007, in Simpson and Whiteside 2012:3). *Super* in *superdiversity* denotes hyper, while *super* in *supervernacular* may be construed to mean *trans* The latter can be construed to refer to movements across regions and semiotic boundaries. In short, the *super* in *superdiversity* does not have the same meaning as the *super* in *supervernacular*. The *super* in *supervernacular* resonates with notions such as *trans-languaging* and *poly-languaging*.

Although it is not clear what *languaging* means in *trans-languaging*, let alone *poly-languaging,* if *supervernacular* is based on *superdiversity* then the differences in the meanings of *super* in *superdiversity* and *supervernacular* have to be addressed; otherwise, *supervernacular* might be misleading. This is not to say that *supervernacular* cannot be used to refer to both *hyper* and *trans*. I am, however, extremely uncomfortable with the notion of diversity when used to refer to 'mass movements' for three main reasons. First, writing from a vantage perspective of being an immigrant in a rural university which seeks to bring to fruition diversity, I keep asking myself whether it is not the case that diversity, as articulated by Vertovec, Blommaert and Rampton, is a version of a description of reality that can only be advocated by those who are part of the powerful elite, such as researchers. Second, those of us who have spent most of our professional lives outside our countries of origin find that diversity may be extremely uncomfortable, because it is typically others who do so. It is the powerful who celebrate the notion of diversity; those of us from other parts of the world feel the idea of diversity is a careful concealment of power differences. When we celebrate mass movements we need to be able to distinguish between those who are compelled by circumstances to travel and those who do so willingly. *Superdiversity* contains a powerful sense of social romanticism, creating an illusion of equality in a highly asymmetrical world, particularly in contexts characterized by a search for homogenization. Third, I find it disconcerting, to say the least, to have an open celebration of diversity in societies marked by violent xenophobia, such as South Africa; at least two chapters in this volume are based on

68

South Africa (Steyn http:www.mmg.mpg.de/research/all-projects/super-diversity-south Africa accessed December 18.2012). Furthermore, diversity stresses the differences between individuals, languages, groups, etc. Whether we are diverse or not depends on the power of the social microscope being used. It is ironic that while sociolinguistics is celebrating diversity, super or not, other strands of research that also address issues surrounding migration, real or imagined, seem to be returning to a notion of assimilation:

> Examining public discourse in France, public policy in Germany, and scholarly research in the United States, I find evidence of a modest "return of assimilation" in recent years. Yet what has returned, I emphasize, is not the old, analytically discredited and politically disreputable "assimilationist" understanding of assimilation, but a more analytically complex and normatively defensible understanding. (Brubaker 2004: 5)

Ultimately, it is worthwhile to stress that notions about diversity are extremely powerful when used as metaphors to describe species. The danger we have to guard against in this case is one in which we unintentionally biologize a social phenomenon! If a social phenomenon is biologized, then social intervention is likely to be construed negatively because it will be interfering with a natural ecology.

A Short Historical Statement
Mass movement of populations is not new to Africa, so if diversity is accentuated by migration, then prior to colonialism there was considerable migration; however, it is framed as nomadism! The differences lie in the terminology: people moved—they simply did not need passports! 'African

69

history, like that of any other continent, reveals plenty of population movements linked to multiple factors such as nomadism, rural exodus, economic migrations and conflicts' (Canut 2009:92).

A Minor Quibble: 'A Storm in a Tea Cup'

I strongly support Blommaert and Rampton's (2011, 2012) project of creating new terms as a strategic way of facilitating understanding and visualizing sociolinguistic patterns, which cannot be easily understood using existing frameworks. Existing terms are construed as failing to capture the diversity that is rapidly enhanced by new, relatively cheap technology, including cell phones. Even though I support Blommaert and Rampton's project, I have a couple of minor concerns that I outline as part of the commentary in the conclusion to this book. Blommaert and his other associates, Dyers, Velghe, and many others, employ the term *supervernacular* to refer to a widespread usage of sociolinguistic resources that are not constrained by 'territorial fixedness, physical proximity, sociocultural sharedness and common background' (Blommaert 2011:3).

Blommaert and Rampton (2011) challenge us to frame *supervernaculars* in a wide range of ways. The term *supervernaculars* may be understood to refer to 'semiotic codes, chat codes, gaming codes, standard codes, mobile texting, mini-languages, or as a global medialect of condensed abbreviated English' (McIntosh 2010) and many others. Mobile texting is an example of a *supervernacular* code. In light of Blommaert's argument, the idea of a *supervernacular* code may perhaps be a contradiction because *supervernaculars* are meant to capture rapid and complex variations that cannot be explained through conventional frameworks when languages are understood as codes. However, by describing texting, e-mail messaging, and codes as *supervernacular*, traditional linguistic conventions are rein-

70

troduced into the analysis. An example of the problematic nature of moving beyond code-based framing of language is elegantly captured in a quotation about, paradoxically, the search for a metalanguage that goes beyond orthodox linguistic terms (whatever that may mean): 'A hybrid combination of linguistic forms (cf. "multi-racial"/"multi-ethnic"... straightforwardly identifiable *lexically, phonologically and grammatically/syntactical) elements of language*' (Rampton 2011: 289).

On the one hand there is a strong impulse to move beyond the notion of codes; on the other there is a powerful counterforce that restates characteristics of codes—lexical, phonological, grammatical, and syntax elements. Perhaps the notion of a *supervernacular* may not be as radical as we are led to believe because it is based on conventional notions of language, a position reinforced when Blommaert states that '*supervernacular* have all the attributes of a language' (Blommaert 2011:4). It is based on what Harris refers to as 'segregationist' linguistics (Pablé and Hutton 2015; Makoni 2011, 2012).

The search for invariant rules in *supervernaculars* reflects the extremely powerful nature of the ideologies of code-based views of language. These views lead to a search for invariant rules, efforts to establish fixed meanings, and efforts to consolidate form-meaning relationships. This quest seems counterintuitive in a framework that is seeking to describe wide circulations of semiotics. The trans-movements and circulations of 'semiotic codes' should render it difficult, if not impossible, to predict the meanings that the discourse practices. The challenge in *supervernacular* inspired research is how to introduce and sustain notions of indeterminacy and unpredictability that are consistent with the ideological impulse toward mass movements, while still distancing it from code-based views of language.

If *superdiversity* is taken seriously at an epistemological level, then a diversity or multiplicity of interpretations of signs must be accepted, if not encouraged. It is conceptually self-contradictory to argue for the importance of *superdiversity* in theory but fail in practice to seriously take into account inconsistency and contradictory interpretations that are consistent with common functioning of anthropolinguistic communication: communication involves vagueness, contradictory meanings and inconsistency between form and meaning which demand frequent reinterpretation in light of pragmatic cues which bring into focus and stabilize forms in context.

I find the notion of a *supervernacular* extremely complicated, not only because of the relationship it has with traditional notions of codes and orthodox ways of framing language, but also because I am not certain how the notion of *vernacular* is comprehended in *supervernaculars*, a situation rendered extremely difficult because of the many different meanings of the term *vernaculars* in sociolinguistics. Mufwene (1998) enumerated at least six different ways in which the idea of a vernacular can be defined:

(i) primary
(ii) native
(iii) indigenous language variety
(iv) vernacular may be a standard, and the best exemplar is definitely written.
(v) non-standard language varieties
(vi) a continuum ranging from basilectal to colloquial varieties.

Regardless of whether the list above is exhaustive or not (which it is unlikely to be), the critical issue for me is exploring the implications for sociolinguistics if *super* is added to *vernaculars* and if *vernaculars* are defined with more than one meaning.

If *super* in *supervernacular* means *trans* and vernaculars are understood as non-standard, then the only way I can easily understand *a supervernacular* is to argue that *supervernaculars* are manifestations of non-standard language varieties that can either be spoken or written. If *super* means *trans*, the term *supervernacular* might be equivalent to *transidiomatic expressions*. If *super* in *supervernacular* is understood in the way it is understood in *superdiversity* as 'hype', then a *supervernacular* may mean a *hypervernacular* whose intensity of variation may be characterized and situated along multiple continua, analogous to the meaning of vernacular in (vi).

(i) *Supervernaculars* 'have all the features we commonly attribute to "languages"'
(ii) *Supervernaculars* only occur as dialects
(iii) *Supervernaculars* and their dialects

In (i), *supervernaculars* are languages plus something else. I am not clear what constitutes (all) the features 'we commonly attribute to language'. (i) does not clarify the issue for me because what I regard as attributes of language may be based on what we understand to be a theory of language and communication. From an integrationist perspective (Makoni, 2011, 2013), the following might be regarded as attributes of language: indeterminacy in the relationship between form and meaning, language as a myth, communication as central, and language as an extra. The challenge for me is whether I can integrate the idea of a *supervernacular* within integrationism, and if so, how?

(ii) is difficult to fully comprehend. If *supervernacular* can only occur as dialects, this undermines the very essence of the rationale for creating a term such as *superver-nacular* and its intellectual apparatus.

From *Supervernaculars* to Polylanguaging in Superdiversity

The complexity in having a grasp of *supervernaculars* is that in some cases there is a subtle shift from *supervernaculars* to *superdiversity* and the idea of polylanguaging is introduc-ed, as in '*Polylanguaging* in Superdiversity' (Jørgensen *et al* 2011) and 'Superdiversity on the Internet: A case from China' (Wang and Varis 2011). It is critically important to observe that the shift here is from vernacular to *superdiver-sity*, conflating distinctions between diversity and vernacu-lars. The argument that *polylanguaging*, also referred to in-terchangeably as *polylinguistic*, can be situated in *superdi-versity* begs the question: what is the postulated relationship between *polylanguaging* and *supervernaculars?* To address this issue, given that *polylanguaging* can be situated in *superdiversity*, one must make sense of what *languaging* means in a wide range of terms. *Polylanguaging, translang-uaging*, and others may be taken as equivalents. *Polylang-uaging* does not resolve the issue because the term *languag-ing* is in itself ambiguous and has been used in many diffe-rent and, at times, conflicting ways.

Concluding Remarks

Emerging sociolinguistic frameworks have not been as suc-cessful (at least, at this stage, to me) in their description of African contexts. It is, therefore, appropriate to reflect on Canut's (2009: 93) comments:

> It is only when speakers move about or meet a stranger that they become conscious of their particu-lar linguistic features and the processes of compari-son and transformation are put in place leading to the

overlap of different varieties which cannot be categorized.

I would like to bring my chapter to an end by citing some of the categories in a recent paper by Rampton (2011) that are becoming important, defining features of the emerging sociolinguistic subfield and that demand a sophisticated reading which include: *"multi-ethnic adolescent heteroglossia, heteroglossic speech stylization"*, *"contemporary urban vernaculars"*, *"polylingual languaging"*, *"youth language"*, *"community English"*, *"multiracial vernacular"*.

References

Blommaert, Jan and Ad Backhus (2011). "Repertoires revisited: Knowing language in super-diversity" *Working Papers in Urban Language and Literacies,* 67.

Blommaert, Jan and Ben Rampton (2011). "Language and Superdiversity. Special issue" *Diversities* 13, 2.

Blommaert, Jan and Ben Rampton (2012). "Language and Superdiversity" *MMG Working Paper,* 12-05.

Canut, Cecile (2009). "Discourses, community, identity: Processes of linguistic homogenization in a city (the case of Bamako, Mali" In: *The Languages of Urban Africa,* ed. Fiona McLaughlin. Indiana University Press, pp.86-102.

Chomsky, Noam (1986). *Knowledge of Language: Its Nature, Origins and Use.* New York: Praeger.

Creese, Angela and Blackledge, Adrian (2010). "Translanguaging in the bilingual classroom: A pedagogy for learning and teaching?" *Modern Language Journal,* 94(1), pp.103-115.

Davidson, Donald (2002/1986). *Subjective, Intersubjective, Objective.* Oxford: Oxford University Press.

García, Ofelia (2007). Foreword.In: *Disinventing and*

Reconstituting Languages, eds. Sinfree Makoni and Alastair Pennycook. Clevedon: Multilingual Matters. pp.xi-xv.

García, Ofelia (2009). *Bilingual Education in the 21st Century: A Global Perspective.* Malden: Wiley-Blackwell.

Harris, Roy (1999). "Integrational linguistics and the structuralist legacy" *Language and Communication* 19, pp. 45-68.

Harris, Roy (2000). *Rethinking Writing.* London: Athlone Press.

Harris, Roy (2011). *Intergrationist Notes and Papers 2009-2011.* Brighton: Gamlingay.

Jacquemet, Marco (2005). Transidiomatic practices: Language and power in the age of globalization. *Language and Communication* 25, pp.257-277.

Johnstone, Barbara (1996). *The Linguistic Individual: Self-Expression in Language and Linguistics.* Oxford: Oxford University Press.

Jørgensen, Jens Normann (2008). "Polylingual languaging around and among children and adolescents. *International Journal of Multilingualism* 5(3), pp. 161-176.

Jørgensen, Jens Normann, Martha Sif Karrebæk, Lian Malai Madsen, and Janus Spindler Møller (2011). "Polylanguaging in superdiversity. *Diversities* 13 (2), pp.23-38.

Khubchandani, Lachman (1997). *Revisualizing Boundaries: A Plurilingual Ethos.* New Delhi: Sage.

Lantolf, James P. and Steven L. Thorne (2006) *Sociocultural Theory and the Genesis of Second Language Development.* Oxford: Oxford University Press.

Makoni, Sinfree (2013). "An integrationist perspective on colonial linguistics" *Language Sciences* 35, pp.87-96.

Makoni, Sinfree (2011). "Sociolinguistics, colonial and postcolonial: an integrationist perspective" *Language Sciences* 33(4), pp.680-688.

Maryns, Katrijn and Jan Blommaert (2002). "Pretextuality and pretextual gaps: On re/defining linguistic inequality" *Pragmatics* 12(1), pp.1-30.

Maturana, Humberto R. and Francisco J. Varela (1998). *The Tree of Knowledge: The Biological Roots of Human Understanding.* Boston: Shambhala.

Mignolo, Walter D. (1996). "Linguistic maps, literary geographies, and cultural landscapes:Languages, languaging, and (trans)nationalism" *Modern Language Quarterly* 57, 2: 181-196.

Mignolo, Walter D. (2000). *Local histories/Global Designs.* Princeton: Princeton University Press.

Møller, Janus and Jens Normann Jørgensen (2012). "Enregisterment among adolescents in superdiverse Copenhagen. *Tilburg Papers in Culture Studies*, 28.

Orman, Jon (2012). "Not so super: The ontology of 'supervernaculars'" *Language and Communication* 32(4), pp.349-357.

Pablé, Adrian and Christopher Hutton (2015). *Signs, Meaning, and Experience: Integrational Approaches to Linguistics and Semiotics.* Berlin: De Gruyter.

Ramanathan, Vaidehi (2009). "Silencing and languaging and the assembling of the India nation-state: British public citizens, the epistolary form, and historio-graphy" *Journal of Language, Identity, and Education* 8, pp.203-219.

Rampton, Ben (2011). "From 'multi-ethnic adolescent heteroglossia' to 'contemporary urban vernaculars'" *Language and Communication* 31(4), pp.276-296.

Seargeant, Philip and Caroline Tagg (2011). "English on the internet and a 'post-varieties' approach to language" *World Englishes* 30(4), pp.496-514.

Swain, M. (2006). "Languaging, agency and collaboration in advanced second language proficiency" In: *Advanced Language Learning: The Contribution of Halliday and Vygotsky,* ed. H. Byrnes, London: Continuum. pp.95-108.

Swain, Merrill (2009). "Languaging: University Students Learn the Grammatical Concept of Voice in French" *Modern Language Quarterly* 93(1), pp.5-29.

Swain, Merrill (2010). "Self-scaffolding mediated by languaging: Microgenetic analysis of high and low performers" *International Journal of Applied Linguistics* 20(1), pp. 23-49.

Vertovec, Steven (2007). "Super-diversity and its implications" *Ethnic and Racial Studies* 29(6), pp.1024-1054.

IV

From Human Linguistics to System 'D' and Spontaneous Orders: An Approach To The Emergence Of Indigenous African Languages

Abstract

Recently language practices have been viewed from many different perspectives; translanguaging (García and Kleyn 2016), codemeshing (Canagarajah 2013), superdiversity (Blommaert and Rampton 2011), metrolingualism (Penny-cook and Otsuji 2015). All these different frameworks are motivated by an acute awareness of the imperative to adequately capture some of the contemporary sociolinguistic diversities sweeping through both rural and urban global communities or capture the diversities which historically occurred but were missed in the analysis of African sociolinguistic landscapes because of the analytical frameworks we used. All the frameworks underscore the need to expand the 'epistemological repertoires' (di Carlo 2017:1) which we are currently deploying. On the one hand, this paper follows in the similar vein to the aforementioned research in its search to expand analytical epistemological repertoires to describe sociolinguistic diversities. On the other hand, the line of thinking adopted in the paper is different from the other frameworks because it is situated in African socio-historical contexts and places emphasis on how indigenous languages, by and large, were designed and subsequently appropriated by African speakers as first languages. The paper explores the implications of a human linguistic perspective which places significance on individuals over language in language planning.

Introduction[1]

Our main objective is to explore the implications of adopting a 'human linguistics' (Yngve, 1996:80) perspective on language planning in Africa. From such a perspective 'language is not a thing that leads a life of its own outside and above human beings, but it has true existence only in the individual, and all changes in the life of a language can only proceed from the individual speaker' (Yngve 1996: 28). In a 'human linguistics' perspective it is people and the activities that they are engaged in which should be central to a study of language so from such a perspective the primary goal of language planning in Africa would be to promote and change the political and economic status of people by enhancing the nature of communication between them. Enhancing communication between people is valuable because 'communicative tasks are often subtasks of non-linguistic tasks ... and interface naturally with practical affairs (Yngve and Wasik, 2004: 23), so the ultimate objective of 'human linguistics' is to enable people to carry out their activities, and language is a sub-task within that process, language cannot exist in 'splendid isolation' (Yngve and Wasik, 2004: 23). Language cannot be walled from other semiotic practices. In a 'human linguistics' perspective in which people are of primary importance, people are seen as using language and not language users. To call people language users is therefore 'perverse' because we are defining people in terms of language (Yngve, 1997: 77).

Many scholars working on Africa have observed frequently that African governments are either reluctant or un-

---

[1] This is an analytically expanded version of a chapter which first appeared as: Sinfree Makoni and Pedzisai Mashiri, "Critical historiography: does language planning in Africa need a construct of language as part of its theoretical apparatus?" in Makoni, S & Pennycook, A. (2006) *Disinventing and Reconstituting Languages*. Clevedon. Buffalo.Toronto. Multilingual Matters.

willing to comprehensively implement language policies that seek to promote what are regarded as indigenous languages (Stroud 2001). The alleged failure by African governments to implement such language policies is attributed to their preference for English or French, which in turn is construed to be a result of neo-colonialism. Unfortunately, that argument is historically wrong. The argument is based on the assumption that one of the primary objectives of colonial governments was to promote either English or French. The argument is not historically valid because colonial governments were much more inclined to promote African languages than either English or French. Contrary to the neo-colonial argument it was African parents who strongly argued for the use of English in education (Summers, 2000; Makoni and Truddell, 2006). The main thrust of our argument in this article, is however, not on the historical aspect of language planning, illuminating though such an analysis might be, but on the theoretical notion of language and by extension multilingualism in African language planning and the implications of reframing language from a 'human linguistics perspective' in language planning in Africa.

The oft-reported failure of African language planning policies in Africa has paradoxically created unique opportunities for us to critically examine some of the assumptions made about African languages. The lack of success of language planning policies in Africa is not due to an unwillingness or inability on the part of the African governments to implement language policies but is due to a theoretical tendency to treat African languages as if they were real objects. We are neither the first nor the only scholars to be skeptical about the belief that languages are entities in the real world; such skepticism has rarely been articulated in African language policy and planning contexts.

Our position is not that we should dispense with language planning as an enterprise in Africa, but that we should reorient ourselves away from a reification of languages as if they existed in the real world, towards frameworks whose primary objectives would be, first, to promote people, and second enhance communication between them. African linguistics language planning projects carried out from a human linguistics perspective should lead us to reformulate our questions even in other areas going beyond the notion of African languages.

We could say that we are interested in how children learn to talk and that we are also curious about how the way we view the world [and we could add people —SM] depends on the ways we have to talk about it (Yngve, 1996: 73).

A success of language planning projects requires at the very least moral and intellectual courage to dispense with the notion of language in African sociolinguistics.

The position we are adopting is the converse of conventional models of language planning, whose objective was to promote the status of languages; such models do not pay adequate attention to how people talk about the world and each other and language emerges from such interaction and is not pre-given in advance of human encounters. We are arguing that changes in the status of language can occur as a result of changes in the social, political and economic status of its speakers. The converse does not necessarily occur. People's social-economic status will not necessarily improve because the status of their language has been changed. Recognizing and attributing official status to language does not improve the social and political status of indigenous peoples.

If our conceptualizations of African languages are to change, we have to disinvent the discourses of African languages and we have to analyze not only our discourses about Africa but how our discourses are (mis)appropriated or subverted by local people. For disinvention to take place it is necessary to intervene at a level of discourse, at the level of representations, and by implication at the level of the conceptualization of African languages and by extension what it means to be an African which includes the status of and the relationship between African language practices and the supernatural and 'the curse of the undeadvoices' (Perley 2012:133). The ultimate objective of disinvention is to facilitate alternative ways of framing and conceptualizing African languages, and dispensing with the notion altogether and laying a bold ground work for a language-free African epistemological sociolinguistic context. In the interim because of the continuing hold of the notion of language over our imagination of Africa we are left with the alternative to disinvent five dominant ways of conceptualizing African languages.

- Linguistic diversity as enumerability
- The naming game
- Conceptualizing African languages
- Constructing indigeneity; and
- Dictionaries as discourse and as a theory of African languages.

The arguments we are putting across are not necessarily unique to Africa, although they may assume heightened significance in Africa. Not only may they resonate with minority language experiences in Europe and other ex-colonial situations such as India, they are also clearly relevant in the so-called Global South (Kerfoot and Hyltenstam 2017; and Jo Arthur and Chimbutane 2015).

Linguistic diversity as enumerability
In this section of the article we analyze the role of enumeration in the conceptualization of African diversity. Greenberg

(1966) in *Languages of Africa* estimates that there are about 800 different languages. Crystal (1997: 316) places the number at about 2000. Mann and Dalby's (1987) estimate is relatively higher than that of Crystal. They suggest that Africa has approximately 2550. There is an on-going debate among linguistics, anthropologists, aid groups, educational planners and African governments on the exact number of African languages. Even well-established linguists, with extensive experience in Africa working in a single polity, seem to be undecided about the exact number of languages. For example, Whitely 1974 assigns 47 languages to Kenya on page 21, and then he mysteriously reduces the number to 34 on page 27. According to the Kenyan government, Kenya has a total of 39 languages (Njoroge, 1986: 330). Estimates for Malawi vary between 12 and 35; such a wide variation is not peculiar to Malawi. Estimates for Zambia vary even more widely. Sometimes it is claimed there are 20 languages in Zambia, at other times 73 (Williams, 1992).

The variability in the number of African languages is not peculiar to either southern or eastern Africa. Grimes (1974) estimates the number of languages in Cote d'Ivoire to be 58. A year later, the 1975 official census reports that Cote d'Ivoire has a total of 69 languages. The Summer Institute of Linguistics, an organization which has extensive experience in the codification of African languages, in 1995 listed a total of 84 languages for Cote d'Ivoire, 10 non-indigenous and one extinct (Djite, 1993: 16). The controversy about the number of African languages foregrounds important theoretical issues that have a direct bearing on applied areas such as language planning and language in education. It is highly unlikely that we will ever come to a general agreement on the exact number of African languages.

Mühlhäusler (1996: 36), with his mind focused on the Pacific region suggests that the lack of agreement on the numbers of languages does not so much reflect the inability of linguists to distinguish between communalects, languages and dialects but the non-existence of languages as constructed in a formal western sense. Although Mühlhäusler did not have Africa in mind, his mind is equally relevant there. Paradoxically, the discrepancy and controversy in the number of African languages is not an unfortunate situation. It is indeed a situation which should be encouraged. It compels us to rethink some of the foundational concepts in African linguistics such as whether we indeed need notions about language as a way to frame and describe African socio-linguistic contexts.

The numbers game in African languages is symptomatic of the powerful influence of census ideology in African linguistics. Census ideology is the backbone of the enumerative modality, one of the five modalities used to frame colonial and post-colonial narratives about Africa. Other modalities are historiographic, observational/travel modality, survey modality, museocological (Cohn,1996: 8).

The enumerative modality unlike other modalities is based on the idea that African languages can be converted into countable forms, are describable, and can thus be prescribed. In short, the enumerative modality is predicated on the belief that languages in general, but African speech forms in particular can be contained and controlled. In order for the counting to take place, the languages are labeled, even though "naming languages is a type of consciousness, an artifact embedded in the consciousness of western formal education, in a continent in which a majority are not formally literate in a western sense" (Makoni et al 2003). Ideologically, the numbers play a dual role. In some cases, the numbers are used to oppress the speakers of these languages, while on the other hand some linguists evoke the same numbers to demand redress and compensation.

The naming game
In this section we illustrate how the notion that languages
have names emerged, and the impact naming has on ways in
which African linguistic maps are drawn and perhaps construed. Because the linguanyms often coincided with ethno-
nyms the Shona spoke Shona, the Zulu spoke Zulu, the
Bambara spoke Bambara the production of linguistic maps
also produces ethnic maps simultaneously. We illustrate how
the naming, cataloguing and classifying was part of a project
of developing encyclopaedic colonial inventories (Fabian,
1986). Linguistically, the variability in the number of languages is in part a consequence of the different names assigned to the 'same' speech variety at times even within the
same polity resulting in counting the same speech variety
more than once, thus inflating the number of African
languages (Djite, 1993; 2008).

Because some of the African languages are spoken
and used in a number of different polities, they have not surprisingly multiple names. For example, a Zulu-based pidgin
spoken in mining towns in southern and central Africa, dero-
gatively referred to by European colonialists as either 'kitch-
en kaffir' or 'mine kaffir' is referred to as Fanakalo in South
Africa, Chilapalapa in Zimbabwe, Chikabaga in Zambia,
Kitanga in the Congo. There is also a tendency to regard
mutually-intelligible languages as distinct because they are
historically associated with different political dispensations
some of which predate colonialism. For example, Kirundi
and Kinyarwanda owe their identities to different kingdoms
that have evolved into modern Burundi and Rwanda (Ma-
sangara, 1997: 385).

There is also a discrepancy between the names used
by linguists and those used by speakers themselves. The
names used by applied linguists have generally been the
versions created by colonialists; this is not surprising since,
in Africa, applied linguistics is heir to colonialism. In ethnic-

86

methodological terms, the names of the languages used by colonialists and applied linguistics do not necessarily correspond with those used by speakers themselves. For example, Djite cites two examples of languages spoken in west Africa, Guere and Wobe, which on the basis of ostensible objective linguistic criteria can be treated as different languages, but are regarded as the 'same' language by Guere and Wobe speakers themselves. According to the speakers, the distinction between Guere and Wobe exists in the language of the white man but speakers identify themselves with the bigger Akan community (Djite, 1989: 6).

Evidence of the impact of European colonialism in shaping Africa's linguistic map is widespread across Africa and is not confined to west Africa only. In some cases, the names were not only imposed, but were pejorative as well. The pejorative nature of the labels did not escape the colonialists themselves. For example, Springer writing in 1909 about chiShona in southern Africa comments "various terms have been invented by the white man, the most well-known being chiSwina, meaning, the language of the filthy people (Springer 1909: 4). In Malawi, the missionaries and early explorers were responsible for giving the language chi-Chewa the name chiNyanja during the pre-colonial era (Mvula,1992: 45). Mvula recounts how early Portuguese explorers entered south eastern Africa in the Quelimane region where they came across the Maravi or Chewa people. The Marawi people were nicknamed amaNyanja since they lived in the area near the lake or shire river, commonly referred to as Nyanja. Hence amaNyanja meant people of the lake and chiNyanja the language of the lake people Mvula,1992 45. In 1968 four years after independence, Malawi replaced the name chiNyanja with chiChewa.

The arguments by (Djite 1989, Springer 1905 and Mvula 1992), among others underscore the need to pay close attention to how speakers construct their languages, and the

87

need to build descriptions and classifications that take into account the perspectives of the users, as part of decolonizing the thinking that shaped the so-called indigenous languages. The perspectives of the users normally reflect the nature of the social relationships among the speakers from the 'allegedly' different groups (Hymes 1983), unlike those used by linguistics which are ostensibly built on objective linguistic criteria whose accuracy is open to question. The legacy of objectivism is apparent in how African speech forms are divided into distinct languages and languages are further divided into 'families'. At times the languages are traced to a common ancestor, a Proto-Bantu (Guthrie, 1972) or Ur-Bantu. Proto-Bantu and Ur-Bantu are historical reconstructions, linguistic fictions and not real languages. They are reconstructions based on the assumption that all Bantu languages developed from a common ancestor.

The analysis of the neo-Grammarian Carl Meinhof demonstrates that Bantu languages are 'related' and belong to the same family and that there was historical continuity with proto-Bantu. The comparative method which was applied to African languages, has been used in other regions of the world—for example, in the pacific region (Crowley, 1989). The classification excluded 'mixed languages', contact, vehicular languages, creoles, which went undescribed because they were treated as ideologically marginal. They were ideologically marginal becauae they were used mainly between Africans and not between Africans and Europeans (Errington, 2001: 29). The reconstruction of proto-Bantu languages also created a linguistic interpretation of history, based on an idealization of historical processes, a simple juxtaposition of present states and hypothetical states without any reference to intermediate states. Thus, a whole range of data endowed with variation has been excluded from historical analysis. Cohn levels a much more powerful critique of the comparative method when he writes

The power of comparative method was that it enabled the practitioner to classify and control variety and difference. At a phenomenological level the British discovered hundreds of languages. As with genealogies, which could represent all the members of a family or descent group visually as a tree with a root, trunk, branches, and even twigs, so could dialects and languages be similarly represented and grouped. Significantly, the trees always seemed to be northern European ones, like oaks and maples, and the British never seemed to think of using the most typical south Asian tree, the banyan, which grows up, out, and down at the same time. (Cohn 1996: 55)

Bantu languages are the biggest language group within the Niger-Congo group of languages. The Niger-Congo is the biggest 'language family' (Hurst forthcoming) in Africa south of the Sahara, and so (it is claimed) is spoken by about 260 million people in western, central, eastern and southern Africa (Webb and Kembo-Sure, 1999:33). The linguistic relationship between the languages is apparent if the words used for the same concept are analyzed.

The discourse of language classification of African languages is an object of analysis because as a type of discourse, it shapes our images of and conceptualizations of African languages (Blommaert 2008). From a feminist perspective, the discourses on the classification of African languages are quite striking. Family imagery is used to enframe relationships between African languages. The metaphor of a family is an extremely powerful and emotive one even when used analytically (Irvine and Gal, 2000). Unfortunately, as an idiom it might be ill suited to describe relationships between languages because like any metaphor it carries baggage, extra implications about languages and their speakers—such as whether those speakers share a common interest, whether they are co-participants in some global community, and whether their participation is inevitably differentiated according to a social hierarchy. In some cases, related languages are described as 'sister' languages. The feminization of languages is taken to an extreme extent when languages such as Hausa are said to be 'impregnated with semiticism'.

Methodologically, the classification of African languages into distinct, hermetically sealed units (Makoni 1998), although ostensibly based on objective linguistic data, unfortunately excludes the perspectives of the speakers. It furthermore conceals the role of the analysts. Linguistic objectivism arises from a double demand. On the one hand, the analyst is expected to be objective, while at the same time s/he is expected to be immersed in local life. The labels and names assigned to the languages subsequently shape the sociocultural identities of speakers of African languages. The issue, therefore, is not one of simply getting the right name for what one speaks, but an awareness of the constitutive nature of naming. The labels are not merely descriptive, but they are constitutive (Danzinger, 1997) resulting in Africans seeing themselves through colonial lenses.

Historically, such invented labels are frequently mobilized in nationalistic and ethnic politics. For example, Webb (2003: 289) remarks on a growing consciousness of linguistic identity in South Africa producing self-identifying labels such as 'I speak Tswana' yet as van Warmelo (1974: 74) cited in Herbert,1992:2) rightly observes, it is difficult to draw any real boundary between Tswana and Northern Sotho, and Northern Sotho is so diverse that one may question its relevance as a single category.

Conceptualizing African Languages

Conceptually, African linguistic diversity is an artifact of constructing separate languages whose boundaries may not necessarily have any social functional reality. A demarcation based on purely linguistic criteria does not necessarily translate into boundaries of communication (Djite,1993). If the African map was designed on the basis of communication rather than imagined language differences it would be relatively easy to produce workable solutions (Djite, 1993). In the African continent, the issue of redrawing African linguistic boundaries has ramifications that go beyond language. Chimhundu argues:

> What Europeans actually did when they partitioned Africa was effectively to stop the perpetual movements of groups of people. The result was to freeze the geopolitical and ethnopolitical linguistic maps which the Europeans themselves created by their own rules during the early stages of colonial rule. African linguists and historians need to look at these maps again (Chimhundu, 1985: 89).

Stroud (2001) elaborates on the lack of fit between the construct of language and multilingual environments. He argues that the construct of 'language' may be poorly attuned to multilingual developing nations. The construct of multilingual networks may be suited to describe the nature of African language practices that one encounters within African contexts. African speakers "move into, between, and across many different semiotic practices, exhibiting multiple and varied practices of language use, such as language crossing and mixed registers" (Stroud, 2001: 350). Interest in the problematic nature of language has implications on other areas of sociolinguistics such as Linguistic Human Rights. Some of the Rights discourses seem to treat language as

91

having an ontological validity independent of the discourses in which the discourses are embedded. The meaning of 'language', its significance, is strongly contested; it is the outcome of divergent and conflicting ideological positions. The word language is used in several senses and it is not obvious that the senses are compatible with each other. Language is construed as a

> natural phenomenon, the object of science, a type of faculty, a type of system, as voluntary behavior, as something used, as something taught and learned, as having learned elements, as having patterns, as something spoken, heard, and learned as something processed, as something cognized and structured, as something produced and comprehended as data (Yngve,1996: 10)

It is not clear that each of the aforementioned notions of language necessarily complements with the notions of linguistic rights. Stroud (2000) tries to resolve the problematic nature of the notion of language by proposing the notion of 'linguistic citizenship'. This is a potentially useful framework since it enables Stroud to reframe language in a way which emphasizes how 'language', its meanings and significance, is a very much constrained and contested object and the sociohistorical outcome of debate, legislation, divergent ideologies and social conflict. The notion of linguistic citizenship is a powerful corrective that challenges the overwhelming hold of a structuralist view of language, a view which has a powerful impact on how African languages are imagined. If our imagination of African sociolinguistics is organized around discrete, countable, unitary languages, we end up conjuring up an image if exceptional linguistic African diversity (Breton, 2003: 204) which may lead us to formulate inappropriate language policies.

Constructing Indigeneity

Mudimbe, in *The Invention of Africa* and subsequently in *The Idea of Africa,* argues compellingly that the idea of Africa was an invention (Mudimbe, 1988, 1994). He argues that the invention was carried out through a deployment of a series of Eurocentric and conceptual tropes and discourses commencing with Greek narratives about Africa, through to anthropology and missionary discourses and philosophy. Africa was therefore being imagined and embedded in foreign discourses. Even though the idea of Africa as an invention is widespread in African Studies, indigenous languages in African linguistics have been treated as if they were primordial. This has had major policy implications in which the goal of the projects was the promotion of the so-called indigenous languages. In the following section we argue that the ways in which indigenous languages were constructed are an invention. The process of invention is not restricted to the colonial era, as the construction of the chiChewa in Malawi and Runyakitara in Uganda demonstrates. Bernstein illustrates how during the heydays of the Buganda kingdom, Runyakitara was regarded as a single language, but after the advent of missionaries, it was divided into two. In the early period after the attainment of Ugandan independence in the 1970's, it was further subdivided into four separate languages. Currently there are efforts to reduce it into a single language! The history of the Runyakitara illustrates how a single language goes from one to two to four and then looks like it's getting back to one again. (Bernstein, 1998).

The concept of indigenous languages is one of the key tropes through which African sociolinguistics is narrated and imagined. Its significance is evident in how it is frequently evoked to frame decisions on language policy and planning in Africa. In terms of language planning when African countries are officially selecting language policies they typically select to choose among three options:

1.	opt for a colonial language
2.	opt for an ex-colonial language
3.	choose a combination of indigenous and ex-colonial languages.

The main objective of this article is not to debate whether or not English can still be defined as a colonial language although that could be an interesting issue in its own right but to argue that the opposition between English and African languages, frequently constructed as one between colonial and indigenous languages, is conceptually flawed and is historically unsustainable. Because the so-called indigenous languages are colonial inventions themselves. The concept of indigenous languages is a postcolonial response to varieties of languages emerging as a consequence of Africa's engagement with colonialism. Indigenous languages are therefore a post-colonial prism through which pre-colonial Africa is imagined.

Paradoxically, the languages that are defined as indigenous in postcolonial Africa were constructed as inauthentic during the colonial era by missionaries, their African assistants, colonial administrators and local Africans themselves. For example, Africans referred to the version of chiShona used in the educational system as chibaba—the language of the priests. Baba was used here to refer to priest. The priests were even more candid about the inauthentic nature of the indigenous languages by referring to chiShona as Jesuit language (Ranger, 1995). It is these indigenous languages that were framed as colonial languages and not English by educated Africans (Ranger, 1985).

The process of invention was not restricted to colonial Africa; it was part of a general process in British colonialism. Breckenbridge and van der Veer, writing about India comment in ways that resonate with African experiences:

"The very languages that are called 'native' are products of an intricate dialectic between colonial projects of knowledge and the formation of distinctive group identities" (Breckenbridge and van der Veer, 1993: 6). In southern Africa sociohistorical investigations of languages like Tswana, Zulu, Xhosa, Tsonga and Ndau were recently reconstructed, hence in need of disinvention and reconstitution (Makoni, 1998, 2003; Cook, 2002; MacGonagle, 2001).

The process of invention, unlike most other language standardization situations, was not one of converting a linguistic continuum into discrete languages, but that of actively creating 'ideal' languages (Eco, 1995) which reflected more European epistemology than prevailing local social realities (Harries, 1995: 40). The creation resulted in a production of African languages that were not anybody's mother tongue. Invented African languages have their socio-genesis as second languages. In Zimbabwe the creation of complex orthographical rules (word division) and spelling was part of the harmonization of chiShona by Clemente Doke (1931). The chiShona language committee and Fortune (1972) produced a type of chiShona that no one used successfully outside the context of an examination (those who use it are likely to view it more as a second language than as a first language).

The process was not one of simply reducing African speech forms, but in Harries' (1989:87) felicitous terms, that of 'compiling' an inventory of linguistic forms and regulating meaning through the production of dictionaries. For example, Swiss missionaries created a language called Tsonga as a lingua franca for "a dauntingly confusing pot-pourri of refugees, drawn from the length and breadth of colonial south-east Africa, who shared no common language and lived in scattered villages that were independent of one another" (Harries, 1995: 29). Tsonga is currently spoken in northern and eastern Transvaal in South Africa and the southern part of Mozambique. The people who occupied this region were not a coherent social and linguistic reality. They were made up of refugees from a series of political and ecological upheavals prompted by Gaza civil wars in the 1860's and the Shakan refugees (hence Harries' assertion that there were a pot-pourri of refugees).

After the compilation of a linguistic inventory, currently referred to as Tsonga, it was subsequently reintroduced into the area to give what was originally a heterogeneous area the appearance of linguistic coherence. The term Tsonga is Zulu in origin, and literally means conquered peoples. The inhabitants of this geographical region were then for practical purposes appropriated by an indigenous language assigned to them. The important issue to emphasize here is that the missionaries through their positivistic orientation to language failed to see that the linguistic inventories to be subsequently referred to as languages were human constructs that were not scientifically objective. "Unlike microbes or river mouths, the Ronga and the Thonga/Shangaan languages were not awaiting discovery; they were very much the invention of European scholars and perhaps even more so of their African assistants" (Dwyer, 1999). The compiled inventories which were to subsequently pass for languages were to subsequently shape the oral languages, particularly for those who were to be educated initially through the medium of indigenous languages. Historically, the compiled inventory called Tsonga was to subsequently have three discrete dialects as part of its development.

The compilation of the inventory was part of an imperial hegemony, an attempt to control and bend African realities to suit European epistemology (Harries, 2001: 410) which created a context in which descriptive appropriation could become an avenue for linguistic imposition (Fabian, 1986). Did the missionaries, colonial administrators, and their African collaborators succeed in shaping African realities to suit European epistemology? The answer has to be a qualified no. Even hegemony has its limits, as Said with his mind on a different context, said:

> ... reality is neither at the individual's command (no matter how powerful) nor does it necessarily adhere more closely to some people's mentalities than to others. The human condition is made up of experience and interpretation, and these can never be completely dominated by power; they are also the common domain of human beings in history.
> (Said, 2003)

The process of creating 'new' versions of African languages entailed not only developing an orthography but constructing grammatical rules and regulating words through lexicography. "Once established, the grammatical rules were sub-sequently portrayed as operating autonomously of their creators. Their person-made origins were forgotten and were conceived as givens operating according to the laws of science" (Harries, 1995: 43). According to Irvine, because of academic pressures for objectivity in linguistic science, the personal, or socially situated character of authors and speakers disappeared—or was made to disappear—from African linguistic analysis at both the speaker end and the linguist end, in pursuit of a science of language, pursued within the conditions of an imperial system (Irvine 2001: 87).

From a constructionistic perspective, the danger of effacing the social situated nature of knowledge construction is that a constructed linguistic phenomenon assumes ontological status independent of the analysts and producers. The constructed knowledge is presented as natural knowledge. Colonial knowledge is made to pass for official knowledge (Prah, 1999).

From the perspective of the missionaries and colonial administrators they owned 'Tsonga' and used their control and influences over the colonial state to promote their versions of African languages in collaboration with missionary-educated Africans. The monopoly held by the mission and later by the government, over the publications of Tsonga books and African books crucially shaped and determined what Africans read. In colonial applied linguistics, as in anthropology and folklore, Africans were readers, consumers of texts (Yankah, 1999). They generally were not expected to be authors (Irvine, 2000). They were expected to be compliant natives (Said 1997: 172).

Print literacy was taught so that Africans could read the Bible not so that they would write books of their own. Africans might be translators, interpreters or copyists; they might offer (oral sermons) to fellow Africans (if supervised), but they were not to sermonize to fellow Europeans, or hold authority over them (Ranger 1995; Irvine, 2001: 80). When Africans were subsequently to be writers they did so initially based on colonial epistemological assumptions. For example, using 'invented languages' and 'dialects', Africans produced 'tribal pasts', and 'tribal histories' (Ranger, 1985: 15). Europeans tried to shape how Africans conceptualized themselves by articulating European world views through African linguistic forms, a process analogous to what Franz Fanon (1967) called *Black Skin White Masks*.

Dictionaries as Discourse and as a Theory of African languages
The notion of 'dictionaries as discourse' is unusual because it runs counter to assumptions about dictionaries and language. Dictionaries are widely regarded as a type of list or listing whose organizational principles differ substantially from discourse in everyday sense (de Beaugrande, 1997). The discrepancy recedes, however, if we define discourse

not as an artifact of language based on the model of every-day conversation, but as a communicative event among participants. We shift our focus from tangible artifacts of paper and ink, over to compilation and use of dictionaries as communicative occasions occurring under characteristic circumstances (de Beaugrande, 1997; Benson, 2001). In an African context, dictionary production has to be understood within a broader context of colonialism, neo-colonialism and Black Elite supremacy.

The development of lexicography in African applied linguistics has been driven by Christianity, colonial expansion, and anthropology—rendering any avoidance of a discussion of political imperialism in African applied linguistics an intellectual impossibility. Recently lexicography has been driven by developments in descriptive linguistics, specifically corpus linguistics (Prinsloo and de Schruyver, 2001, 2002). Corpus linguistics has led to a launching of ambitious lexicographical projects. To date corpora have been developed for at least 15 different languages including Ciluba, Swahili, ChiShona isiZulu and isiXhosa.

Most of the early dictionaries in African languages were bilingual for example, one of the earliest dictionaries (published before Johnson's famous English dictionary) was a quadrilingual dictionary comprising of Italian, Latin, Spanish, and kiKongo (1650). Other significant bilingual dictionaries include Biehler's *English-Chiswina dictionary* (1927), his *Shona Dictionary* (Biehler, 1950) and a Zulu/Kaffir dictionary (1953). Lexicographical research is increasingly becoming monolingual.

The shift from bilingual dictionaries to monolingual dictionaries warrants an explanation. Most of the bilingual dictionaries were modelled around European languages; bilingual lexicography created a space that enabled Europeans to exercise authority over African languages. Monolingual dictionaries enabled African scholars to exercise counter authority to 'write back'. In an intellectual context in which bilingualism is celebrated, it is impossible to resist the tendency to villainize monolingualism. It is necessary to take cognizance of the intellectual strategies that the researchers are pursuing to avoid an uncritical celebration of bilingualism. A shift from bilingual to monolingual dictionaries is taking place against a background in which the relationships between African expertise and western scholarship are radically being reconfigured. Ranger made an astute observation when he commented:

> in contemporary Africa and Asia expatriate scholars have to accept partnership or apprenticeship as condition of doing research as part of an effort to replace old colonial relations of dominance.
> (Ranger, 1995: 272).

The temerity to insist that Western scholars serve as apprentices to African scholars as a prerequisite for carrying out research is taking place in a context in which paradoxically, powerful donor agencies exercise an influence over African intellectual agenda in ways more powerful than in earlier decades.

African applied linguists, as with other African intellectuals, are concerned that their agenda is in danger of 'being domesticated' (Hyden 1993: 252) by outsiders, a majority of whom do not empathize with their predicaments. Because they cannot always represent themselves, they continue seeing themselves through other people's lenses, images and an external intellectual idiom. The apprehension which African scholars feel has to be understood within a context in which most of what the West knew about the non-western world, it knew in a framework of colonialism and approached the African subjects in a position of dominance. It is this position of dominance that African scholars are

100

seeking to challenge as they insist on making research apprenticeship a precondition for research involvement by Europeans in Africa.

Dictionaries during the colonial era were part of a process that encouraged Africans to internalize European epistemology about themselves, creating a new view about their current affairs and superimposing new values on their past (Makoni, 2003: 142). These dictionaries invented fresh and ideologically laden relationships between words and meanings giving European meanings to African words. The internalization of European epistemology by African-educated speakers resulted in rural and educated Africans not being able to readily relate to each other's world views, although ostensibly speaking the 'same' language. Diction-aries in the colonial era can be constructed as a perfect example of Bentham's Panopticon (Foucault, 1977). An analysis of dictionaries written between 1890 and 1931 in Southern Rhodesia (now Zimbabwe) demonstrates the role of dictionaries in providing an important epistemological and Foucauldian lens through which African societies were observed, surveyed and controlled. Hartman in his 1893 dic-tionary translates 'gentleman' as *murungu* which in Shona vernacular referred to whites, thus implying that the only people who could be gentlemen were Europeans. Incidental-ly, a century later after Hartman's dictionary, Mawadza (2000: 95; Mashiri, 2003:1123) demonstrate that urban Shona has now the same meanings as the ones invented by Europeans in the formations of meanings of African words.

The colonialists were preoccupied with raising reve-nue through wage labor and at times imposing hut taxes on Africans. People who refused to be engaged in wage labor were defined as lazy or dishonest. Holy Spirit was translated in Shona as *mudzimu unoyera*. *Mudzimu* in African cosmo-logy refers to the spirit of the deceased. Other dictionaries went so far as to define God as *mudzimu*, an inaccurate

101

interpretation that is inaccurate even from an Africanist perspective. Because *mudzimu* is an intermediary and not an ultimate being.

Jeater aptly describes the process that took place in the embedding of European epistemology and cosmology in African languages when she comments thus:

> To find a word for god or sin or spirit in a local vernacular that did not do damage to the concept as understood by Christians was a powerful method of forcing missionaries to think deeply about the spiritual ideas of those they hoped to convert, and so as to identify points of connection, entry points between the two cosmologies. The missionaries were not just recreating the languages in textual form, making decisions about phonetics, orthography and word division based on European languages, they were bending the vernaculars to their will and making them do new things. The language projects were important, not because they helped missionaries to converse with Africans, but because they enabled them to appropriate African languages and to reinvent them within Christian tradition.
> (Jeater, 2000: 457).

An analysis of colonial dictionaries demonstrates that there was a systematic effort to bend African words to express European epistemological views. Unlike other African scholars (Mazrui and Mazrui, 1988) we are arguing that colonial images are covertly inscribed in the so-called indigenous languages. The argument that indigenous languages have been bent to embody European meanings clearly has implications on how relationships between 'signifier' and 'signified' within those languages can be conceptualized. From the perspectives of the compliers of colonial diction-

102

aries, the relationships between signifier and signified were clearly not arbitrary but were socially motivated.

A different set of claims is being made for dictionaries designed on electronic corpora; "Compiling and querying electronic corpora has become a sine qua non as an empirical basis for contemporary linguistic research" (de Schryver and Prinsloo, 2000: 89). Taking the suggestions of some of the key protagonists of corpus linguistics and lexicography seriously we query some of the claims of corpus linguistics as a type of dictionary discourse. Electronic corpora aspire to build corpora that are both representative and balanced and are based on authentic as opposed to invented data.

The categories of analysis ('authentic', 'representative', 'balanced') are terms of reference used in relation to English corpus linguistics, but they have been a source of much controversy (Sinclair, 1991; McCarthy and Carter 1995; de Beaugrande, 2001; Widdowson, 2000). The terms are potentially ethnocentric because more research has been carried out on corpora in English. Conceptualizations about English corpora are unintentionally being foisted on corpora of other languages (Makoni and Meinhof, 2003). Hegemony is being defined here as the imposition on African languages of staple discourses associated with English. The danger of the hegemonic relationships is not only the unwitting imposition of English discourses on African languages but that the nuances within English discourses are stripped of that complexity when transferred to other languages.

The discourse of dictionaries conjures the idea that there are texts that make up the corpora on which dictionaries are based are 'representative' of the language in use. The corpus is therefore presented as representative of language in use, when it is, in reality, a collection of texts, a magna vocabulary. The magna vocabulary of the corpora that form the basis of the dictionaries cannot be said to be representative of any language because they do not constitute the vocabulary of any native speaker. If the dictionaries are based on 'texts' as contained and assembled in a corpus, then the meanings are derived from the texts and not directly from language in use because in a written ecology languages are 'measured by authoritative collections' and not by how they are used. Because magna vocabulary as contained in dictionaries has an authoritative status, it entrenches a prescriptive tendency within language.

The blurring of the distinction between language as actually used and language as assembled in a collection of texts is an artifact of language as an Autonomous Text in which the meaning is encoded in a text, and no other information is necessary for its interpretation, such as who the speaker is, whom she is addressing (who else may be listening, the mood of the speaker, etc.). ATs are typically used to encode and decode propositions, and to communicate factual information. "The nearest approximations to AT language can be—and are sometimes—spoken, its prototypical medium is writing. The spoken forms are derivative. AT languages are not natural languages" (Grace). If AT languages are not natural languages, then the language in corpora cannot be read as exemplars of authentic language. They are an artifact of an AT language.

The development of metalinguistics is necessary because it is difficult to separate our knowledge of African languages from the categories used to describe them. In other words, it is difficult to maintain a clear distinction between language under description from the language of description. Or maintaining a distinction between language and metalinguistics (Harris 1981). If a language cannot be successfully separated from its metalinguistics, and the metalinguistics we are using in African languages has come to us English via Latin, it means we are viewing African languages through the prism of English. Consequently

African languages in such contexts cannot be said to be equal to English or French. If the objective of language planning is to promote African languages so that they are equal to English, then the intervention has to take place at an analytical level in terms of how we construe and frame African languages (Makoni and Pennycook 2006; Makoni and Pennycook 2012).

Toward disinvention and reconstituting African languages; spontaneous orders

In the following section we argue against a pluralistic view of multilingualism as providing building blocks of disinvention. One of the most articulate proponents of African multilingualism was the late Neville Alexander (1998; 2000) who among other things argued for viewing African multilingualism as a resource, a view best encapsulated by his astute rhetorical move that turns the Tower of Babel inside out when he talks not about the Tower of Babel but the power of babel. The metaphor of indigenous languages as a resource has not gained much traction from the people on whose behalf it was being articulated. To argue, for instance that the language which one neither speaks nor understands is a resource makes sense if one subscribes to a notion of universal ownership of resources. From the perspective of those that speak the language, however, it sounds strange to insist that one has a claim to a language that one does not even speak and might not even have any intention of learning. Universal ownership will in such cases be construed as a strategy to conceal the control of the world's resources including language by a small but powerful group of people in a globalizing world.

Even though we are critical of the pluralistic view of multilingualism articulated in the language as a resource metaphor, we concede that multilingualism in Africa has to some extent succeeded in so far as it has forcefully drawn our attention to the potential beneficial impact of African languages in education, health, and the economy. The multilingual argument has also forcefully drawn our attention to the fact the acquisition and use of English is not necessarily a panacea to Africa's social and educational challenges. Unfortunately, the multilingual argument has severe limitations apparent in its failure to gain much traction among Africa's urban poor who in spite of the rhetoric of indigenous languages as a resource, are shifting away from so-called resources towards urban vernacular (Cook, 2002; Ngom, 2005; Mufwene, 2002).

In spite of the way multilingualism has enhanced our understanding of the language situation in Africa, the epistemological construction of language in African multilingual contexts is questionable. The issue is not only epistemological: it has real effects in so far as the way languages are constructed has an impact on the material life circumstances of Africans. Firstly, in what sense is Africa a Power of Babel? In a massive Pan African Project Prah (1999) directly challenges the idea of a Tower of Babel that forms the basis of Alexander's arguments. He argues that over 80% of Africans speak no more than twelve key languages or clusters that are 85% mutually intelligible. It is not clear however, what criteria he uses to determine what constitutes a key language. Prah is also making questionable assumptions. He is basing his argument on the belief that it is languages which are mutually intelligible as if languages were things which were animate and had lives of their own (Yngve, 1996: 29).

Kwesi Prah is inadvertently defining Africans in terms of Western framings of language. He has succumbed to the powerful belief in the existence of African languages as entities in the real world. Starting from the assumption that African languages exist, the main objective of his research project is to improve the linguistic description. Improving the description of African languages does not resolve Africa's sociolinguistic problems if African languages are a Western illusion foisted on African sociolinguistic contexts. Prah is therefore taking for granted the very building blocks that his theory should subject to critique. He has succumbed to 18th and 19th century Western philosophical assumptions about language and consequently fails to question the validity of a concept such as language, and by extension other constructs frequently used in a description of African languages such as phonemes, phonology, words, grammars etc. If African linguistics is to make progress we therefore need not better descriptions but better questions about the very basis of the concepts we are using. The critique is necessary because "while physicists study objects of the real world given in advance, language is not an object given in advance that can be studied scientifically" (Yngve, 1996: 69).

The starting point for a disinvention project should be the mixtures rather than indigenous languages, and the ability of Africans to draw upon linguistic material from different social/linguistic systems to communicate. Comaroff and Comaroff (1991) demonstrate how the ability to mix and draw from different languages and semiotic systems, which is being widely reported is not novel. It was characteristic of Africa's social and linguistic behavior even in pre-colonial Africa. Mixing is therefore socially embedded in Africa's historical and contemporary social experiences of language.

If Africans are shifting away from indigenous languages towards urban vernaculars, it is therefore a contradiction to argue that the promotion of indigenous languages facilitates the retention of African cultural practices. A disinvention project has to address the factors that facilitate a shift towards urban vernaculars and explore the implications of the shift on language planning projects. The shift is not

107

necessarily a bad thing, if indigenous languages are associated with specific ethnicities and conservative social and political ideology while on the other hand, urban vernaculars are an "embodiment of the hybrid identity of city dwellers ... where people from different ethnic and religious backgrounds may be unified" (Ngom, 2005: 284). Urban vernaculars are also used in rural communities by rural people seeking to project an urban identity. The fact the urban vernaculars are also used in rural shows the importance of combining both urban and rural social histories in Africa because many Africans live in both places simultaneously, suggesting that distinctions between rural/urban, indigenous and modern might not be very productive ways of handling African sociolinguistics (Coquery-Vidrovich, 2005; Cook 2002).

Another major advantage of using urban vernaculars as a basis for disinvention project is their extensive use by urban African youth. The African youth constitutes a majority of most African countries, so the language which they use rapidly spreads to the rest of the population (Salm and Falola 2005). From a critical historiographical perspective, it is important to stress two important factors. Cities in Africa have always played a crucial role in the formation of new ethnicities and languages in the socio-historical linguistics of Africa. Swahili is the best example, of a city language, was most likely born before some of the invention of indigenous languages whose invention was a consequence of colonialism (Coquery-Vidrovitch, 2005).

Most language-planning projects in Africa are based on the notion of the state. We need to move beyond a state-centric perspective of language planning. By this we mean shifting away from the perspective of those who are representing the state or the language policy towards those who are subjects of the activation. (Williams, 1992: 178). While the state and linguists might frame their discourse in terms of language, non-linguists might frame their activities in terms of communication. In a disinvention project we are arguing that most of the subjects of the language policy are likely to have social networks which extend to rural communities as well.

It is important to shift away from state-centric orientations because most states might be dysfunctional while cities constitute important hubs of social and political energy in Africa. "Cities most of the time, exist as leading to or incorporated into a network of paths, roads, railways, rivers resulting in a network of other cities: what we call in French *tissu urbain*" (Coquery-Vidrovitch, 2005: xx). Cities have a long and complicated history in Africa. Some African cities predate colonialism. The first urban revolution in Africa occurred when prehistoric hunting and gathering societies became sedentary, which allowed domesticated agriculture. "Cities thus became multipurpose centers from the beginning. This was the case of Jenne-Jeno in the Niger River valley, at the dawn of the 1st century" (Coquery-Vidrovitch, 2005:17).

A disinvention program has to be able to take into account the historical and contemporary realities we have been describing above as a starting point, rather than accepting assumptions about the promotion of indigenous languages based on the belief that they are promoting unitary and discrete phenomena with objective realities rather than fuzzy-edged constructs (Gardner-Chloros, 1995). A view of indigenous languages as unitary constructs is part of a legacy of the construction of African languages in the 19th century, which has the effect of reifying languages (Errington 2001; Williams,1992). The tendency to reify languages leads to a reformulation of ineffective strategies to redress inequalities because the social status of speakers of the language or variety is construed as derived from the language itself rather than the social status of those who speak

109

the language (Williams, 1992). If the status is attributed to the language rather than the speakers, the logical but wrong strategy would be to change the status of the languages as a strategy for shifting the status of the speakers of those languages. We are arguing that changes in the status of the speakers of the variety of the language in question will most likely contribute towards a shift in the status of the language spoken by group whose status has changed. The converse does not necessarily apply. A shift in the status of the language does not necessarily result in the shift of the status of the speakers. Theoretically, we are therefore arguing for an African linguistics that seeks explanation in terms of people, who they are, where they live, their migration and so on (Yngve,1986).

> We could say that we are interested in how it is that people differ in the way they talk in different parts of the world, and how it is that we differ in the way we talk from previous generations. All this would be easily understandable to the general public and so to our new students: it can be said without obscure references to Language. (Yngve, 1996: 73)

If our argument is valid, then the failure of the multilingual movement in Africa frequently lamented by many scholars should be welcomed because advocates of multilingualism inadvertently sought to continue a top-down tradition of colonial thinking which does not take into account the perspectives of those who are the targets of the policy.

Orthodox sociolinguistic research in Africa is likely to describe Africans as multidialectal/multilingual, but we feel that a notion of verbal repertoire is more appropriate because the speech forms individuals use may be drawn from languages which the speaker can use and deploy but does not have full and comprehensive command over.

From verbal repertoires to System 'D' and spontaneous orders.
In the conclusion we argue that what is required is a System 'D' approach to language practices. The term System 'D' is a slang phrase with roots in Francophone Africa and the Caribbean in the French word *débrouillards*. *Débrouillards* is used to describe effective, self-motivated, resourceful, ingenious and creative people. System 'D' takes as its basic premises the idea that every human being is an expert in his or her own existence. It is a framework from which to challenge notions of expert status but not to do away with them completely but mitigates the potential tyranny of colonial expertise. Methodologically, in System 'D' each individual travels a unique sociolinguistic journey and no two individuals have identical social trajectories, and travel provides each person with social, economic and cultural capital thus the importance of building a historical perspective in the analysis of every individual's language practices.

References
Arthur, Jo and Chimbutane, F. (eds) (2015) *Bilingual Education and Language Policy in The Global South*. London: Routledge
Alexander, N. (1992) "South Africa: harmonizing Nguni and Sotho" in N. Crawhall (ed) *Democratically Speaking: International Perspectives on Language Planning*. Cape Town: National Language Project, pp. 56-68.
Alexander, N. (2000) *English Unassailable and Unattainable. The Dilemma of Language Policy in Education in South Africa*. Praesa Occasional Papers 3. Cape Town/Praesa/University of Cape Town.
Ashcroft, G. Griffiths and Fiffin, H. (1989) *The Empire*

111

Writes Back: Theory and Practice in Postcolonial Literature. London and New York: Routledge.

Benson, P. (2001) *Ethnocentricism and the English Dictionary*. London Routledge.

Bernstein, B. (1971) *Class, Codes and Control* vol. 1. London: Routledge and Kegan Paul

Bernstein, J. (1998) "Runyakitara Uganda's new language" *Journal of Mutilingual and Multicultural Development* 19 (2) pp.93-108.

Biehler, E. (1927) *English-chiSwina Dictionary* [S.l.]: The Jesuit Fathers

Biehler, E. (1950) *A Shona Dictionary with an Outline Shona Grammar*. (Rev edn) The Jesuit Fathers.

Blommaert, J. (2008) "Artefactual ideologies and the textual production of African languages" *Language and Communication*, 28(4) pp.291-307.

Blommaert, J. and B. Rampton (2011) "Language and superdiversity" *Diversities: an Online journal published by UNESCO.*, vol.13(2) pp.1-23

Breton, R. (2003) "Sub-Saharan Africa" in R. Breton (ed) *Languages in a Globalizing World* (203-217). Cambridge: Cambridge University Press.

Breckenbridge, C. and van Der veer, P. (eds) (1993) *Orientalism and the Postcolonial Predicament*. Philadelphia. University of Pensyslvania Press.

Canagarajah, S. (2013) *Translingual Practice Global Englishes and Cosmopolitan Relations*. London and New York: Routledge.

Chimhundu, H. (1985) "Early Missionaries and the ethnolinguistic factor during the 'invention' of tribalism in Zimbabwe" *Journal of African History* 33, pp.87-109.

Chimhundu, H. et al (2001) *Durmazwi guru rechiShona*. Harare: College Press.

Cohn, B. (1996) *Colonialism and its Forms of Knowledge:*

The British in India. Princeton,NJ: Princeton
University Press
Comaroff, J. and Comaroff, J. (1991) *Of Revelation and
Revolution: Christianity, Colonialism and
Consciousness in South Africa.* Chicago: Chicago
University Press.
Cook, S. (2002) "Urban language in a rural setting: the case
of Phokeng, South Africa" in G. Gmelch & W.P.
Zenner (eds.), *Urban life: Readings in the
Anthropology of the City*, 4th edn., pp. 106–114,
Waveland Press, Prospect Heights, IL
Coquery-Vidrovitch, C. (2005) "Introduction: African
spaces: History and culture" In J. Salm and T. Falola
(eds) *African Urban Spaces in Historical Perspec-
tives.* (pp xi-xv) Durham, NC: Carolina Academic
Press.
Crowley, T. (1989) *The Politics of Discourse: The Standard
Language Question in British Cultural Debates.*
London: Macmillan.
Crystal, D. (1997) *English as a Global Language.*
Cambridge: Cambridge: Cambridge: University
Press.
Danzinger, K. (1997) *Naming the Mind: How Psychology
Found its Language.* London: Sage.
de Beaugrande, R. (1997*) New Foundations as a Science of
Text and Discourse.* Stanford: CT: Ablex.
de Schruyver, G. and Prinsloo, D.J. (2000) "Electronic
corpora as a basis for the compilation of African
dictionaries: The macrostructure" *South African
Journal of African Languages* 20(4), pp.291-309.
Di Carlo P. (2017) "Towards an understanding of African
endogenous multilingualism, ethnography, language
ideologies and the supernatural" *The International
Journal of the Sociology of Language,* 254, pp.139-
163

Djite, P. (1993) "Correcting errors in language classification. Monolingual nuclei and multilingual satellites" *Language Problems and Language Planning*. 12 (1), pp.1-13.

Djite, P. (2008) *The Sociolinguistics of Development in Africa.* Clevedon. Buffalo. Toronto. Multilingual matters.

Doke, C. (1931) *Report on the Unification of Shona Dialects.* London: Stephen Austin and Sons.

Dwyer, D. (1999) The language/dialect problem. www.http://www.msu.edu-lgDialPr.htm.

Eco, U. (1995) *The Search for the Perfect language.* Oxford: Basil Blackwell.

Errington, J. (2001) "Colonial linguistics" *Annual Review of Anthropology* 30, pp.19-30.

Fabian, J. (1986) *Language and Colonial Power.* Cambridge: Cambridge University Press.

Fanon, F. (1967) *Black Skin, White Masks.* New York: Grove Publishing.

Fardon, R. and Furniss, G. (eds) (1994) "Introduction: Frontiers and boundaries: African languages as political environment" In R. Fardon and G. Furniss (eds) *African Languages, Development and the State* (pp. 1-13). London: Routledge.

Foucault, M. (1977) *Discipline and Punish: The Birth of the Prison.* London: Allen Lane.

Fortune, G. (1972) *A Guide to Shona Spelling.* Harare. Longman.

Garcia, O. and Kleyn, T. (2016) *Translanguaging with Multilingual Students: Learning from Classroom Moments.* New York: Routledge.

Gardner-Chloros, P. (1995) "Code-switching in community, regional and national repertoires. The myth of discreteness of linguistic varieties" In L.Milroy and P.Muysken (eds) *One speaker, Two languages:*

Cross-disciplinary Perspectives on Code-switching.
(pp 68-90) Cambridge: Cambridge: University Press.

Grace, G. WWW at http:ww2hawaii.edu/-grace. Accessed 01.06.06

Greenberg, J. (1966) *Languages in Africa.* The Hague: Mouton.

Grimes, J.E. (1974) *Word Lists and Languages.* Ithaca. NY: Cornell University. (Technical report of the National Science Foundation, 2).

Gumperz, J. (1972) "The communicative competence of bilinguals" *Language and Society* 1 (1) pp.143-154.

Guthrie, M. (1972) *Comparative Bantu: An Introduction to the Comparative Linguistics and Prehistory of the Bantu Languages* (4 vols). Farnborough: Gregg Press.

Hadebe, S., Mpofu, N., Maphosa and Khumalo, L. (2001) *Ischazamazwi se siNdebele.* Harare: College Press.

Harries, P. (1988) "The roots of ethnicity: Discourse and the politics of language construction in South Africa" *African Affairs,* 87(346), pp.25–52

Harries, P. (1995) "Discovering languages the historical origins of standard Tsonga in southern Africa" In R.Mesthrie (ed) *Language and Social History* (pp. 154-176). Cape Town: David Philip.

Harries, P. (2001). "Missionaries, marxists and magic: power and the politics of literacy in south-east Africa" *Journal of Southern African Studies,* 27(3), pp.405-427.

Harris, R. (1981) *The Language Myth.* London: Duckworth.

Hartman, A.M. (1893) *Outline of a Grammar of the Mashona Language.* Cape Town: St.Leger Printer.

Herbert, R.K. (1992) "Introduction: Language in a divided society" In R.K Herbert (ed) *Language and Society in Africa: The Theory and Practice of*

Sociolinguistics (pp 11-19) Johannesburg:
Witwatersrand University Press.

Hayden, G. (1993) "The challenges of domesticating rights
in Africa" In R.Cohen, G.Hayden and W.P. Nagan
Human Rights and Governance in Africa (pp 256-
281) Gainsville: University of Florida Press.

Hurst, E. et al. (forthcoming) *The Oxford Guide to Bantu
Languages.* Oxford: Oxford University Press.

Hymes, D. (1983) *Studies in the History of Linguistic
Anthropology.* Amsterdman; John Benjamins.

Irvine, J. (2001) "Style as distinctiveness: the culture and
ideology in linguistic differentiation" In P.Eckert and
J.Rickford (eds) *Style and Sociolinguistic Variation.*
Cambridge: Cambridge University Press.

Jacquement, M. (2005) "Transidiomatic practices. Language
and power in the age of globalization" *Language and
Communication.* 25, pp.257-277.

Jeater, D. (2000) "Speaking like a native" *Journal of African
History.* 43, pp.449-468.

Kerfoot, C. and Hyltenstam, K. (2017) *Entangled
Discourses: South-North Orders of Visibility.*
London: Routledge

Lupke, F. and Storch, A. (2013) *Repertoires and Choices in
African Languages.* Boston and Berlin. De Gruyter:
Mouton

McCarthy, N. and Carter, R. (1995) "Spoken grammar:
What is it and how can we teach it?" *ELT Journal*
49(3), pp.207-218.

MacGonagle, E. (2001) "Mightier than the sword: The
Portuguese pen in Ndau History" *History in Africa*
28, pp.169-186.

Makoni, S. (1998) "African languages as European scripts:
The shaping of communal memory" In S.Nuttal and
C. Cotzee (eds) *Negotiating the Past: The Making of*

Memory in South Africa. (pp.242-248) Oxford: Oxford University Press.

Makoni, S. (2003) "From misinvention to disinvention. Multilingualism and the South African Constitution" In S.Makoni et al (eds) *Black Linguistics: Language, Society and Politics in Africa and the Americas*. (pp. 132-153). New York: Routledge.

Makoni, S. and Meinhof, U. (2003) "Introducing applied linguistics in Africa" *AILA Review*. 16, pp.1-13.

Makoni, S. and Truddell, B. (2006) "Complementary and conflicting discourses of Diversity in language Planning" *Per Linguam* 22(2), pp.14–28.

Makoni, S. and Pennycook, A. (2012) "Disinventing Multilingualism. From Monological Multilingualism to Multilingua Francas" In M. Martin-Jones, A. Blackedge and A. Creese (eds), *The Routledge Handbook of Multilingualism*. Abingdon: Routledge. pp.167-183.

Mann, M. and Dalby, D. (1987) Online at www.geocities.com/athens/academy/8919/olmes/2htm.

Masagara, N. (1997) "Negotiating the truth through oath forms" *Journal of Multilingual and Multicultural Development*. 18(5), pp.385-400.

Mashiri, P. (2003) "Managing face in urban public transport: Polite request strategies in Commuter Omnibus Discourse in Harare" *AILA Review* 16, pp.120-126.

Mawadza, A. (2000) "Harare Shona slang. A linguistic study" *Zambezia* 27(1), pp.93-101.

Mazrui, A.A. and Mazrui, A.M (1998) *The Power of Babel: Language and Governance in the African Experience*. Chicago: University of Chicago Press.

Mudimbe, Y.V. (1994) *The Idea of Africa: Gnosis, Philosophy and the Order of Knowledge:* Bloomington: Indiana University Press.

Mufwene, S. (2002) "Colonization, globalization and the

future of languages in the 21st century" *International Journal of Multicultural Societies* 4, pp.165-197.

Mühlhäusler, P. (1996) *Linguistic Ecology: Language Change and Linguistic Imperialism in the Pacific Region*. New York: Routledge.

Mvula, E.T. (1992) "Language Policies in Africa: the case for chiChewa in Malawi" In R.K Herbert (ed) *Language and Society in Africa. The Theory and Practice of Sociolinguistics*. (pp.37-47). Johannesburg: Witwatersrand University Press.

Ngom, T. (2005) "Linguistic and sociocultural hybridization in Senegalese urban spaces" In T.Falola abd S. Salm (eds) *Urbanization and African Cultures* (pp. 279-295). Durham, NC: Carolina Academic Press.

Njoroge, K. (1986) "Multilingualism and some of its implications for language policy and practices in Kenya" In A.Davies (ed) *Language in Education in Africa* (pp. 327-353). Edinburgh: Centre of African Studies, University of Edinburgh.

Pennycook, A. and E. Otsuji (2015) *Metrolingualism: Language in the City*. London and New York: Routledge.

Perley, B. (2012) "Zombie Linguistics: experts, endangered languages and the curse of undead voices" *Anthropological Forum* 22(2) pp.133-149.

Prah, K. (1999) *African Languages for the Mass Education of Africans*. Cape Town: The Centre for the Advanced Study of African Societies.

Phillipson, R. (2003) *English only? Challenging Language Policy*. London: Routledge.

Prinsloo,D.J. and Gilles-Mauricede Schryver (eds), Pieter S.Groenewaldetal. (dictionary committee) (2000). *SeDiPro 1.0, First Parallel Dictionary Sepêdi-English*. Pretoria: University of Pretoria.

Prinsloo, D. and de Schruyver, G-M. (2001) "Corpus based

activities versus intuition -based compilations by lexicographers, the Sepedi-Lemma sign list as a case in point" *The Nordic Journal of African Languages* 10(3), pp.374-398.

Prinsloo, D.J. and de Schruyver, G.-M. (2003) "Non-word error detection in current South African spell checkers" *Southern African Applied Linguistics and Applied language Studies.* 21(4), pp.307-326.

Skutnabb-Kangas, T. (2003). "Linguistic diversity and biodiversity: The threat from killer languages" In C. Mair (ed) *The Politics of English as a World Language: New Horizons in Postcolonial Cultural Studies.* (pp.31-52). Amsterdam: Rodopi.

Soynika,W. (1987). "Banquet Speech" In W. Odelberg (ed) *Les prix Nobel = The Nobel Prizes 1986.* Stockholm: Nobel Foundation.

Spear, T. (2003) "Neo-nationalism and limits of invention in British colonial Africa" *Journal of African history* 44, pp.3-27.

Thomas, N. (1994) *Colonialism's Culture: Anthropology Travel and Government,* Oxford: Polity Press.

Vansina, J. (1990) *The essential Wallerstein.* New York: New York Press.

Woolard, K. (2004) "Is the past a foreign country? Time, language origins and the nation in early modern Spain" *Journal of Linguistic Anthropology* 14(1), pp.57-80.

Yngve, V. (2004) "Issues in hard-science linguistics" In V.Yngve and Z. Wasik (eds) *Hard-Science Linguistics* (pp 27-35). New York: Continuum.

V

Multilingualism:
Spontaneous Orders And System D
A Concluding Note

I would like to express my gratitude to the editor of this Special Issue for the opportunity to reflect on the articles. Even though this volume covers a wide range of issues, it has one underlying principle: diversity. Diversity is viewed through a number of prisms, including, but not restricted to home language, multilingualism, and lingua franca. In this concluding commentary, I analyze the nature of the prisms through which diversity is framed in the papers and the consequences of such an analysis on sociolinguistic practices.

One of the powerful arguments made through the issue is the value of multilingualism, reflected in the notion of lingua franca. That multilingualism can serve as a critique of the idea of pluralization of singularity or the tendency to view languages as hermetically sealed units that can be separated from each other is now well-known. The issue therefore should not be that lingua franca renders it hard to count the number of languages, but the countability of languages which should never have been an important issue in the first instance.

From multilingualism to System D
If languages are not discrete entities, then they are not autonomous and cannot be separated from individual and community experiences, history, geography, and context. Fur-

thermore, if languages are not discrete, the underlying principle in notions about phonology being distinct from phonetics, lexis from semantics, and form from meaning are difficult to sustain. The idea of multilingualism has to be treated extremely circumspectly otherwise it might end up not being as productive as originally intended.

Multilingualism has to be treated carefully and we have to avoid celebrating it without providing a systematic analysis of terms such as repertoires, resources, diversity, and related terms. Furthermore, multilingualism as a way of framing sociolinguistics is founded on the assumption that it is the idea of a code-ideology, also referred to as monolingualism, that constitutes a problem because it cannot capture the complex social dynamics of current societies.

I prefer the term 'System D' as an alternative to multilingualism because while multilingualism may lead us to concentrate on notions about languages, irrespective of whether we are referring to repertoires, resources, supervernaculars and other related terms, it is still language which is central to the frameworks. Instead of multilingualism, and other relatively new terms, I prefer the term 'System D' because it draws our attention to individual abilities, to respond to challenges, to improvise, and be creative in resolving social and linguistic problems. 'System D' therefore provides us with an opportunity to pay attention to what we actually do in resolving problems or challenges we are confronted with in postcolonial contexts. It is particularly relevant to complex urban contexts because it captures human capacity to think quickly, and at times in unorthodox ways when getting a job done under severe time pressures. The term 'System D' has been used by Robert Neuwirth (2006) but was brought into wide circulation by Anthony Bourdain (2006) in his book on travels and food. The term 'D' originated from the French noun *débrouillardise* or *démerde*

(French slang). 'D' is a shorthand to make do, to manage, especially in adverse situations.

From multilingualism to spontaneous order
Generally, I agree with the contributors about the conceptual limitations of the notion of discrete languages. I, however, feel that the implications of this critique of languages as discrete have not been fully articulated and a positive path has not been proposed. I would like to propose that we consider drawing on metaphors from other areas of scholarship such as Economics in order to develop our ideas further. An attractive position to pursue is the idea of 'spontaneous order'. A 'spontaneous order' enables us to capture the degree to which language, like other issues, is a product of human action, and not a consequence of a pre-designed plan. Language in education is apparently based on a notion of language as a pre-designed plan thus contrary to the idea of 'spontaneous order'. The idea of a spontaneous order renders it feasible to capture and create a latitude for human action all be it within physical, political, and physiological constraints (En.wikipedia.org/spontaneous-order, 23 June 2014). 'Spontaneous orders' are scale-free and are neither controlled nor controllable by anyone. If languages are 'spontaneous orders,' neither fully controlled nor controllable, the construct poses a serious challenge to language teaching and language planning which are in varying degrees based upon the assumption that language is controllable and its scale can be determined.

I am not arguing that language education requires both notions of monolingualism and multilingualism. What is required is an awareness that:

> language appears as something different depending how we look at it. Objectification of language as a thing—makes particular problems appear to demand

123

urgent rectification. But how far is the problem "language" or the way we are thinking about languages? (Fardon and Furniss 1994, 9).

If the nature of language depends upon how it is perceived, because language is not a natural object, then language teaching is itself a projection of a specific view of language. In other words, when we are teaching and indeed researching language, we are advancing specific views about language and society.

Identity
Identity is widely used in African Studies. Because of the weight of the identity regime there are two main features that Brubacker (2004, Stoler 2002) regards as relevant: 'strong and weak identities.' Strong identity refers to a consistency in the nature of social and behavioral practices including language performance. On the other hand, 'weak identity' is a flexible, fluid, and adaptable usage of identity. Strong identity is essentialist, whereas weak identity is founded on 'soft' social constructivism in which individuals choose an identity by exercising individual agency. This means an individual is not trapped by the history and contemporary nature of their identity. The capacity and latitude of individuals to express and shape their identity is restricted by the fact that agency and the choices they make are constrained by a combination of linguistic, historical, and social factors. Paradoxically, if identity were completely free, the social and linguistic practices would be uninterruptable; after all, choice is meaningful if it is restricted as Brubacker cautions: 'If identity is everywhere it is nowhere' (2004, 29). The key issue, however, is the issue of identity which we project as scholars. Perhaps even more important, the identity trope is a reflection of a crisis of elitist middle-class

scholars. I doubt whether the low rural class Africans feel that identity is an important matter to consider.

Ownership

Ownership irrespective of whether it is partial or full can be fruitfully understood when it is situated in social theory and in historical and contemporary contexts. From the point of view of legal theory, if language is open-access it can be collectively owned because it is fundamentally non-property. The converse is also the case, that if language is a closed system, its ownership can be dominated by specific people or groups (as argued below).

Home language

One of the recurring themes in language education is the importance of home language. It is now commonly accepted that cognitive advancement occurs when students are taught in their home language. The idea of home language reflects a nationalistic view of language in which each group owns its artifact called "language," a phenomenon similar to each group's ownership of other symbols, such as land, country, etc. If home language is one of the symbols of nationalism, promotion of home language is a powerful mechanism for the advocacy of nationalism. Any nationalistic movement may have unintended effects, some of which may be negative. Therefore, language teaching, particularly the promotion of home languages, must assess whether the benefits of language teaching in a home language outweigh any negative effects.

While the promotion of a home language may be controversial, the presence of indigenous perspectives about language should not be. For example, in indigenous communities, knowledge of language may entail capabilities to sing in that language, and in many cases, knowledge of indigenous language does not necessarily mean the language is

125

easily understandable to outsiders. Teaching and promotion of indigenous languages, however, involve the exact opposite – transparency within the language – and are restricted to writing, reading, and speaking. Promotion of indigenous languages should, therefore, include the ways in which we seriously try and capture the conflicting meanings of language practices, the diversity in the interpretation.

Super-vernacular and super-diversity

Super-diversity is increasingly becoming a popular framework used in the analysis of language practices; even though it is not discussed in this Special Issue, it is quite clear that it overshadows some of the discussion. I am uncomfortable with the idea of diversity, even more so than super-diversity because it celebrates differences and, thus, reinforces social, ethnic, and class differences rather than challenging the elitism implied. Superdiversity does not make a distinction between claims and sociolinguistic facts. I seriously wonder whether users of the so-called super-diversity regard their sociolinguistic research as diverse. In other words, discussions of super-diversity are etic but presented as if the material is emic.

Anglo-American

The geographical and geo-linguistic space covered by the Special Issue is impressive. However, the papers are unintentionally constrained by Anglo-American frameworks. It would have been enlightening to explore the nature of language planning practices that cut across a geo-linguistic space in different geographical areas, particularly former Portuguese colonies. Lusophone countries provide a fascinating approach to language challenges, particularly the impact of Lusitanization (i.e., the spread of Portuguese colonial ideology) as a framework in former Portuguese colonies. This approach would have provided an additional lens through which to frame colonial and ex-colonial language practices because of the increasing importance of Brazil over Portugal in the spread of Portuguese.

Conclusion
In this informal commentary, I have provided an account that, I hope, complements the approaches adopted in the Special Issue.

References
Bourdain, Anthony (2006). *The Nasty Bits, Collected Varietal Cuts, Usable TRIM, Scraps, and Bones.* New York: Anchor.

Brubacker, Roger (2004). *Ethnicity Without Groups.* Cambridge, MA: Harvard University Press.

Fardon, Richard, and Furniss, Graham (1994). *African Languages, Development and the State.* London: Routledge.

Neuwirth, R. (2006). *Shadow Cities: A Billion Squatters, a New Urban World.* London: Routledge.

Stoler, Anne (2002). *Carnal Knowledge and Imperial Power: Race and the Intimate in Colonial Rule.* Berkeley: University of California Press

VI

Romanticizing Differences And Managing Diversities: A Perspective On Harmonization, Language Policy, And Planning

Preamble

Harmonization and other sociolinguistic variants (e.g., unification, soft harmonization, natural harmonization, core, and cluster) are metaphors that describe a series of interlocking metalinguistic processes through which common vocabulary or structure for a putative language is created. Metalinguistic processes are neither historically new nor restricted to Africa. Even though harmonization is situated in this special issue in African contexts (with the exception of one paper on China), five key principles arise whose relevance resonates beyond historical and contemporary Africa: (1) community participation in harmonization projects, (2) the role and status of harmonization as a strategy to facilitate social equality, (3) management of diversity, (4) harmonization and the development of epistemology of African languages, and (5) the adequacy of harmonization as a method of historical analysis.

First, it is plausible to argue that harmonization projects are likely to fail if communities do not participate actively in such projects. While this may be true, the converse does not necessarily always apply. In other words, community involvement in harmonization and related projects does not necessarily guarantee the success of such projects (Dobrin 2008). Second, while one of the most powerful arguments supporting harmonization is the benefits of language development, it does not necessarily result in social equality. In some cases, paradoxically, it may even accentuate differences within communities. Third, harmonization creates intellectual opportunities to manage diversity, serving as an important counterpoint to a romantic celebration of diversity apparent in some African sociolinguistic projects. Diversity in harmonization is construed as problematic. Fourth, harmonization provides opportunities to explore the relationship between language and epistemology. By tracing the discursive trajectories of philosophies and metaphors about language, harmonization creates an intellectual space that renders it feasible to outline the development of philosophical thoughts in African sociolinguistics. Fifth, because of a 'linguistic turn' in African history, harmonization, as a form of linguistic analysis, is a form of historical practice. Harmonization's effectiveness as a method of historical study, inter-alia, is one of the primary issues addressed in this special issue.

In light of the above introduction, I explore the implications of harmonization for language policy, history, and philosophy in Africa using Zimbabwe, South Africa, Sudan, and Senegal as case studies. In these case studies, I draw upon a diverse range of materials, including language reports, controversies among African intellectuals in local African newspapers, and academic material on the topic. I conclude this introductory essay with a brief description of the articles in this special collection and the ways their contributions substantiate the complex relationship among harmonization, politics of language, and language policies in Africa. Specifically, I address the following questions and organize my introduction around them:

1. What is the relationship between harmonization and

unification, and what are the implications of that
relationship for language policy?
2. What is the relationship between harmonization and
standardization, and what are the implications of that
relationship for language policy?
3. What is the relationship between harmonization and
individual and social identities, and what are its
implications for language policy?
4. What is the role of language academies and the State in
promoting harmonization, and what are implications
of such politics for language policy?
5. What is the nature of community participation in
development of indigenous languages?

Harmonization, unification, and language policy
The term *harmonization* was rarely used in colonial linguistics but was foreshadowed by the term *unification*. While both terms may be considered semantically identical, they are ideologically different. Unification of African languages as a discourse strategy is part of the universe of colonialism or a form of 'vernacular construction' in terms of colonial discourses, while harmonization is part of a discourse that seeks to contain and reverse the effects of colonialism's legacy. Unification and harmonization, therefore, have different ideological and discursive statuses, histories, and trajectories in African sociolinguistic thought. The degree to which harmonization succeeds in containing the legacy of colonialism is a moot question, as I illustrate in this introduction.

The unification of African languages or dialects entailed 'aligning' different orthographies, integrating multiple orthographies, or establishing common linguistic features. The most well-known examples of harmonization are the unification of Shona dialects (Doke 1931) and *Union Igbo*. Another meaning of *harmonization* is the one associated with Prah (2008) in which harmonization is defined as made up of combining dialects into mutually understood languages or clustering dialects into 12 mutually understood (written) languages.

Unification of languages or dialects is apparently aimed to produce 'economies of scale,' which will make producing material in African languages attractive to publishers, thereby enhancing literacy in those languages. In the colonial period, unification was construed as both a linguistic and political project. For example, the unification of Shona dialects can be taken as a strategy to facilitate colonial administration and control of Africans. The ways in which the social and linguistic aspects of linguistic unification and harmonization were realized differed, depending upon the dynamics and politics of each context. In light of these dynamics, I have opted to illustrate my argument using a number of case studies: Zimbabwe, South Africa, Sudan, and Senegal.

Colonial Rhodesia and the unification of Shona
Colonial Rhodesia aptly illustrates issues about the 'unification of Shona dialects' (Doke 1931) and the role of individual linguists, missionaries, and the colonial state in facilitating unification. The title of the Doke (1931) report, *Report on the Unification of the Shona Dialects*, suggests that the dialects were being unified, not the languages themselves (if such a distinction is epistemologically possible). The Doke report is an excellent example of colonial government intervention into African sociolinguistics in Rhodesia. In the report, it is made clear that these efforts were 'carried out under the auspices of the Government of Southern Rhodesia and the Carnegie Corporation' and were presented to the Colonial Rhodesia Legislative Assembly in 1931 (Doke 1931). The fact that unification was sponsored by the Southern Rhodesian government reflects its institutional

status and its relevance as one of the instruments used by the colonial government not only to manage but also to constrain diversity. That the project was also funded partly by the Carnegie Corporation (CC) is also significant because the CC was supposedly a philanthropic organization seeking to fund research and improve social advancement in Canada and then-British colonies. However, this objective was broad enough to include projects such as the Doke report that appear to improve the welfare of Africans immediately or in the long term. The CC's funding of the Doke report reflects the complex relations between colonialism, on the one hand, and philanthropic concerns with colonialism, on the other.

In the table of the contents of Doke's (1931) report, the metalanguage about language is imprecise and used inconsistently. For example, reference is made to 'language-groups' and 'dialects': the *Zezuru*, *Karanga*, and *Manyika* language-groups. Surprisingly, the terminology changes from pages 119–135 of the report, where there is a shift to *Manyika* or *Zezuru*. At a conceptual level, the indeterminacy in the use of the categories 'group,' 'language,' and 'dialect' in a report, which has significant importance in the discursive history of Shona, reflects inconsistency and ideological conflicts. The term *Shona union* is, at times, used alternatively with *union Shona*, masking tensions within colonial discourses about language practices encapsulated in terms such as 'language-group,' 'language,' and 'dialects.' This inconsistency is not peculiar to colonial missionary encounters but also recurs in other reports and in radical postcolonial African scholarship on language harmonization. The inconsistency and widespread nature of the terms relating to harmonization are apparent in the use of alternative and perhaps conflicting terms such as 'soft harmonization,' 'natural harmonization,' 'core languages,' and 'language clusters.' The inconsistency and multiple uses of categories render it difficult to navigate both colonial and postcolonial scholarship on harmonization. Regardless of how the terms were used, they had clear social impact and influenced colonial and postcolonial elite/nationalist government to manage and organize African communities.

In Rhodesia, there were a number of different missionaries, including Anglican, Dutch, and American. Each missionary station developed its version of Latinate orthography and spelling in the late twentieth and early twenty first centuries. In some cases, Rhodesian orthographies were modeled on those from other geographical regions, particularly East Africa. In rare cases, individual missionaries invented their own orthographies, a situation that was not peculiar to Rhodesia/Zimbabwe. The illustration below captures the relationship between different missionaries and geographical regions from which they operated and sub-ethnicities in which they were located:

Zezuru Roman Catholic Church and Wesleyan Methodist
    Church
Ndau American Board Mission and American Methodist
ChiManyika Anglican
Kalanga London Missionary Society
Karanga Dutch Reformed Church

In such cases, unionization of languages was prompted by a standard language ideology that sought to establish uniformity over variation, the underlying assumption being that diversity has to be managed and unionization was implemented as a diversity management strategy. Paradoxically, unification or creation of standardized languages enhanced sociolinguistic diversity in speech practices. The varieties that formed the basis on which the orthographies were produced were versions of Shona or African languages spoken by missionaries and referred to as (*chibaba*) in colonial Rhodesia. Missionary speakers of *chibaba* were second language

134

speakers of African languages and, therefore, bilingual. In simple terms, the orthographies produced were solely based on Europeanized varieties of African languages. Yet *chibaba* was widely used when it was subsequently framed as an indigenous language and used as a medium of instruction in schools. *Chibaba* and *union Shona* contributed to the emergence of a diaglossic situation that might not have existed prior to African/missionary encounters. While missionary engagement with Rhodesia enhanced linguistic diversity, it also limited it. The construction of African grammars for individual dialects reduced the diversity within African communities because diverse languages were described using the same template that, ultimately, was drawn from Latin. However, the *chibaba* example shows that Europeans were 'authorities' in a development of orthographies, coining terms, compiling dictionaries and grammars, translating books in particular the Bible.

Identities and wars over diacritics
In Rhodesia, early efforts to address perceived problems arising from orthographic variation were addressed at a religious conference in 1909. Efforts to create a written standard orthography (i.e., to harmonize different orthographies) did not succeed because of differences between religious denominations about which orthography to adopt. Each denomination identified intensely with its own orthography and felt that selecting a single orthography or integrating them was impossible. Put differently, there was tension between standardization and variation; similar conflicts occurred in other contexts as well.

After the failure of the 1909 religious conference to create a union Shona, Doke, a linguist from Witwatersrand, was tasked with standardizing Shona. He based his integration of Shona largely on *Manyika* and *chiZezuru,* excluding other dialects such as *Ndau* and *Kalanga*. The latter was

135

assigned as a dialect to another language: Ndebele spoken in Southwestern Zimbabwe. Phonetic and phonological properties and a major component of *chiNdau* were also excluded from union Shona. At a lexical and idiomatic level, union Shona was based largely on *chiZezuru*, which de facto approximated closely union Shona. Since *chiNdau* speakers and *Kalanga* speakers did not constitute a major basis for the construction of union Shona, speakers of those dialects could be construed as having been discriminated against.

Another important consequence of the Rejaf conference (Abdelhay et al. 2013) that had long-term effects was the exclusion of Arabic as a medium of instruction in south Sudan, thus enhancing the image of a Christian/English/African South, as opposed to an Arab/Islamic North. The 1929 Rejaf conference was the third to address issues about language in education and orthographies for the Sudan and Northern Uganda. Ongoing conferences in 1918, 1927, and 1929 (the Rejaf conference) were designed to address language in southern Sudan (Miner 2003).

The Rejaf conference was attended by representatives from different African colonies, such as Uganda and the Belgian Congo. It was chaired by M.M.J. Matthew, then Secretary for Education and Health in the Sudan; delegates from six different missions; and Westermann, an expert in linguistics who had studied Shilluk, a language spoken in Southern Sudan. The conference was instructed to achieve the following:

1. To make recommendations as to whether a system of group languages could be selected as a medium of instruction.
2. To explore the possibility of a *unified system of orthography* (emphasis mine).
3. To explore cooperation in textbook production and the developments of templates for a 'skeleton grammar,'

reading books, and primers that would facilitate standardization of the curriculum across language groups.

Even though most of the deliberations about creating a unified system of orthography took place without any substantial input from Africans, a 'close reading' of Westermann reflects tensions between designing orthographies that would serve the interests of Europeans and those systems that would serve the interests of Africans:

> The script we want to introduce is intended for use *by* Africans, not for use by Europeans who want to learn the language. We should keep this constantly in mind. It means that we should try to look at the problems from *the African's point of view*, not from our own. His difficulties are *not always ours*; we are to remember that our views on orthography are *hopelessly* restricted by the *history* of orthography of our European languages. (Westermann in Rejaf 1928, pp. 14–15, as cited in Miner 2003)

Westermann (1928, as cited in Miner 2003) makes an apt point when he draws attention to the absence of African voices in conferences, even those addressing issues that would have a substantial impact on their sociolinguistic, educational, and political lives. There were, however, no monolithic missionary/colonial voices, as the Westermann quotation above expresses. Similarly, even when Africans were engaged in sociolinguistic issues, there was no monolithic African voice on issues relating to language harmonization. The multiplicity of missionary/colonial voices and African voices complicated relationships between colonialism and African resistance, and the nature of the politics of each participant cannot be easily read from the position they adopted toward issues about language in language policy. Ironically, even when Africans, largely African elites, were involved, sharp and, at times, acrimonious controversies arose. For example, the Nhlapo-Rabaroko debate in South Africa during the apartheid regime reflects the degree and extent to which there was no monolithic African voice on harmonization of African languages and its suitability as an instrument of language policy.

The Nhlapo proposal and recurring controversies about harmonization

Nhlapo (1953) is well known in southern African sociolinguistics literature for his proposal to unify Nguni languages, on the one hand, and Sotho languages, on the other. The proposal generated acute controversy and acrimonious debate led by Raboroko (1953). Jacob Nhlapo (also affectionately referred to as 'Dr. Degrees' by his friends and acquaintances because of the many degrees he had either acquired or had conferred on him) is well known for his contribution to language policy, particularly his proposal that all major languages be systematically combined into a single language, "the throwing of Bantu languages into one pot" in the 1944 pamphlet *Bantu Babel: Will the Bantu Language Live?* Reviewing that pamphlet Dhlomo excitedly described Nhlapo's argument that Xhosa, Zulu, and other intermediate languages such as Swazi and Ndebele be *made into one language*: "...People who speak or write Xhosaised Zulu and Zuluised Xhosa should be encouraged and not condemned. They are forerunners to the harmonized Nguni languages" (Dhlomo 1944, also quoted in Masilela, n.d.). Nhlapo (1953) elaborated his argument about the unification of Nguni languages in a short essay entitled "The Problem of Many Tongues" in the monthly magazine *Liberation* in August 1953. The essay elicited vicious reaction by Raboroko (1953) in the September 1953 issue of *Liberation*. In "The

Linguistic Revolution" Raboroko described Nhlapo's proposal of throwing Bantu languages into one pot as "preposterous and impracticable." The Nhlapo/Raboroko debate and the intellectual history of South Africa, when compared with that of Shona in Zimbabwe, demonstrate the extent to which the same sociolinguistic situation may yield different outcomes. For example, Shona was regarded as a continuum, while in South Africa, the policies produced speech forms that were construed as different languages.

The idea of harmonization generated controversies even in post-apartheid South Africa when it was revived by Neville Alexander, who proposed that it become the basis of language policy in South Africa. The underlying assumption in Nhlapo/Neville Alexander (see Heugh, 2016) seems to be that language diversity is impracticable as a site of language policy; diversity needed to be managed. Harmonization would reduce the extent of diversity, rendering the policies much more manageable. Nhlapo, and to some extent Alexander, seem to have been concentrating on language as a system—as forms that can be integrated.

The response by Sizwe Satyo, a specialist in African languages at the University of Cape Town, to Nhlapo/Alexander at the University of Cape Town is indicative of the challenges African scholars faced regarding issues about harmonization and the challenges that diversity poses for the framework. Satyo proposed a much more watered-down version of harmonization that he referred to as 'soft harmonization.' For Satyo, it was not necessary to develop and harmonize African languages because the processes of harmonization had already taken place, rendering efforts to harmonize them unnecessary. If harmonization had to take place, Satyo argued, it had to be a bottom-up policy, unlike that proposed by Nhlapo/Alexander. In both proposals, the voices and participation of local communities are erased from view. Arguably, however, local communities played a more significant role in 'soft harmonization' because the objective was to describe language practices as they were–forms of 'pan-ethnic vernaculars'–and not as idealized artifacts, as in the Nhlapo/ Alexander framework.

Arabic, indigenous orthography and Latin alphabet: the case of Senegal

In African scholarship, there has been a general conviction of the cognitive and social benefits of using *indigenous* African languages in literacy and schooling. The case of Senegal compels us to adopt a much more nuanced view of this argument. In most cases, indigenous refers to language, not locally created orthographies, as the Senegalese case illustrates. In Senegal, the *Mande* and *Nko* were literate using Nko orthography indigenous to Senegal. Between 1958 and 1968, sharp controversies arose about orthography: whether to use *Ajami* (an Arab-based orthography), a Latin orthography, or indigenous orthography in Senegal. Two other idiosyncratic scripts, as pointed out earlier, were constructed and disseminated by a tailor and a selftaught Arabist. One of the most powerful arguments for the use of *Ajami* was that a relatively large number of Senegalese were literate in a variety of *Ajami* that had been adapted to the Wolof, Pulaar, and Mandingo languages. A relatively small minority of Senegalese learn to read and write in French; from such a perspective, one would have imagined that *Ajami* and not a Latinate-based orthography would have been used.

Contrary to expectations, a national language policy was proclaimed in support of a Latinate based orthography. Issues about orthography were so socially divisive that the Senegalese Supreme Court had to intervene. Such sharp controversies arose over the use of diagraphs that their use was subsequently determined by the Senegalese Supreme Court Decree No. 71,566 of May 1971, which adopted the

140

'one letter for one sound' principle for the six Senegalese languages. The Senegalese Supreme Court's intervention and ruling in favor of the 'one letter one sound' principle reflects its beliefs about the importance of standardization as a primary feature of language. The 'one letter one sound' policy and the use of a Latinate orthography did not, however, change or affect actual writing practices because the writing of some Senegalese drew bits and pieces from different orthographies. The Senegalese case illustrates the degree to which language policy pronouncements are, at times, aimed at unscrambling writing practices and producing idealized forms of writing wherein only one orthography is used at a time, not a combination of different orthographies. From a Senegalese perspective, harmonized practices were interpreted as problematic, while, in other contexts, the absence of harmonization was a source of problems, as the Pan Africanist perspective discussed below shows.

Pan African approaches to harmonization
While most of the projects on language unification and harmonization that I have discussed so far dealt with specific countries or regions, the 'harmonization project' led by Ghanaian sociologist Kwesi Prah was much more ambitious. Pan-African in scope insofar as it attempted to describe and outline principles along which harmonization may be developed in Africa, this project, on which Prah has been working for the last quarter century, was prompted by the need to develop policies and literacy materials that could be widely used across different polities of the African continent. Extensive usage of literacy materials was limited by the linguistic diversity within Africa. Prah (2008) argued that among 600–700 million Africans, 80–85 % speak 15–17 'core' languages either as first, second, or third languages. An example of a language 'cluster' can be illustrated by Gbe/Ewespeaking peoples, who can be found along the

141

West African coast from Ghana, Togo, Benin, and the Nigerian border. The cluster includes Aja in Badagry/Nigeria, Aja, Mina and Fon in Benin, Mina and Ewe in Togo and Ewe in Ghana (Prah 2008). Another example that easily forms a cluster is Ndebele speakers, who can be found in South Africa, Botswana, Lesotho, Swaziland, and Zimbabwe. The presence of a limited number of 'core' languages makes introduction of literacy much easier, and perhaps the fewer languages spoken by relatively large numbers of people makes producing literacy material more attractive to publishers than producing written materials that are used by a small number of people. Kwesi Prah deserves credit for his harmonization project and his proposition for rendering diversity in Africa manageable and beneficial to Africans and perhaps more economically attractive to publishers.

Because of the importance of Prah's project, it is necessary to evaluate some of the main principles on which it is founded. While Prah might be correct about the number of core languages and the percentages of Africans who speak them, how he arrived at the figures he treats as factual is not empirically self-evident. Efforts to establish common principles of mutual intelligibility are important insofar as they attempt to build consistency in measuring intelligibility; thus, it behooves him to explain theoretically why he arrived at an 80 % cutoff point. Another primary theoretical advantage of Prah's project is how he uses the same framework and instrumentation in different contexts. The use of the same instruments gives the project a high degree of reliability, but unfortunately, the sociolinguistic validity of the project becomes suspect because the methodology does not seem to be sensitive to context. As a result, he ends up in a situation that he may not have found productive: a one-size-fits-all approach. Prah is clearly writing from a managerial position in which counting and innumerability are critically important. The identification either of core languages or dialects that can be made into clusters is conceivable if one subscribes to the positivistic assumption that languages are external and independent of their users. The concepts of 'core' and cluster are 'akin' to the metaphor of languages, which, like the former, tries to capture the nature of the relationships between languages. The difference, however, is that Prah postulates social relationships between languages while the family metaphor biologizes relationships between languages.

Reflections
In this special issue, I have explored the nature of the construct of harmonization by situating it within different historical and contemporary contexts, ranging from late 19th century Sudan to contemporary Chinese feelings about harmonization. In the issue, it was apparent that harmonization could be used both to serve issues about 'governmentality' (Foucault 1978/1982, p. 43) during colonial rule and, at times, to mitigate the effects of colonialism. The analysis, however, also illustrated that there are no uniform and monological voices about the value and significance of harmonization, either during the colonial era or in postcolonial Africa. Harmonization has been proposed as a way to accomplish many language planning objectives. In some cases, such as the formation of *union Igbo* and *union Shona* (also referred to as *Shona union*), which were legislated in the ninetieth and early twentieth centuries, the long-term effects of the formation or birth of the languages are real and apparent, as captured in language materials and tests. In other cases, such as Kwesi Prah's project, it is still too early to be fully aware of the impact because such projects vary in their uptake.

In spite of these factors, one major intellectual theme runs through most of these projects. The emphasis has been on the role and status of African languages within African languages (i.e., whether, African languages were to be theoretically amalgamated or kept as separate entities) and not in relationship to European languages. There is, contrary to expectations, very limited preoccupation with multilingualism. The closest reference to bilingualism is when Raboroko (1953) in his response to Jacob Nhlapo (1953) argues for the importance of bilingualism. The bilingualism he had in mind, however, was between African languages (e.g., Xhosa and Swahili). The issue in this case is not the practicality of using Swahili as a second language in southern African contexts but, rather, that English is erased from such discussion and is, thus, discursively constructed as irrelevant. The issue is not whether European languages would serve as national languages or whether the rights of African languages have to be maintained or advocated for. The issue that preoccupied most harmonizationists as analysts or practitioners was how to manage diversity, which, at times, was construed as negative, as illustrated in the following quotation from the Nhlapo reference

> When the question of reducing Ibo in Nigeria to writing, the multiplicity of its dialects reared its head. Each tribal group wished to have its dialect written. The writer in the language decided on 'Union Ibo' which was a fusing of the various dialects whose vocabularies became contributions to the combined language. *Union Ibo* was taught in schools and was used in the translation of the Bible.

One of the primary critiques of harmonization projects is the lack of robust community involvement in them. While this argument is clearly welcome, the converse does not necessarily apply. In other words, community involvement in issues directly affecting them does not necessarily result in successful uptake of the projects in the long term.

From a Western perspective, the lack or withdrawal of out-side expertise and involvement might be regarded as valuable because it shows respect for a community's autonomy. However, in some cases, that community may construe withdrawal from the projects as lack of commitment to a project that outsiders themselves have initially set up and in which the communities might not have had any strong interest in the beginning, as Bashkow (2006) observed with Papua New Guinea:

> While well-meaning westerners are intensely concerned to respect the dignity—implying autonomy—of people they see as poor or subaltern, Papua New Guineans often interpret westerners' hesitancy to involve themselves in their affairs as disdainful aloofness, one that leads people to draw negative inferences about their own moral worth.
> (Bashkow 2006, as cited in Dobrin 2008, p. 307)

Bashkow's observation raises some skepticism of statements such as the following, which have tended to be regarded as axiomatic:

> It is only if indigenous speech community itself desires and initiates efforts toward language survival that such programs should exist or would have any chance of success. (Hinton 2001, p. 5, as cited in Dobrin 2008, p. 303)

> Only the indigenous community itself can save its language. (Crystal 2000, p. 111, as cited in Dobrin 2008, p. 303)

> The overall success of any revitalization program depends on the motivation of the future speakers and

community which supports them. (Grenoble and Whaley 2006, p. 20, as cited in Dobrin 2008, p. 303)

Even if the issue of community involvement or lack thereof is resolved, a number of critically important issues remain. For example, involvement in indigenous communities is founded on a philosophical assumption that the notions of language, language proficiency, etc., between even Western-trained linguists are identical to those of the local indigenous communities. Yet as Makoni and Severo (2015) argue, 'language' may be understood as singing traditional and religious indigenous songs to carry local cultural meanings that are not comprehensible to those who do not belong to the local indigenous communities. In such situations, efforts to harmonize orthographies may not necessarily result in preservation of the communities' cultural practices because they tend to override existing forms of writing.

Interest in promotion of indigenous languages that entails complex harmonization of dialects does not necessarily result in protection of indigenous cultures and may fail to appreciate the complex ways that communities use language practices and resist appropriation of new ways of discourse practices to protect their indigenous practices. This creates a conundrum for scholars because, while the intervention may be motivated by desires to protect or enhance the communities' capabilities to function in contemporary societies, indigenous communities may view their resistance to exactly the same projects, which are proposed for their advancement, as depriving them of a sense of self-preservation!

Descriptions of articles in the issue
This special issue is made up of five articles, excluding this introductory essay. The articles range from an analysis of theoretical issues relating to harmonization in Africa to perspectives about harmonization from outside Africa, in this

case China. In the first article in this collection, Heugh writes on the many different ways in which linguists in southern Africa have written about harmonization. Her paper is unique insofar as it gives insights into the nature of the debates among linguists on issues relating to harmonization. Heugh's paper is followed by Banda's that describes the nature of harmonization projects in cross-border languages. He uses harmonization as a framework on which regional language and cross-border language policies could be grounded. His main focus is on southern Africa, but given the pervasive nature of cross-border languages, Banda's contribution is relevant to many geographical regions in East, West, and North Africa. Chebanne's paper is interesting as it tries to both focus on a specific group, the Khoi-San, whose work might not be very well known in many parts of the world and to illustrate the extent to which harmonization may facilitate local development of the Khoi-San communities. The final article by Wang, Juffermans, and Du is on Chinese perspectives on harmonization. This paper explores the ways in which harmonization is framed culturally and used as a political instrument of power by the Chinese government. The authors, however, finally demonstrate the degree to which the Chinese may deploy and undermine the policing powers of the Chinese government through the use of the Internet.

Acknowledgments

I'd like to express my sincere thanks to Kaushalya Perera who managed and successfully adminis-tered the project.

References

Abdelhay, B., Makoni, B., & Makoni, S. (2013). "A very 'oily' sociolinguistics of the "New Sudan": Old wine in new bottles" In N. Kamwangamalu, R. Baldauf, & R. Kaplan (Eds.), *Language planning in Africa: Cameroon, Sudan, and Zimbabwe*. London: Routledge.

Dhlomo, I.E.H. (1944). "Weekly review and commentary" *Ilanga lase Natal* March 18, 1944 (published under the pseudonym of "Busy-Bee") Viewed 22 June 2020: http://pzacad.pitzer.edu/NAM/newafrre/writers/hdhlomo/weekly/18-3-44.gif

Dobrin, L. (2008). "From linguistic elicitation to eliciting the linguist: Lessons in community empowerment from Melanesia" Language, 28(2), pp.300–325.

Doke, C. (1931). *Report on the unification of the Shona dialects: Carried out under the auspices of the Government of Southern Rhodesia, presented to the Legislative Assembly*. Southern Rhodesia: Mercury Press.

Heugh, K. (2016). "Harmonisation and South African languages: twentieth century debates of homogeneity and heterogeneity" *Language Policy* 15, pp.235-255.

Makoni, S., & Severo, C. (2015). "Lusitanization and Bakhtinian perspectives on the role of Portuguese in Angola and East Timor" *Journal of multilingual and Multicultural Development*, 36(2), pp.151–162.

Miner, E. (2003). "The development of Nuer linguistics" Retrieved from http://www.dlib.indiana.edu/collections/nuer/edward/linguistics.html

Nhlapo, J. (1944). *Bantu Babel: Will the Bantu Languages Live?* Cape Town: The African Bookman. (The Sixpenny library, Vol. 4)

Nhlapo, J. (1953). "The problem of many tongues"

148

Liberation: a journal of democratic discussion, 4 (August), pp.13-14.

Masilela, Ntongela (n.d.). "Jacob N. Nhlapo" Retrieved from http://pzacad.pitzer.edu/NAM/newafrre/writers/nhlapo/nhlapoS.htm

Prah K. (2008) "Language, Literacy and Knowledge Production in Africa" In: Hornberger N.H. (eds) *Encyclopedia of Language and Education*. Boston: Springer.

Raboroko, P. (1953). "The linguistic revolution" *Liberation: a journal of democratic discussion,* 5 (September), pp.14-19.

VII

Disinventing and (Re)Constituting Languages

(with Alastair Pennycook)

Abstract
In this paper we argue that although the problematic nature of language construction has been acknowledged by a number of skeptical authors, including the recent claim in this journal (Reagan, 2004) that there is no such thing as English or any other language, this critical approach to language still needs to develop a broader understanding of the processes of invention. A central part of our argument, therefore, is that it is not enough to acknowledge that languages have been invented, nor that linguistic metalanguage constructs the world in particular ways; rather, we need to understand the inter-relationships among metadiscursive regimes, language inventions, colonial history, language effects, alternative ways of understanding language, and strategies of disinvention and reconstitution. Any critical (applied) linguistic project that aims to deal with language in the contemporary world, however estimable its political intent may be, must also have ways of understanding the detrimental language effects it may engender unless it confronts the need for linguistic disinvention and reconstitution.

Introduction

In the first issue of this journal, Reagan (2004) proposed that "there is, or at least there may well be, no such thing as English. Indeed, my claim is even a bit stronger than this— not only is there no such thing as English, but there is arguably no such thing as Russian, French, Spanish, Chinese, Hindi, or any other language" (p. 42). To back up this provocative claim, Reagan argues that the notion of languages as fixed entities is problematic from both an historical and a social point of view. Historically, "language—*any* language —is constantly changing, and in flux, and thus any effort to demarcate the boundaries of a particular language are inevitably at best able to provide a snapshot of the language at a particular time and place" (p. 44); and socially, language varies across contexts, speakers, classes, genders and so on. A language, he suggests, is "ultimately a collection of idiolects which have been determined to belong together for what are ultimately non- and extra-linguistic reasons" (p.46). He concludes by arguing for a form of critical language awareness which employs a constructivist epistemology in order to "reject the positivist objectification of language, in favour of a more complex, sophisticated and nuanced view of language" (p. 56).

In this paper, we intend to push these insights further by exploring in greater depth the processes of linguistic invention and reinvention. We start with the premise that *languages*—and the *metalanguages* used to describe them— are inventions. By making this claim we are pointing to several interrelated concerns: First, languages were, in the most literal sense, invented, particularly as part of the Christian/colonial project. Second, in a parallel process, a linguistic metalanguage—or as we prefer, given its broader coverage, a *metadiscuscursive regime* (Bauman & Briggs, 2003, p. 299)—was also invented. Thus, alongside the invention of languages, an ideology of languages as separate and enumerable categories was also created, an ideology founded on a nominal view of language. An extreme extension of this nominal view of language enumerability arises when languages are treated as institutions, a view reinforced by the existence of grammars and dictionaries (Joseph, 2004). Third, these inventions have had very real and material effects, determining how languages have been understood, how language policies have been constructed, how education has been pursued, how people have come to identify with particular linguistic labels. And finally, as part of any critical linguistic project, we need to disinvent and reconstitute languages, a process that may involve becoming aware of the history of invention, and rethinking the ways we look at languages and their relation to identity, geographical location and other social practices. Given that we acknowledge the very real contemporary effects of these inventions, our intention in disinvention is not to return to some edenic pre-colonial era, but to find ways of rethinking language in the contemporary world.

It is our contention that although some of these themes have attracted attention over the years—the invention of languages is reasonably well documented, and the problematic assumptions underlying the metalanguage of linguistics has not escaped the attention of some linguists (e.g., Harris, 1980, 1981; Mühlhäusler, 1996) —the *interrelationship* between these elements, and the development of strategies for moving forward, have not been adequately considered. A central part of our argument, therefore, is that it is not enough to acknowledge that languages have been invented, nor that linguistic metalanguage constructs the world in particular ways; rather, we need to understand the interrelationships among metadiscursive regimes, language inventions, colonial history, language effects, alternative ways of understanding language, and strategies of disinvention and reconstitution. Any critical (applied) linguistic

153

project that aims to deal with language in the contemporary world, however estimable its political intent may be, must also have ways of understanding the detrimental language effects it may engender unless it confronts the need for linguistic disinvention and reconstitution.

Invention, imagination, construction

Terence Ranger's (1983) *The Invention of tradition in colonial Africa* is the Ur-text of invention (Spear, 2003, p. 5). The concept of invention is relevant to both colonial and contemporary postcolonial and metropolitan contexts. Conceptually, the notion of invention was initially used by Ranger to describe "not the invention of African traditions but how colonial authorities adopted recently constructed British institutions of the regiment, public school, country house, civil service and imperial monarchy to establish a feudal patriarchal ethic of African subordination." Yet, linking a notion of invention in overly simple terms to colonialism runs the danger of creating an impression that it was only colonial agents that were actively involved in the invention process, and that the process of invention culminated at the end of the colonial epoch. Such a view would be unhistorical. Vaughan (2003), for example, describes how contemporary elites in postcolonial Africa create their past as an "imaginative adaptation of Yoruba indigenous political structures (particularly Yoruba chieftaincy) to the processes of state formation in Nigeria in which Yoruba elites consistently deployed subjective interpretations of their past to construct structures and ideologies of power" (Spear, 2003, p. 11).

Our understanding of invention links closely with what Blommaert (1999, p. 104) calls 'discovery attitude', the defining aspect of which is the myth that Africa prior to colonization was a blank slate on which Europeans had to map their categories. The categories which were created included names of ethnic groups, languages, and how they were to be described. Everyone who had some knowledge of Africa could present his/her knowledge of them as 'discovery'. Another concept related to 'invention' is Edward Said's 'being there' (Said, 1985, pp. 156-7). The very fact of having been present in Africa, the Middle East, India, South East Asia—irrespective of length of stay or nature of association—is deemed adequate to claim 'knowledge' of the native languages and cultures. Missionaries, administrators and other colonial functionaries wrote grammars and textbooks which were based on very particular constructions of languages rather than the local languages used by the natives themselves, contributing to the Christianization of 'indigenous' languages (Isichei, 1995; Renck 1990). In some cases what were subsequently referred to as 'indigenous' languages were the variants which the missionaries themselves spoke in their exchanges with Africans, and not what the Africans spoke with each other. And Africans through their reactions were clearly aware how the codified languages constituted new languages. As Rusike commented,

> No African was given a seat in the unification committee and the use of the results is that the newly formed language is all a mixture of Xhosa, Zulu, Ndebele, Kitchen kaffir, Nyanja and English. To my mind it's not Shona language that the white people are trying to force but a white man's language. (Rusike, *Bantu Mirror* 1934)

Descriptions of indigenous languages reflected the internal referential discourse of the missionaries and the administrators in their discussions of the colonized, rather than the language use of the colonized. In the Christianization of indigenous languages, it was the analyst's individual competence and not necessarily those of the 'native informants'

155

which formed the basis of the description of so-called 'indigenous' languages. "Missionaries did not describe (or even learn) African languages because 'they were there'; their linguistic, scholarly work was embedded in a communicative praxis which had its own internal dynamics. In very broad terms, it was characterized by a gradual shift from descriptive appropriation to prescriptive imposition and control" (Fabian, 1986, p. 76).

The notion of invention is thus in a number of ways akin to Homi Bhabha's (1994) discussion of narration (*narrating the nation*) and Benedict Anderson's (1983) 'imagined community'. Contrary to Ranger's auto-criticism of the complexity of the concept of 'invention,' there are substantial similarities between 'invention' and Benedict Anderson's 'imagined communities': both point to the ways in which nations are imagined and narrated into being, and both stress the role of language, literacy, and institutions in that process. Ranger prefers Benedict Anderson's 'imagined community' because it effectively captures the multidimensionality of the process of invention. Unlike Anderson, however, we regard both languages and nations as being co-constructed dialectally, and thus concur with Joseph (2004) in his critique of the one-sidedness of Anderson's formulation: "Anderson's constructionist approach to nationalism is purchased at the price of an essentialist outlook on languages. It seems a bargain to the sociologist or political scientist, to whom it brings explanatory simplicity not to mention ease. But...it is a false simplicity. National languages and identities arise in tandem, dialectically, if you like, in a complex process that ought to be our focus of interest and study" (Joseph, 2004, p. 124).

The advantage of the term 'invention' is that it points to specific contexts—as well as the specific agendas and conceptual beliefs—in which institutions, structures, language and languages are produced, regulated and constituted.

156

For example, the invention of some African languages, such as Tswana, Shona, and Tsonga (mainly used in southern Africa) was based upon the Herderian view that was a significant part of the German Intellectual Romantic movement in which language, race and geographical location were constructed as indivisible. These conceptual insights have encouraged us to explore the essential contradictions in colonial rhetoric between preserving the past, promoting economic development and protecting Africans and other colonized people from the traumas of modernity. These contradictions were eloquently captured in colonial disdain for the 'detribalized' or 'trousered' Africans who responded most enthusiastically to the 'colonial civilizing mission'. 'Trousered' Africans, who were more likely than not to be educated, were held in disdain because they were treated as 'mimics' or 'hybrids' parodying white discourse (Jeater, 2004). The term hybrid was being used negatively to refer to the appropriation which took place in moments of encounter between Africans and whites (see Young, 1995). When the colonizers appropriated material from encounters they were not regarded as hybrids. The term hybrid was thus restricted to appropriation by the colonized 'trousered' Africans.

The insights from invention can serve as a critique of some aspects of language 'endangerment' as articulated by Nettle and Romaine (2000), Crystal (2000), and Skutnabb-Kangas (2003), amongst others. Currently, there is a discernible shift away from indigenous languages towards urban vernaculars in Africa. While some linguists may regard the shift as regrettable because it constitutes a form of endangerment, from an invention perspective, promoting the continued use of the indigenous languages constitutes a retrospective justification of colonial structures. While the shift from 'indigenous' languages to urban vernaculars may also be read as catastrophic from the perspective of some linguists, those who shift from indigenous languages to urban verna-

157

culars may construe the shift as a reflection of a creative adaptation to new contexts (Makoni & Meinhof, 2004). The advantage of the notion of 'invention' is that it provides opportunities for social intervention, and counter-practices through disinvention. For example, the widespread use of urban speech forms which are ontologically inconsistent with notions of 'language as hermetically sealed units' (Makoni, 1998) challenges existing dominant ideologies which constrain official policies, particularly in South Africa.

The conceptual orientations which we adopt in disinvention may also vary depending upon the problems we are seeking to address. Language planning debates have tended to think and articulate their positions in terms of solutions. Through disinvention we prefer to argue that it is more realistic to think in terms of viable alternatives than solutions. The conceptual alternatives which we propose might vary between situations. For example, in some situations the viable solution may lie in essentializing mother tongues, in other cases, in problematizing them (Pennycook, 2002). The ideology of invention serves as a critique of language imposition or linguistic imperialism, not in the sense that dominant languages are imposed on minority groups, but rather in the sense that the imposition lies in the ways in which speech forms are constituted/constructed into languages, and particular definitions of what constitutes language expertise are construed and imposed.

Inventing languages
An important starting point for understanding the invention of language is within the broader context of colonial invention. Our position that languages are inventions is consistent with observations that many structures, systems and constructs such as tradition, history, or ethnicity, which are often thought of as natural parts of society, are inventions of

a very specific ideological apparatus. To claim authenticity for such constructs, therefore, is to become subject to very particular discourses of identity. That is to say, while lived contemporary practices may create an authenticity of being and identification with certain traditions, languages and ethnicities, the history behind both their construction and maintenance needs to be understood in terms of its contingent constructedness. A great deal of historical work has drawn attention to the common project of the invention of history (the processes by which we establish legitimacy, lineage and linkage by reference to a constructed past (see Hobsbawn, 1983; Ranger, 1983, Wallerstein, 1999)). As Cohn (1996) and Wallestertein (1999) argue, a major aspect of the British colonial project in India was to turn Indian language, culture and knowledge into objects of European knowledge, to invent an India not in Britain's image but in Britain's image of what India should be like. Similarly, Mudimbe (1988) discusses in detail the ways in which Africa was invented. This project of invention needs therefore to be seen not merely as part of European attempts to design the world in their own image, but rather as part of the ideology of countability that was a cornerstone of European governance and surveillance of the world.

This process reached its peak in the late 19th and early 20th centuries. As Ranger (1983) puts it, "The 1870's, 1880's and 1890's were a time of a great flowering of European invented traditions—ecclesiastical, educational, military, republican and monarchical. They were also the time of the European rush into Africa. There were many complex connections between the two processes" (p. 211). As Ranger suggests for Africa and Cohn (1983) for India, the invention of traditions became a crucial part of colonial rule as Europeans sought to justify their presence and redefine the colonized societies in new terms. Hardt and Negri (2000) explain: "British administrators had to write their own 'Indian history' to sustain and further the interests of colonial rule. The British had to historicise the Indian past in order to have access to it and put it to work. The British creation of an Indian history, however, like the formation of the colonial state, could be achieved only by imposing European colonial logics and models on Indian reality" (p. 126).

It was the metadiscursive regimes of European thought that produced the histories and languages of the empire from the materials they found in the field. One of the great projects of European invention was Sir George Abraham Grierson's massive Linguistic Survey of India, completed in 1928. A central problem for Grierson, as with many other linguists, was to decide on the boundaries between languages and dialects. Dialects tended to be considered spoken forms, while languages were accorded their special status according to other criteria such as regional similarities, family trees, or literary forms. One of the problems with this, however, was that while people had terms for their 'dialects'—or at least terms for other people's dialects (their own just being considered the way one speaks) —they did not have terms for these larger constructions, 'languages'. As Grierson explained:

> Few natives at the present day are able to comprehend the idea connoted by the words "a language." Dialects they know and understand. They separate them and distinguish them with a meticulous, hair-splitting subtlety, which to us seems unnecessary and absurd; but their minds are not trained to grasp the conception, so familiar to us, of a general term embracing a number of interconnected dialects... It thus follows that, while the dialect-names in the following pages have been taken from the indigenous nomenclature, *nearly all the language-names have had to be invented by Europeans.* Some of them, such as

"Bengali," "Assamese," and the like, are founded on words which have received English citizenship, and are not real Indian words at all; while others, like "Hindostani," "Bihari," and so forth, are based on already existing Indian names of countries and nationalities. (Grierson, 1907, p. 350; emphasis added)

While it is interesting at one level to observe simply that the names for these new entities were invented, the point of greater significance is that these were not just new names for extant objects (languages preexisted the naming), but rather the invention and naming of new objects. The naming performatively called the languages into being. Crucial here, too, we can see the dismissal of local knowledge as 'hair-splitting subtlety' and an inability to grasp the concepts borne by superior European knowledge. As suggested above, this invention of Indian languages has to be seen in the context of the larger colonial archive of knowledge. The British, as Lelyveld (1993) points out, "developed from their study of Indian languages not only practical advantage but an ideology of languages as separate, autonomous objects in the world, things that could be classified, arranged, and deployed as media of exchange" (p. 194). This whole project was of course a cornerstone of the Orientalist construction of the colonial subject. Orientalism, suggests Ludden (1993), "began with the acquisition of the languages needed to gain reliable information about India. Indian languages became a foundation for scientific knowledge of Indian tradition built from data transmitted to Europeans by native experts" (p. 261).

At the heart of the problem here is the underlying ideology of countability—what we call *census ideology* in sociolinguistics. The idea of linguistic enumerability is based on the dual notions of both 'languages' and speakers of those languages being amenable to counting. It has been

161

widely attested that there is a massive disparity between the number of languages that linguists believe exist and the number of languages that people report themselves as speaking. The Christian language preservation society Ethnologue for example, notes the disparity between the 6800 languages that exist in the world by their reckoning, and the 40,000 names for different languages that exist if you ask non-linguists to name languages (Ethnologue website). Nevertheless, many linguists interested in preservation are content to deal in terms of enumerative strategies which have the effect of reducing sociolinguistics to the level of arithmetic: "Over 95% of the world's spoken languages have fewer than 1 million native users; some 5000 have less than 100,000 speakers and more than 3000 languages have fewer than 10,000 speakers. A quarter of the world's spoken languages and most of the Sign languages have fewer than the 1,000 users, and at least some 500 languages had in 1999 under a hundred speakers" (Skutnabb-Kangas, 2003, p. 32). Mühl-häusler (2000) views this position as a continuation of the tradition of segregational linguistics, which insists that "languages can be distinguished and named" (p. 358).

To abstract languages, to count them as discrete objects, and to count the speakers of such languages is to reproduce a very particular enumerative strategy. Yet the enumeration of speakers of a language is founded on a "monolingual norm of speakerhood" (Hill, 2003, p. 128), a paradoxical state of affairs given that this speakerhood model seems to play a key role in shaping our images of the world, particularly in multilingual contexts (see Ethnologue). In order to make the languages countable, census ideology is crucial because of the role it has played in the colonial imaginary (Anderson, 1991; Appadurai, 1993; Leeman, 2004). A major problem, then, with current approaches to diversity, multilingualism, and so forth, is that they all too often start with this enumerative strategy: How many

162

languages are there in the world? It is our contention that while opening up questions of diversity with one hand, at the same time such strategies are also reproducing the tropes of colonial invention. By rendering diversity a quantitative question of language enumeration, such approaches continue to employ the census strategies of colonialism while missing the qualitative question of where diversity lies.

Metadiscursive regimes and epistemic violence
The invention of 'metadiscursive regimes' to describe language and languages has implications for both language (as a general capacity) and languages (as entities). That is to say, although we acknowledge that all humans have language, the way in which both senses of language are understood is constructed through a particular ideological lens dependent in a large measure on specific 'metadiscursive regimes', and the analysts' cultural and historical 'locus of enunciation' (Mignolo, 2000, p. 116). These metadiscursive regimes are significant because linguists, more than any other 'scientists' create the objects of analysis through the nature and type of 'metadiscursive regimes' which form the basis of their analysis. Disinvention here is tied to a question of rethinking understandings of language (for example, language as medium of communication (see Kyeyune, 2004, for a recent use of the medium metaphor), an unfortunate metaphor excluding as it does other more creative uses and ways of thinking about language). Drawing attention to such metaphors is an important disinventive strategy aimed at finding a way in which linguists and applied linguists can avoid being imprisoned by their own semiotic categories.

In order to understand the development of these regimes, we need to return, as with the invention of languages reviewed above, to the historical origins of modes of thought. In their discussion of the work of Bruno Latour (1993) and Michel Foucault (1970), both of whom, in their different ways, sought to understand how it is that we came to be modern, Bauman and Briggs (2003) suggest that Latour "misses language, that is, the role of its construction as autonomous and the work of purification and hybridization this entails in making modernity" (p. 8). By viewing language as only a mode of mediation between the primary domains of science and society, Latour remains "simply modern here, having succumbed to the definition of language as real and its relegation to the role of carrying out particular modernist functions, such as conveying information" (p. 8). They argue, therefore, for "the full recognition of language as a domain coequal in this enterprise with Latour's society and nature" (p. 10). Meanwhile, while Foucault (1970) acknowledged the significance for modernity of the construction of language as a separate realm in the 17th century, Bauman and Briggs contend that he constructs too unified a view of language. By contrast, as they show, it was the struggles over the construction of language in relation to questions of social difference that led to the particular making of language and its role in the production of modernity: "While Foucault's account of language thus provides an excellent starting point for discerning how reimagining language was crucial for imagining modernity, we suggest that the story needs to be retold if its broader significance—particularly for understanding how modernity produces and structures inequality—is to become more intellectually and politically accessible" (p. 10).

For Bauman and Briggs, the key question is how modernism (through the work of philosophers such as Locke) created language as a separate domain, how "language came into being" (p. 7), and "the process involved in creating language and rendering it a powerful means of creating social inequality" (p. 9). This, then, is a crucial step prior to the rise of the European nation state's production of languages as separate, distinct, national entities. This latter point has been widely discussed and observed, from Anderson's discussion of the role of language in the construction of the nation state (though, as suggested above, he fails to observe that this was a bi-directional construction, language constructing nation and nation constructing language) to observations such as Mühlhäusler's (2000) that "the notion of a 'language' is a recent culture-specific notion associated with the rise of European nation states and the Enlightenment. The notion of 'a language' makes little sense in most traditional societies" (p. 358). Bauman and Briggs, however, are pointing to the period that preceeds this, when language itself was constructed as an entity separable from the social world. Crucial to this project was Locke's "positioning of language as one of the three 'great provinces of the intellectual world' that are 'wholly separate and distinct'" (Bauman & Briggs, 2003, p. 299). As they go on to explain, "Separating language from both nature/science and society/politics, Locke could place practices for purifying language of any explicit connections with either society or nature at the center of his vision of modern linguistic and textual practices" (p. 299-300).

This construction of language as an autonomous object is challenged both by the integrational linguistics of Harris (1980, 1981, 1998), as well as research on 'critical localism' (Geertz, 1983, Canagarajah, 2002), which seeks to understand how language may be understood differently in different contexts. Harris has argued that linguistics (or segregational linguistics as he calls orthodox linguistics) has profoundly misconstrued language through its myths about the autonomy, systematicity and rule bound nature of language, its privileging of supposedly expert, scientific linguistic knowledge over everyday understandings of language, which, following Geertz, we are referring to as 'local knowledge'. "An integrationalist redefinition of linguistics" Harris (1990) suggests, "can dispense with at least the fol-

165

lowing assumptions: (i) that the linguistic sign is arbitrary; (ii) that the linguistic sign is linear; (iii) that words have meanings; (iv) that grammar has rules; and (v) that there are languages" (p. 45). As both Mühlhäusler (2000) and Toolan (2003) argue, an integrational view of language, suggests not merely that language is integrated with its environment, but rather that languages themselves cannot be viewed as discrete items, rejecting "as a powerful and misleading myth, any assumption that a language is essentially an autonomous system which humans can harness to meet their communicational needs" (Toolan, 2003, p. 123). Thus drawing on Harris's work (e.g., 1998), this version of linguistic ecology takes seriously Harris's claim that "linguistics does not need to postulate the existence of languages as part of its theoretical apparatus" (Harris, 1990, p. 45). As Harris goes on to argue, the question here is whether

> the concept of 'a language,' as defined by orthodox modern linguistics, corresponds to any determinate or determinable object of analysis at all, whether social or individual, whether institutional or psychological. If there is no such object, it is difficult to evade the conclusion that modern linguistics has been based upon a myth. (p. 45)

Discussing language use in Papua New Guinea, Romaine (1994) asks how we come to terms with the problem that speakers may claim to speak a different language when linguistically it may appear identical. She goes on to point out that the 'very concept of discrete languages is probably a European cultural artifact fostered by procedures such as literacy and standardization. Any attempt to count distinct languages will be an artifact of classificatory procedures rather than a reflection of communicative practices" (p. 12). If the notions of language which form the basis of

166

language planning are artifacts of European thinking, language policies are therefore (albeit unintentionally) agents of the very values which they are seeking to challenge: "Like hygiene (the control of diseases often introduced or spread by colonization), 'vagabondage' and alcoholism, the language question belonged to those problems of largely European making whose real importance lay in the fact that they legitimized regulation from above" (Fabian, 1986, p. 82). Branson and Miller (2000) stress that we "must not only revel in linguistic difference but cope with that difference analytically. Let us recognize the culturally specific nature of our own schemes and search for new modes of analysis that do not fit other languages into a mould but rather celebrate and build on their epistemological differences" (p. 32). We broadly concur with these positions but want to push them further: Unless we actively engage with the history of invention of languages, the processes by which these inventions are maintained, and the political imperative to work towards their disinvention, we will continue to do damage to speech communities and educational possibilities.

Towards disinvention and reconstitution
In the disinvention project we are therefore not merely reiterating the generally accepted notions that languages have fuzzy boundaries, that the distinction between language and dialect is arbitrary, as is frequently stated in conventional sociolinguistics. Rather, we want to argue that the concept of language, and indeed the 'metadiscursive regimes' used to describe languages are firmly located in western linguistic and cultural suppositions. They do not describe any real state of affairs in the world, i.e they are not natural kinds (Danzinger 1998): they are only convenient fictions to the extent that they provide a useful way of understanding the world and shaping language users, and they are very inconvenient fictions to the extent that they produce particular and limit-

ing views on how language operates in the world. In response, we want to propose neither a view that we need better descriptions nor more acknowledgement of fuzziness, but instead (strategies of) disinvention.

The view of language we are suggesting here has major implications for many of the treasured icons of liberal - linguistic thought. Not only do the notions of language and languages become highly suspect, but so do many related concepts that are premised on a notion of discrete languages, such as language rights, mother tongues, multilingualism, or code-switching. It is common in both liberal and more critical approaches to issues in sociolinguistics to insist on plurality, sometimes strengthened by a concept of rights. Thus, there are strong arguments for mother tongue education, for an understanding of multilingualism as the global norm, for understanding the prevalence of code-switching in bi- and multilingual communities, and for the importance of language rights to provide a moral and legal framework for language polices. Our position, however, is that although such arguments may be preferable to blinkered views that take monolingualism as the norm, they nevertheless remain caught within the same paradigm. They operate with a strategy of pluralization rather than a questioning of the inventions at the core of the whole discussion. Without strategies of disinvention, most discussions of language rights, mother tongue education or codeswitching reproduce the same concept of language that underlies all mainstream linguistic thought: multilingualism therefore simply becomes a pluralization of monolingualism.

Sonntag (2003) makes a similar point when she argues that the rights-based approach to support for linguistic diversity and opposition to the English-Only movement "has not fundamentally altered the American projection of its vision of global English ... because a rights-based approach to promoting linguistic diversity reinforces the dominant liberal democratic project rather than dismantling it" (p. 25). The point here, then, is that while on the one hand seemingly promoting a progressive, liberal cause for diversity, rights and multilingualism, at the same time, by employing the same epistemologies on which monolingualism and the denial of rights have been constructed, such arguments may do more to reproduce than oppose the conditions they object to. As Rajagopalan (1999) suggests, "the very charges being pressed against the hegemony of the English language and its putative imperialist pretensions themselves bear the imprint of a way of thinking about language moulded in an intellectual climate of excessive nationalist fervour and organized marauding of the wealth of alien nations, an intellectual climate where identities were invariably thought of in all-or-nothing terms" (p. 201). Thus, as Sonntag goes on to argue, "the willingness to use the language of human rights on the global level to frame local linguistic demands vis-à-vis global English may merely be affirming the global vision projected by American liberal democracy" (p. 25).

Our argument, then, is that just as languages were invented, so too were related concepts such as multilingualism, additive bilingualism, or code-switching. Language planning policies seeking to promote additive bilingualism are founded upon a very specific view of language, a view which takes languages to be 'entities' which, when accessed, will then be beneficial to the speakers. Thus although they tend to be projected as if they were goals which language planning policies must seek to achieve, additive bilingualism or multilingualism must also be understood as particular ways of thinking about language. Language planning research therefore needs to focus not only on the political contexts in which it operates, but also on the nature of the concepts of language which underpin the different policy options, to question not only the *realpolitik* but also the *real-linguistik* of the 20th century.

169

In our view there is a disconcerting similarity between monolingualism and additive bilingualism in so far as
both are founded on notions of language as 'objects'. By
talking of monolingualism, we are referring to a single entity, while in additive bilingualism and multilingualism the
number of 'languagethings' has increased. Yet the underlying concept remains unchanged because additive bilingualism and multilingualism are at best a pluralization of monolingualism. The current valorization of multilingualism, furthermore, seems to exclude the reactions of language speakers to situations in which their languages are being learnt by
others. Renck (1990), with a Papua New Guinea context in
mind, suggests that speakers may erect boundaries around
their own languages to limit the degree to which their languages may be learnt by others; in such situations one's own
language is a form of safeguard, a secret which is lost when
the language is used by other groups. While from an academic perspective, multilingualism might be construed as progressive, speakers of some of the local languages may regard
the learning of their own languages by others as constituting
a violation of their private space.

In the context of South African language policy
Makoni (1998a) argues that "emerging discourses about
multilingualism derive their strength through a deliberate
refusal to recollect that in the past multilingualism has always been used to facilitate the exploitation of Africans" (p.
244-245). Proponents of multilingualism seem to suffer from
a process of 'historical amnesia' (Stuart Hall, 1997, p. 20),
in which they believe that just because they have started
thinking about the idea, so the idea has just begun. Furthermore, proponents of multilingualism are the ideological captives of the very system which they are seeking to challenge.
"The battle for independence" suggests Makoni (1998b) "is
simply not won by opting for vernaculars over English as
normally articulated in the decolonization literature ... From

UNESCO to the multicultural lobby the potential negative effects of learning through vernaculars assigned to speakers is not addressed as it is assumed that it is cognitively and emotionally advantageous that a child learns through such a medium, overlooking as it does the colonized images encoded in such versions of African vernaculars" (pp. 162-163).

More importantly, in disinvention we are seeking to provide alternative ways of understanding some of the frequently reported problems about language planning. For example, it is frequently suggested that in a lot of cases, particularly in Africa, parents may object to their children being taught in their mother tongues. The refusal to be taught in their mother tongue is treated as the legacy of colonialism. We would like to adopt a different perspective. Some indigenous communities object to being taught in 'their mother tongue' because schooling is perceived not as the place where knowledge is transmitted, but as a point of contact between the 'indigenous world and the white-man's world'. Nonindigenous languages (i.e., European languages) are regarded as central to that contact. Education and the transmission of knowledge from the perspective of indigenous communities take place in the oral tradition in the home. While indigenous communities regard schools as sites of contact between indigenous communities and the 'white-man's world,' education being understood as taking place at home, western scholarship takes the opposite view, defining what indigenous communities regard as education to the relegated status of socialization (Reagan, 1996).

More recently, the scramble for African languages has been dominated by a discourse of promotion and development (promotion of the languages, not a promotion of the speakers of those languages (see Simire, 2004, for a recent example)). The concept of language which forms the basis of the notion of language in language development is taken for granted. Our argument, however, is that unless we explore in much greater detail the material and political consequences of ways of talking and thinking about language, we will be unable to avoid unfortunate situations in which it is the languages which are developed rather than its speakers, and more resources are spent on languages than individual speakers as is apparent in the South African interest and commitment to multilingualism. Further, such a way of thinking in which languages are independent of their speakers may lead to situations in which rights are attached to languages rather than to speakers. When descriptions of language hegemony (language rights, linguistic imperialism and the like) reify those languages rather than account for the language users, when languages are developed and promoted without consideration of the speakers of those languages, and when all this is done within a framework for understanding languages that constructs, objectifies, and normalizes those languages, then languages as inventions are being privileged over humans as agents. Descriptions of languages may disable the very speakers to which these languages are attributed. Our view of disinvention as a strategy is one in which languages are subordinate to their speakers, rather than hegemonic over individual speakers.

Disinvention and applied linguistics
Our interest in the applied linguistic effects of invention is therefore concerned with the ways in which applied linguistics has adopted and perpetuates particular versions of language through its many arms of language imposition, amongst which language learning, translation, language policy and language testing are some of the most significant. The numerous discussions of linguistic imperialism, for example, tend to focus on the imposition of dominant languages such as English. But such a dominant focus overlooks other possibilities of imposition, such as how learning less widely spread languages might in itself be used as a form of

172

linguistic imperialism, particularly when the 'target' language is the primary language of the less powerful, as is the case, for example, when the colonizer learns the language of the colonized. Jeater (2002) cogently demonstrates how the learning of African languages by European missionaries and administrators was aimed at creating opportunities through which European thinking could be articulated through African speech forms. The 'bilingual' colonizer may participate in far more insidious forms of imperialism than the 'monolingual' colonizer.

Translation from English into local African languages was a political exercise, as was translation from African and Indian languages into English (see e.g. Niranjana, 1991). It was not merely a neutral technical exercise, as illustrated in the case of chiShona spoken in southern Africa. The general tendency was to use very few words to communicate a wide range of English words in translation. For example, *rudzi* serves to translate race, tribe, people, community, nation, despite meaning something akin to 'species'; *mashoko* serves as a translation for almost anything that is written: notes, words, news, items, questions, problems and issues; *nyika* covers Earth, continent, the next world, land and material existence (temporal world), lending credence to the view that English was a much more expressive language than the local African languages. In translation different world views come into contact with each other. In colonial contexts, and in situations in which there is a social hierarchy (and most societies have one form or other of a social hierarchy), translation—particularly when translating from a 'stronger' language into a weaker one—entails simulating the original and expressing it in a different language.

Anthropologists and professional translators typically translate a foreign culture into their mother tongues; in colonial and some postcolonial contexts, the translation is from one's mother tongue into a second language—let's say from

English into Swahili, from Afrikaans into Zulu. In such cases translation involves inscribing European norms and values into the local language. The process of translating from English into Zulu is different from that of translating Zulu into English. In the former it entails inscribing European views into Zulu, while in the latter it involves an adjustment of Zulu to fit into English without English necessarily being Africanized. The key issue is that the consequences may radically differ depending on whether one is translating from a stronger language into a weaker one, or vice versa. Irrespective of whether the translation is from a stronger language into a weaker one, or vice versa, translation involves one form or other of 'boundary' crossing. The difference however lies in the objectives which the crossing is meant to serve. In translation projects such as Bible translation carried out by the Summer Institute of Linguistics, the 'boundary' crossing is carried out for the purposes of rendering the language a tool for conversion. In cases where the translation is from a relatively weaker language into a dominant one, translation border-crossing may be aimed at understanding the other culture in terms of the dominant.

Language testing also plays a crucial role in this process. It is one of the ways in which languages are regulated and language learning imposed. Language tests privilege particular versions of what constitutes language proficiency/expertise and devalue other types and forms of language expertise resulting in a form of 'epistemic violence' (Spivak, 1993). A key outcome of Shohamy's (2001) argument that a critical approach to language testing "implies the need to develop critical strategies to examine the uses and consequences of tests, to monitor their power, minimize their detrimental force, reveal the misuses" (p. 131) is the need to look at how all forms of language testing imply very particular versions of language. This is not merely a question of a standardized version of a language over other possibilities

174

but the more general denial of difference. For example, in a series of studies of the Kashinawa people, Lyn Mario de Souza (2004) shows that language learning for the Kashinawa people has to be multimodal because knowledge construction for them is predominantly visual. Forms of assessment and indeed language teaching which therefore do not reflect the visual nature of the Kashinawa people's learning orientations are indeed a form of epistemic violence.

We are not only interested in disinventing languages in contexts such as southern Africa, Papua New Guinea, or Indonesia, where the census ideology suggests large numbers of languages are spoken. We also want to argue that this concern over the ontological status of languages affects all contexts of language use. Indeed, there is an urgent need to address not only what are considered 'small languages' but also that mother of all invented languages: English as an International Language (and see Reagan, 2004). Here we want to question both the imagined communication implied by the Myth of English as an international language (Krishnaswamy & Burde, 1998, p. 19) and the equally problematic construction of so-called World Englishes. As Krishnaswamy and Burde (1998) suggest about Indian English, "it is easy to understand why the construct 'Indian English' is easily defined by outsiders like Peter Strevens or Larry Smith and Indians like Kachru who live outside, and so elusive to those who look at it from the inside. Like Indian nationalism, 'Indian English' is 'fundamentally insecure' since the notion 'nation-India' is insecure" (p. 63; see also Dasgupta, 1993, Parakrama, 1995). The pluralization strategies of world Englishes do not do enough to question the central assumptions about language on which they draw. As Canagarajah (1999, p. 180) points out, by "leaving out many eccentric, hybrid forms of local Englishes as too unsystematic" a World Englishes perspective "follows the logic of the prescriptive and elitist tendencies of the center linguists." Just as the notion of multilingualism may leave intact the mono-lingual assumptions about language that it aims to critique, so a World Englishes perspective may support rather than oppose the tenets of centrist linguistics.

For southern Africa we would like to argue that since the notion of what constitutes African languages is open to contestation, the claims being made about the nature of African languages which are ostensibly the basis of African American English and African English need to be clarified. It is not conceptually clear what would constitute African English. And if what constitutes African languages is open to contestation currently, it is difficult to see how specialists in African American vernaculars can claim with such certainty the African language base of African American Vernaculars. For us one way out of the impasse would be to redefine the notions of African language which ostensibly act as a way of imagining African languages: a cross-Atlantic invention of African languages which do not necessarily have to coincide with either historically or contemporary 'objective' descriptions of African languages. Hence the argument that the African language base of African American vernaculars is 'flimsy' at best (McWhorter, 1998) is a fundamental misunderstanding of the socially constructed nature of African languages as Trans-Atlantic inventions.

All societies are in one form of transition and they cannot be changed by using modes of thought which produced the problems with which they are still confronted. Change requires new thought, new ways linguistically of conceptualizing problems. As a South African literary critic and novelist put it:

The past cannot be corrected by bringing to it the procedures and mechanisms and mind sets that originally produced our very perception of it. After all, it is not the past as such that produced the present or

176

poses the conditions for the future ... but the way we think about it. Or even more pertinently, the way in which we deal with it in language. (Brink, 1998, p. 23)

By looking at a wide range of contexts and modes of understanding language, we are arguing for the need to pose fundamental questions for linguists, sociolinguists and applied linguists: If a dominant understanding of language in many parts of the world is a result of the mapping of European colonial and neocolonial constructs onto diverse contexts, how might languages start to look if an alternative conception were mapped back onto the centre from the periphery? For example, what would English look like if we were to analyze it using metadiscursive regimes from languages such Hausa, or if other local perspectives were adopted? What are the political consequences when notions about language in concepts such as language rights, mother tongues, and bilingual education are disinvented?

References
Alexander, N. (1989). *Language Policy and National Unity in South Africa/Azania*. Cape Town, South Africa: Buchu Books.
Anderson, B. (1983). *Imagined Communities: Reflections on the Origin and Spread of Nationalism*. London: Verso.
Appadurai, A. (1993). "Number in the colonial imagination" In C.A. Breckenridge & P. van der Veer (Eds.), *Orientalism and the Postcolonial Predicament: Perspectives on South Asia* (pp. 314-339). Philadelphia: University of Pennsylvania Press.
Bauman, R. & Briggs, C. (2003). *Voices of Modernity: Language Ideologies and the Politics of Inequality*. Cambridge: Cambridge University Press.

Blommaert, J. (1999). "Reconstructing the sociolinguistic image of Africa: Grassroots writing in Shaba (Congo)" *Text* 19(2), pp.175-200.

Branson, J. & Miller, D. (2000). "Maintaining, developing and sharing the knowledge and potential embedded in all our languages and cultures: On linguists as agents of epistemic violence" In R. Phillipson (Ed.), *Rights to language: Equity, Power and Education* (pp. 28-32). Mahwah, NJ: Lawrence Erlbaum Associates, Inc.

Bhabha, H. (1994). *The Location of Culture*. London: Routledge.

Brutt-Griffler, J. (2002). *World English: A Study of its Development*. Clevedon, UK: Multilingual Matters.

Canagarajah A. S. (2002). "Celebrating local knowledge on language and education" *Journal of Language, Identity and Education*, 1(4), pp. 243-261.

Canagarajah, S. (1999). *Resisting Linguistic Imperialism in English Teaching*. Oxford: Oxford University Press.

Chimhundu, H. (1992). "Early missionaries and the ethno-linguistic factor during the invention of tribalism in Zimbabwe" *Journal of African History*, 33, pp. 87-109.

Cohn, B. (1983). "Representing authority in Victorian England. In E. Hobsbawm & T. Ranger (Eds.), *The Invention of Tradition* (pp. 165-209). Cambridge: Cambridge University Press.

Cohn, B. (1996). *Colonialism and its Forms of Knowledge*. Princeton, NJ: Princeton University Press.

Cook, S. (2002). "Urban language in a rural setting, the case of the Phokeng, South Africa" In G. Gmelch & W. Zenner (Eds.), *Urban Life: Readings in the Anthropology of the City* (pp. 106-113). Prospect Heights, IL: Waveland Press.

Crystal, D. (2000). *Language Death*. Cambridge: Cambridge

University Press.

Dasgupta, P. (1993). *The Otherness of English: India's Auntie Tongue Syndrome.* New Delhi, India: Sage Publications.

Danzinger, K. (1997). *Naming the Mind: How Psychology Found its Language.* London: Sage.

De Souza, L. (2004). "A change of skin: Applied linguistics in Indigenous communities in Brazil" Paper presented at the American Association of Applied Linguistics Convention, Portland, US. May 1-4, 2004.

Dixon, R. (1997). *The Rise and Fall of Languages.* Cambridge: Cambridge University Press.

Fabian, J. (1986). *Language and Colonial Power: The Appropriation of Swahili in the Former Congo* 1880-1938. Cambridge: Cambridge University Press.

Fardon, R. & Furniss, G., (Eds.). (1994). *African Languages, Development and the State.* London: Routledge.

Foucault, M. (1970). *The Order of Things: An Archaeology of the Human Sciences.* New York: Vintage.

Geertz, C. (1985). *Local Knowledge: Further Essays in Interpretive Anthropology.* New York: Basic Books.

Grierson, G. (1907). "Languages" In W. W. Hunter (Ed.), *The Imperial Gazetteer of India, vol. 1: The Indian Empire—Descriptive,* New edition (pp. 349-401). Oxford: Clarendon Press.

Hall, S. & Gay, P. (1995). *Questions of Cultural Identity.* Thousand Oaks, CA: Sage Publications.

Hardt, M. & Negri, A. (2000). *Empire.* Cambridge, MA: Harvard University Press.

Harris, R. (1980). *The Language Makers.* Ithaca, NY: Cornell University Press.

Harris, R. (1981). *The Language Myth.* London: Duckworth.

Harris, R. (1988). "Murray, Moore and the myth" In R. Harris (Ed.), *Linguistic Thought in England. 1914-1945* (pp. 1-26). London: Duckworth.

Harris, R. (1990). "On redefining linguistics" In H. Davis &
T. Taylor (Eds.), *Redefining Linguistics* (pp. 18-52).
London: Routledge.

Harris, R. (1998). *Introduction to Integrational Linguistics.*
London: Pergamon.

Harries, P. (1987). "The roots of ethnicity: Discourse and the
politics of language construction in South Africa"
African Affairs, 86, pp. 25-52.

Heryanto, A. (1995). *Language of Development and
Development of Language: The Case of Indonesia.*
Canberra, Australia: Department of Linguistics,
Australia National University. (Pacific Linguistics.
Series D-86)

Hill, J. (2002). "Expert rhetorics in advocacy for endangered
languages: Who is listening, and what do they hear?"
Journal of Linguistic Anthropology, 12(2), pp. 119-
133.

Hobsbawm, E. (1983). "Introduction: Inventing traditions"
In E. Hobsbawm & T. Ranger (Eds.), *The Invention
of Tradition* (pp. 1-14). Cambridge: Cambridge
University Press.

Irvine, J. & Gal, S. (2000). "Language ideology and
linguistic differentiation" In P. V. Kroskrity (Ed.),
*Regimes of Language: Ideologies, Politics and
Identities* (pp. 35-85). Santa Fe, NM: School of
American Research Press.

Isichei, E. (1995). *A History of Christianity in Africa.*
Lawrence, NJ: Africa World Press.

Jeater, D. (2002). "Speaking like a native" *Journal of
African History,* 43, pp. 449-468.

Joseph, J. (2004). *Language and Identity: National, Ethnic,
Religious.* Palgrave: Macmillan

Krishnaswamy, N & Burde, A. (1998). *The Politics of*

Indians' English: Linguistic Colonialism and the Expanding English Empire. Delhi: Oxford University Press.

Kyeyune, R. (2004). "Challenges of using English as a medium of instruction in the multilingual contexts: A view from Ugandan classrooms" In M. Jepkirui & A. Nduku Kioko (Eds.), *New language bearings in Africa* (pp. 77-89). Clevedon, UK: Multilingual Matters.

Latour, B. (1993). *We Have Never Been Modern* (Catherine Porter, trans). Cambridge, MA: Harvard University Press.

Latour, B. (1999). *Pandora's Hope. Essays on the Reality of Science Studies.* Cambridge, MA: Harvard University Press.

Leeman, J. (2004). "Racializing language: A history of linguistic ideologies in the US census" *The Journal of Language and Politics,* 3(3), pp. 507-534.

Lelyveld, D. (1993). "The fate of Hindustani: Colonial knowledge and the project of a national language" In C.A. Breckenridge & P. van der Veer, (eds.), *Orientalism and the Postcolonial Predicament: Perspectives on South Asia,* (pp. 189-214). Philadelphia: University of Pennsylvania Press.

Love, N. (1990). "The locus of languages in a redefined linguistics" In H. Davis & T. Taylor (Eds.), *Redefining Linguistics* (pp. 53-117). London: Routledge.

Ludden, D. (1993)." Orientalist empiricism: transformations of colonial knowledge" In C. A. Breckenridge & P. van der Veer (Eds.), *Orientalism and the Postcolonial Predicament: Perspectives on South Asia* (pp. 250-278). Philadelphia: University of Pennsylvania Press.

Makoni, S. (1998a). "African languages as European scripts:

the shaping of communal memory" In S. Nuttall &
C. Coetzee (Eds.), *Negotiating the Past: The Making
of Memory in South Africa* (pp. 242-248). Oxford:
Oxford University Press.

Makoni, S. (1998b). "In the beginning was the missionaries'
word: The European invention of an African
language: The case of Shona in Zimbabwe. In K. K.
Prah (Ed.), *Between distinction and extinction: The
harmonisation and standardisation of African
languages* (pp. 157-164). Johannesburg: University
of Witwatersrand Press.

Makoni, S. (2003). "From misinvention to disinvention of
language: Multilingualism and the South African
Constitution" In S. Makoni, G. Smitherman, A. Ball
& A. Spears (Eds.), *Black Linguistics: Social and
Linguistic Problems of Languages in Africa and the
Americas* (pp. 132-151). London: Routledge.

Makoni, S. & Meinhof, U. (2004). "Western perspectives on
applied linguistics in Africa" *AILA Review, 17,*
pp.77-105.

Mannheim, B. (1991). *The Language of the Inka Since the
European Invasion.* Austin, TX: University of Texas
Press.

McLaughlin, F. (2001). "Dakar Wolof and the configuration
of an urban identity" *Journal of African Cultural
Studies,* 1(2), pp. 153-172.

McWhorter, J. (1998). *The Word on the Street: Fact and
Fable about American English.* New York: Plenum
Trade.

Mignolo, W. (1995). *The Darker Side of the Renaissance:
Literacy, Territoriality, and Colonization.* Ann
Arbor, MI: University of Michigan Press.

Mignolo, W. (2000). *Coloniality, Subaltern Knowledges,
and Border Thinking: Local Histories/Global
Designs.* Princeton, NJ: Princeton University Press.

Mudimbe, V. Y. (1988). *The Invention of Africa: Gnosis, Philosophy, and the Order of Knowledge.* Bloomington, IN: Indiana University Press.

Mühlhäusler, P. (1996). *Linguistic Ecology: Language Change and Linguistic Imperialism in the Pacific Region.* London: Routledge.

Mühlhäusler, P. (2000). "Language planning and language ecology. *Current Issues in Language Planning,* 1(3), pp. 306-367.

Nettle, D. & Romaine, S. (2000). *Vanishing Voices: The Extinction of the World's Languages.* Oxford: Oxford University Press.

Nhlapo, J. M. (1944). *Bantu Babel.* Cape Town, South Africa: The African Bookman.

Niranjana, T. (1991). "Translation, colonialism and the rise of English. In S. Joshi (Ed.), *Rethinking English: Essays in Literature, Language, History* (pp. 124-145). New Delhi, India: Trianka.

Parakrama, A. (1995). *De-Hegemonizing Language Standards: Learning from (Post)Colonial Englishes About 'English'.* Basingstoke, UK: MacMillan.

Pattanayak, D. P. (2003). "Multilingual contexts and their ethos" In A. Ouame (Ed.), *Towards a Multilingual Culture of Education* (pp. 27-47). Hamburg, Germany: UNESCO Institute of Education.

Pennycook, A. (2002). "Mother tongues, literacy and colonial governmentality" *International Journal of the Sociology of Language,* 154, pp. 11-28.

Rajagopalan, K. (1999). "Of EFL teachers, conscience and cowardice" *ELT Journal,* 53, pp. 200-206.

Ranger, T. (1983). "The invention of tradition in colonial Africa" In E. Hobsbawm & T. Ranger (Eds.), *The Invention of Tradition.* Cambridge: Cambridge University Press.

Ranger, T. (2004). "Nationalist historiography, patriotic

183

history and the history of the nation: The struggle over the past in Zimbabwe" *Journal of Southern African Studies,* 30(2), pp. 215-234.

Reagan, T. (2004). "Objectification, positivism and language studies: A reconsideration" *Critical Inquiry in Language Studies: An International Journal,* 1(1), pp. 41-60.

Renck, G. (1990). *Contextualization of Christianity and Christianization of Language: A Case Study from the Highlands of Papua New Guinea.* Erlangen, Germany: Verlag der Luth.-Mission.

Romaine, S. (1994). *Language in Society: An Introduction to Sociolinguistics.* Oxford: Oxford University Press.

Samarin, W. (1996). Review of Adegbija Efurosibina, *Language Attitudes in Sub-Saharan Africa: A Sociolinguistic Overview. Anthropological Linguistics,* 38(2), pp. 389-395.

Shohamy, E. (2001). *The Power of Tests: A Critical Perspective on the Uses of Language Tests.* London: Longman.

Skutnabb-Kangas, T. (2003). "Linguistic diversity and biodiversity: The threat from killer languages" In C. Mair (Ed.), *The Politics of English as a World Language: New Horizons in Postcolonial Cultural Studies* (pp. 31-52). Amsterdam: Rodopi.

Simire, G. O. (2004). "Developing and promoting multilingualism in public life and society in Nigeria" In M. Jepkirui & A. Nduku Kioko (Eds)., *New Language Bearings in Africa* (pp. 135-148). Clevedon, UK: Multilingual Matters.

Sonntag, S. (2003). *The Local Politics of Global English: Case Studies in Linguistic Globalization.* Lanham, MD: Lexington Books.

Spear, T. (2003). "Neo-traditionalism and the limits of

invention in British Colonial Africa" *Journal of African History*, 44, pp. 3-27.

Spitulnik, D. (1988). "The language of the city: Town Bemba as urban hybridty" *Journal of Linguistic Anthropology*, 8(1), pp. 30-59.

Toolan, M. (2003). "An integrational linguistic view of coming into language" In J. Leather & J. van Dam (Eds.), *Ecology of Language Acquisition* (pp. 123-139). Dordrecht, Netherlands: Kluwer Academic Publishers.

Vaughan, O. (2003). *Chiefs, Power and Social Change: Chiefship and Modern Politics in Botswana, 1880-1990*. Trenton, NJ: Africa World Press.

Wallerstein, I. (2000). *The Essential Wallerstein*. New York: The New Press.

Woolard, K. (1999). "Simultaneity and bivalency as strategies in bilingualism" *Journal of Linguistic Anthropology*, 8(1), pp. 3-29.

VIII

Disinventing Multilingualism
From Monological Multilingualism To Multilingua Francas
(with Alastair Pennycook)

Introduction

Assumptions about the existence of languages and, *ipso facto*, multilingualism, are so deeply embedded in predominant paradigms of language studies that they are rarely questioned. Multilingualism, furthermore, viewed from this perspective, is an indomitably good thing; the task of linguists, sociolinguists, applied linguists and educational linguists is to enhance our understanding of multilingualism, to overcome the monolingual blinkers of Anglo- or Eurocentric thought, to encourage both the understanding of and the practices of multilingualism. The relevance of such models to diverse contexts, however, is often taken for granted. As Haugen once observed

> [t]he concept of language as a rigid, monolithic structure is false, even if it has proved to be a useful fiction in the development of linguistics. It is the kind of simplification that is necessary at a certain stage of a science, but which can now be replaced by more sophisticated models. (1972: 25)

In this chapter we argue that it is indeed time for more sophisticated models, not models that replace monolingualism with multilingualism, as both concepts emerge from the same intellectual context, but rather models that question the very foundations that underpin such linguistic simplifications.

Drawing on different intellectual traditions, from philosophy to anthropology (Davidson1986; Whorf 1988), that have dealt with the existence of languages with some skepticism, we therefore make an unequivocal case that "not all people have 'a language/languages' in the sense in which the term is currently used in English" (Heryanto 1990: 41). To this end we will first turn to the sociohistorical contexts in which notions of languages as "hermetically sealed units" (Makoni 1998) emerged, and how particular understandings of multilingualism emerged as plural monolingualisms. This will be followed by a broader discussion of contexts of diverse language use, where the notion of multilingualism is eschewed in favor of a more comprehensive understanding of the mobilization of diverse language resources. Once we go beyond a framing of languages as discrete entities, it may be plausible to write productively about multilingualism. In order to do so we therefore pose the following three questions:

- If languages are not "primordial," the question is under what sociohistorical contexts did they emerge, what are the philosophical strategies used in their construction and how does invention impact the linguistic practices of the users, and our own understanding of multilingualism?

- What are the metadiscursive regimes (Bauman and Briggs 2003) used in the construction of "languages"? Drawing on examples from different parts of the world, but with a particular focus on Africa, we further ask how diverse communities talk about their languages and what light these metalinguistic framings shed on the "world views," and "orientations" of these communities. What is the impact of particular metalanguages on our understanding of multilingualism?

- If languages do not exist as discrete entities, and language is not universal in the sense of unified systems, how does communication occur in the absence of languages as things?

Framing invention/disinvention: language myths and ideologies

A number of theoretical positions coalesce around a critique of language as discrete, unified systems. Prominent among these is Integrational Linguistics (Harris 2009), and the key claim that the idea of language is a "myth" (see Harris 1980, 1981, 1998, 2009; Harris and Taylor 1997; Pennycook 2007b). In Integrational Linguistics "people use signs in order to communicate," but the signs are not pre-assembled and there is a sharp dissonance between form and meaning. Language from this point of view is so deeply embedded in context that it cannot be separated from it. Communication occurs through a process of mutual adjustment: "when we speak or write, we take those imperfectly remembered prior (a priori) texts and reshape them into new contexts" (Becker 1995:15). Communication may be understood as "multidirectional, interactive, (and) participatory" (Khubchandani 2003), a position quite at odds with a sender/receiver model or "fixed-telementation" in which the thoughts of one person are transported to another through the use of a particular code (Toolan 2009). As Harris (1990: 45) remarks, "linguistics does not need to postulate the existence of languages as part of its theoretical apparatus." Once we make communi-

189

cation central to our thinking, languages may be a "variable extra" (Harris 2009: 44).

A related orientation that also undermines the idea of language as a preformed object is Hopper's (1998) *emergent grammar*, a term borrowed from anthropology (Clifford and Marcus 1986). For Hopper the apparent structure or regularity of grammar is an emergent property that "is shaped by discourse in an ongoing process. Grammar is, in this view, simply the name for certain categories of observed repetitions in discourse" (1998: 156). This is not merely an observation that languages are always changing and that grammar is always therefore, in the longer term, temporary, but rather that the notion of systematicity embedded in the concept of grammar is itself a product of repeated social activity. Language use draws on "lingual memory" shaped in part by each individual's life experiences (Becker 1995; Johnstone 1996). Hence

> there is no natural fixed structure to language. Rather, speakers borrow heavily from their previous experiences of communication in similar circumstances, on similar topics, and with similar interlocutors. Systematicity, in this view, is an illusion produced by the partial settling or *sedimentation* of frequently used forms into temporary subsystems. (Hopper 1998: 157-8)

From this point of view, then, linguistic structure is seen not as an independent set of pre-given laws but rather "as a response to discourse needs" (Bybee and Hopper 2001: 2). "The notion of language as a monolythic system," Bybee and Hopper (2001: 3) go on to argue, "has had to give way to that of a language as a massive collection of heterogeneous *constructions*, each with affinities to different contexts and in constant structural adaptation to usage."

190

Whereas linguists such as Harris, Hopper and Bybee have thus shown good cause to understand language as integrated and emergent (rather than independent or preordained), Yngve's (1996; Yngve and Wasik 2004) critique of linguistics from the point of view of the philosophy of science suggests that unlike other scientific enterprises, linguistics creates its objects anew and shapes the nature of the object of its analysis. According to Yngve, the irony is that language research can make substantial progress when it frames itself not as a science, but situates itself as part of a long tradition of philosophy and grammatical analysis, a tradition that does not claim the existence of language as an object of analysis in advance of its metalanguage. Once we situate linguistics within specific rhetorical or grammatical traditions, rather than a putative science that invents the objects of its descriptions, the culture-specific nature of linguistic inquiry becomes more evident. The immediate relevance of sociolinguistic concepts such as multilingualism thus becomes suspect in diverse contexts (Love 2009). Multilingualism from such a perspective is therefore not a universal category; indeed the very idea that multilingualism could refer to the same thing in diverse contexts of communication is revealed as an absurdity.

Linguistic anthropologists and others studying Creole languages have also cast suspicion on the ways in which languages have been described and mapped onto communities. Le Page and Tabouret-Keller (1985), for example, argue that in extremely complex heterogeneous contexts not every speech event or language will necessarily belong to a nameable language system. Furthermore, speakers may not necessarily have a clearly defined idea of what language they are speaking, and what does or does not constitute "a language." As a result, rather than focusing on languages and their users, we would be better off focusing on the "acts of identity" involved in different interactions. In a related vein, Schiefflien's (1990) research on Kaluli demonstrates that children are not taught language or verbal behavior as such, but rather are taught appropriate social behavior during interactional movements. This perspective echoes research into other post-colonial contexts (see Makoni and Makoni 2010; Pennycook 2010) that suggests that to study language, we always need to incorporate social activity, location, movement, interaction and history, as well as, wherever possible, users' perspectives. The focus of such work is therefore on a human-centered multilingualism as opposed to a language-centered multilingualism. The latter makes a multiplicity of language systems central to its analysis; the former takes the social grounding of human interaction as central.

From the perspective of linguistic anthropology, with a particular interest in the notion of language ideologies, or regimes of language (Kroskrity 2000), the question becomes one of asking how it is that languages are understood locally. As Woolard (2004: 58) notes, such work has shown that "linguistic ideologies are never just about language, but rather also concern such fundamental social notions as community, nation, and humanity itself." For linguistic anthropologists, the problem was that the "surgical removal of language from context produced an amputated 'language' that was the preferred object of the language sciences for most of the twentieth century" (Kroskrity 2000: 5). By studying language ideologies as contextual sets of belief about languages, or as Irvine (1989: 255) puts it, "the cultural system of ideas about social and linguistic relationships, together with their loading of moral and political interests," this line of work has shown the significance of local knowledge about language. At the very least, this sheds light on Mühlhäusler's (2000) point that the notion of a "language" "is a recent culture-specific notion associated with the rise of European nation-states and the Enlightenment. The notion of 'a language' makes little sense in most traditional societies" (Mühlhäusler 2000: 358). Because of the centrality of Eurocentric concepts of language, mother tongues and other monoglot perspectives and related notions "what has passed for a science of language (*including multilingualism*) over the past 150 years has been nothing but an exercise in culture maintenance" (Love 2009: 31, emphasis ours).

Although starting from different theoretical vantage points, these and many other approaches to language study are highly skeptical of the idea of languages as discrete, preformed and independent objects. In order to construct itself as a respectable discipline, linguistics had to make an extensive series of exclusions, relegating people, history, society, culture and politics to a role external to languages: "If the history of a language and its users is not factored into the theory as a primary standpoint" argues Nakata (2007: 37), "then any knowledge generated about that language is flawed." This is not, as Nakata points out, to reject the whole body or work carried out by linguists—this would be foolish in the extreme—but it is to point to the problem that a linguistic focus on formal aspects of a language "fundamentally separates the language from the people; it falsely separates the act of speaking from what is being spoken." For Nakata, at the heart of the problem is the linguistic assumption that languages are "floating in a vacuum, 'ready-made' within a system of phonetic, grammatical and lexical forms and divorced from the social context in which the speech is being uttered."

Such studies assume that language is a "solved problem, a stable and determined entity" (Harpham 2002: ix). As Harpham argues, attempts to pin down languages are hampered because there is both too much and too little information:

Somewhere in the vast domain of linguistics can be found tokens of virtually anything at all, including order, arbitrariness, social cohesion, individual creativity, freedom, the unconscious, excess, nature, culture—anything. That is why all characterizations of the essence or true nature of language are tendentious. (2002: x)

This critique of the notion of separable languages, or the idea that there are "language-free communities" (Heryanto 2007) does not of course in any way suggest that some people do not use language, or because they do not have a view of "a language" that they do not communicate in language. There is very good reason to question common assumptions about the existence of separate, nameable and numerable languages. And thus there is also good reason to question the assumptions that underlie the notion of multilingualism to the extent that the term refers to little more than a plurality of languages. If the status of languages as objects is questionable, so too is their pluralization.

The development of languages: language invention
The construct of "language itself as an all or nothing affair" (Rajagopolan 2007: 194), as well as many of the ideas that are part of this metalinguistic package—standard language, dialect, acrolect, mesolect and basilect, language varieties and so forth—need to be understood as an invention. They are excellent examples of nineteenth-century social and scholarly invention in Europe and colonial contexts (Mudimbe 1988; Spear 2003; Errington 2008). Language invention happens at several levels: the very notion of languages as entities linked to nations, ethnicities, peoples, territories is first of all transported into unfamiliar territory. The local linguistic chaos is then sorted out to fit languages onto categorizations of people, and, where extra work is

needed, languages are specifically created and renamed in order to fit preferred linguistic conditions. Shona in Zimbabwe, for example, was created on the basis of a two-stage process: first, a codification of dialects associated with different missionary stations. Second, the unification of the dialects by colonial linguists (Makoni et al. 2007). Similarly, Mannheim describes the emergence of Quecha in Latin America as a product of Spanish invasion. Prior to the Spanish invasion, the Quecha did not need a construct of language, indeed like many other communities they did not have any specific names to refer to what they spoke (Mannheim 1991). Once this sorting out has been achieved, this invented world of languages and ethnicities is reported as if it were an objective reality that has always been in place (Harris 2009).

Similarly, in Indonesia Heryanto (2007) demonstrates how the notion of "language" did not exist in pre-colonial Indonesia leading him to claim that "language is not a universal category." Of course this does not mean there was no communication prior to the emergence of Bahasa Indonesia as a language, but rather that the idea of language brought in with its introduction, and the appropriation of the notion of *Bahasa* in the process, was a major shift in how language was understood in the region. If language was relevant at all, it was something that was the possession of each individual and not necessarily shared by social groups. From such an individual perspective languages cannot be construed as a collection of objects (Love 2009).

Looking at language descriptions in the same region, van der Tuuk (1971) condemns the pointless attempts to "find a strict system in such language ruins as Javanese and Malay." It is impossible, he suggests, to "represent a language well" unless we disabuse ourselves of the attempt to describe a complete system, for every language is more or less a ruin, in which the plan of the architect cannot be discovered, until one has learned to supply from other works by the same hand what is missing in order to grasp the original design. (ibid.)

If van der Tuuk's view of languages as "ruins" perhaps seems unduly negative, and suggests a possible progression from language to decay, it nevertheless highlights well the fruitless search for order amid a much more chaotic linguistic reality. We also have to appreciate in these and other contexts that many languages, such as Igbo or Yoruba in the nineteenth century had different meanings prior to colonial encounters (Irvine 2009), and that what was understood by many people as their language was simply their description for how they spoke (Crowley 1999).

The process of invention is a complicated one consisting of transforming dialogical and "heteroglossic" material into monological texts (Blommaert 2008). The invented linguistic artifacts were textualized in a wide range of genres: grammatical outlines, grammatical sketches, word lists, orthographies, and so on (Blommaert 2008; Errington 2001, 2008). In this codification process, the serious complexities of different sociolinguistic contexts were reduced through the technical apparatus of monological sociolinguistics into "equally serious simplicities" (Dasgupta 1997: 21). In most colonial contexts, local languages were standardized by outsiders without the direct involvement of the local population, except as informants based on a series of texts, folklore, narratives, and so on (Blommaert 2008). The objective was to produce European bilingual speakers "competent" in the varieties of African languages, which they had created in conjunction with European languages (Fabian 1986; Jeater 2007). The overall effects of this intervention were a European appropriation of and creation of African standardized languages by non-native speakers.

In a bid to regain control of their languages from colonial dictionary makers, local language users increasingly produced monolingual dictionaries, grammars, and so on. Monolingualism became salient as a consequence of an imposed multilingualism when local speakers felt they had lost control of how they were to represent their languages. Such resistance to outsider multilingualism, however, was more random than systematic. The attempts to regain the representation of sociolinguistic situations were limited by the fact that resistance to multilingual grammars and dictionaries by the use of largely monolingual ones was nevertheless conducted by linguistic elites along the lines already laid down for the description of languages. Thus

> the modern language elite, in his role as a liaison between western language values and indigenous language patterns, has appropriated for himself the gatekeeper's privilege of approving or disapproving various shifts being introduced in verbal repertoire. Mostly the elite cartels manage interactions among themselves, very little realizing the indifference of the masses to such endeavors in their everyday speech activity. (Khubchandani 2003)

This process then becomes naturalized so that, for example, the sociolinguistic truism that multilingualism is the natural and common condition for the majority world obscures the implicit language categorizations that lurk behind such apparently descriptive categorizations. What is often overlooked is that multilingualism is a way of thinking, a world view, an intellectual orientation that forces us to look backwards under the burden of a backward-looking metalanguage, which was never designed "for our modern priorities" (Harris 2009

33). The sociolinguistics of multilingualism is thus all too often akin to driving a car on a highway while looking only at the rear view mirror, an activity with the potential to see only what has gone before (which may be catching us up) while risking the dangers of crashing into the diversity of what lies ahead.

Multilingualism or monolingualism of humanity

A central argument in many contemporary accounts of multilingualism is that language research has tended to work with monolingualism as a norm, and that such a construct is inappropriate because a majority, if not most of the people, are multilingual. This line of argumentation, which celebrates the shift or break from monolingualism to multilingualism, does not, from the point of view of disinvention, do enough to question the underlying premises of its own position. It underestimates the social impact and intellectual resilience of monolingual philosophy. Although we share many of the concerns over the monolingual bias at the heart of much research on language, therefore, we are also concerned that the resultant ideas of enumerable languages have the effect of promoting a form of plural monolingualism (Heller 2007; Makoni 1998). The case we wish to make here, then, is that although the critique of monolingualism has taken us some distance, the focus on multilingualism does not take us far enough. One way forward here, in fact, may be described as a return to monolingualism, but a very different monolingualism from the narrow vision that was developed as part of the alliance between linguistics, colonialism, and the nation-state. Rather, a new sense of monolingualism might be envisaged that has at its heart an understanding of diversity that goes beyond the pluralism of multilingualism.

Even if we accept that there has been a conceptual and administrative shift from a focus on monolingualism to multilingualism as reflected in the discourses of much established scholarship (see many contributions to this volume), there is, however, another strand of research that is relatively less well known in colonial and post-colonial contexts, the current impulse of which consists of running by contrast not from monolingualism to multilingualism, but the reverse. The idea of "a language" creates a philosophical bind for sociolinguistics. If we accept the construct of "a language" (albeit a product of complex interplay between sociohistorical factors and politics), then multilingualism may be made up of different autonomous objects, a plural or multiple monolingualism. If, however, we grasp the full implication of the impossibility of the central construct of "a language," it becomes clear that we cannot in fact critique monolingualism as there can be no such thing.

The irrelevance of the monolingual/multilingual dichotomy has also anecdotally been reported in some European contexts. Harris (2009) reports the following anecdote told by Nabokov. He tells us that, when he was a boy, for a number of years he did not grasp that French and Russian were different. "Without realizing it, he was equally fluent in both" (Harris 2009: 29). Most students in early years of schooling attend school without knowing that they are multilingual. Being multilingual is something they discover at school through a radical process that alters their self-perception and identity when pedagogy forces them to discover languages as separate entities. Pedagogy entails teaching a specific view and understanding of language. In such cases pedagogy creates objects: language reinforced by the presence of "subjects" like English, Shona, Yoruba on the timetable alongside mathematics, biology, health science, etc. The idea of "a language" as an educational construct is also reflected in debates as to whether Caribbean Creole (CC) is a variety of English or a separate language. Nero (2006) cites examples of some Jamaican speakers of CC who thought they spoke English until they were assigned to

ESL classes, thus challenging their sense of being native speakers of English.

Although sociolinguists have long had to acknowledge the messiness of the category "language," and have used, for example, notions such as continua to account for the impossibility of imposing borders between creoles and related languages, the Caribbean Creole (CC) example illustrates further how languages are constructs of the frameworks that make them. Clearly, for Jamaicans, Caribbean Creole (CC) was English, whereas their experience when assigned to an ESL class undermines that very same belief. So CC gets caught between speakers' beliefs about what they speak (English), institutional language ascriptions (ESL classes as English is a second language for CC speakers), a fully fledged creole language from the point of view of creole studies, and a subvariety of English that cannot be counted as a world English on a par with Indian or Singaporean English from the point of view of the world Englishes framework. As Mufwene (2001: 107) has noted, "the naming practices of new Englishes has to do more with the racial identity of those who speak them than with how these varieties developed and the extent of their structural deviations." In Liberia, speakers of what some linguistics might call Liberian Pidgin are adamant that what they speak is a variety of English. In Ghana, educated Ghanaian speakers find the reference to what they speak as Ghanaian English as offensive since they perceive their English to be indistinguishable from standard English.

These examples point to several concerns about the linguistic analyses on which many accounts of language in the contemporary world rely. Although the serious study of creoles by linguists and the concomitant acceptance of creoles as languages like any other has been a great advance from earlier views of Creole languages as somehow deficient, the incorporation of these languages into a standard

200

linguistic framework has also caused what Grace (n.d.) calls "collateral damage." By turning them into languages like any other, the very distinctiveness, diversity, and creativity of creoles is reduced to questions of uniformity, origins, and substrata. A similar point is made by Branson and Miller (2007) with respect to sign languages. Although much was gained initially by finally treating sign languages as languages like any other, rather than as mere gesture or the gestural representation of pre-existing languages, much has also been lost by the inability to see their uniqueness as gestural languages that operate spatially and temporally in ways quite different from other languages. The example of Ghanaian English also draws our attention to the need to incorporate local perspective and the locus of enunciation into any analysis of language use: When Ghanaians and indeed other Third World-educated individuals insist that what they speak is English, this does not suggest that they are unaware of linguistic differences between them and other users, but rather that at times the differences are insignificant to them (Rajagopolan 2007).

Lurking behind many of the arguments made in this chapter is the perennial controversial notion of the native speaker. If Indigenous languages were invented and are a fiction, then the languages created cannot have native speakers. They will, however, have people who may claim to be experts in them, and others who resist their formation as part of a prolonged process of disinventing them. The constructed languages may be legitimate in the eyes of political administrators and those who are experts in them, but the notion of a native speaker may be unnecessary. The myth, however, of the native speaker is reinforced by plural monolingual models. The idea of autonomous languages may correspond with that of native speakers but when multilingualism is viewed differently in terms of a lingua franca in which diverse features are blended together, reflecting each indivi-

201

dual's personal experiences, which are inevitably different from one another, then the only reasonable conclusion is to say that each person is a native speaker of what they speak, no more no less.

Plural monolingualism is a powerful ideological position because it is supported by powerful discourses. Plural monolingual discourses are mutually reinforced and complemented by discourses of language rights, which assign rights to individual and autonomous languages (May 2005). The individuality and autonomous nature of language is further consolidated by discourses of language rights in which it is individual languages that have rights assigned to them, which then creates an impression of a language-centered universe where human concerns are of secondary significance (see Blommaert 2008). If the idea of independent languages is not readily applicable to some global contexts, advocates of language rights find themselves in an invidious position of supporting very specific and culturally grounded views of both language and rights as if they were universal.

By promoting "alien" concepts without accommodating the specificities of local interpretation of variants of those concepts, advocates of language rights undermine interests of the communities they seek to serve (May 2005). To some extent human rights discourses are imperialistic insofar as they tend to override other world views and discourses. The language rights discourses sidestep the languages they are seeking to promote by not examining how language rights are interpreted by the vernaculars whose rights they are seeking to advance. As Heller and Duchêne suggest, we need to

> rethink the reasons why we hold onto the ideas about language and identity which emerged from modernity. Rather than assuming we must save languages,

perhaps we should be asking instead who benefits and who loses from understanding languages the way we do, what is at stake for whom, and how and why language serves as a terrain for competition. (2007: 11)

Lingua franca, grassroots and urban multilingualism

Although, as we have suggested, the burden of current research tends towards a pluralization of monolingualism, there are also a number of different ways in which we can move towards a more productive understanding of language use. Fardon and Furniss (1984), for example, propose that multilingualism is "Africa's lingua franca." The view that multilingualism is a lingua franca is in sharp contrast to concepts such as plural/multiple monolingualism. In plural monolingualism languages are distinct, and autonomous, whereas in lingua franca multilingualism languages are so deeply intertwined and fused into each other that the level of fluidity renders it difficult to determine any boundaries that may indicate that there are different languages involved. Hence plural monolingualism is consistent with a model that renders it possible to choose between languages; multilingualism as a lingua franca, by contrast, militates against this trend and conjures a very different notion of "language." In lingua franca multilingualism language is viewed as a multilayered chain that is constantly combined and recombined and in which "secondary" language learning takes place more or less simultaneously with language use. In describing lingua franca multilingualism, Fardon and Furniss point out that language is conceptualized as

a multilayered and partially connected ... chain that offers a choice of varieties and registers in the speaker's immediate environment, and a steadily diminishing set of options to be employed in more distant

203

interactions, albeit a set that is always liable to be reconnected more densely to a new environment by rapid secondary learning, or by the development of new languages. (1984: 4)

This makes the notion of language that forms the basis of all analyses in linguistic theorizing of dubious validity. It is worth observing too that this idea is very different from the current thinking about English as a lingua franca (ELF) (Jenkins 2006; Seidlhofer 2001). Although this understanding of flexible, multiple English may provide a more dynamic model of English than some of the current analyses of varieties of English along national lines, it still keeps in place a notion of English as a language with core and variant properties. As Pennycook (2007b) has argued, there are good reasons to do away with these myths about English (or any other language): to speak of English (as international language, a lingua franca, a second/ foreign language and so forth) is not so much an act of description of linguistic reality as it is a discursive act that brings ideologies of English into being. Canagarajah (2007: 91), by contrast, offers a version of lingua franca English (LFE) that is closer to the position we are arguing for here, suggesting that "LFE does not exist as a system out there. It is constantly brought into being in each context ofcommunication."From this point of view, "there is no meaning for form, grammar or language ability outside the realm of practice. LFE is not a product located in the mind of the speaker; it is a social process constantly reconstructed in sensitivity to environmental factors" (Canagarajah 2007: 94).

Grassroots multilingualism is evident in popular culture, the study of which creates opportunities to advance an analysis of multilingualism that links music, language, paintings, and at times public transport in taxis driven largely by young males in Africa with low levels of formal education.

An analysis that combines these diverse modalities has to be transmodal (Pennycook 2007a; Makoni and Makoni 2009) rather than multimodal (Kress 2003; Kress and van Leeuwen 2001). It has to be transmodal because meanings or communication in such situations are borne out by a complex reading of different modalities, at times reading them against each other, and not separately, which would echo a plural monolingualism. A transmodal analysis should capture the dynamic and evolving relationships between languages and other modalities. The meaning is an evolving art and drama of communication because the semiotic systems are constructed in context and are always in a state of being, inchoate, fragmented, and historically contingent.

From this point of view, an understanding of multilingua francas incorporates not only the linguistic resources speakers draw on but also elements of the accompanying soundtracks. Language use in parts of South Africa may be interwoven with kwaito (a version of South African hip-hop) and its various associations. In such contexts, sampling of sounds, genres, languages, and cultures is the norm (Pennycook 2007a; Alim et al. 2009; Makoni et al. 2010). This view of language is human-centered insofar as it stresses agency (albeit with constraints) and explores how individuals and communities express "voice" (Blommaert 2005), "playing" around with semiotics with fragmented and open designs, which can be manipulated to clarify, obfuscate or make meanings ambiguous (Khubchandani 1997:70;Makoni and Makoni 2010). This ambiguity or meaning obfuscation contrasts sharply with the type of multilingual school language practices "which puts premium on the explicit, unambiguous, overt manifestation through language by laying undue stress on its rationale and overt use" (Khubchandani 1997: 226). This dynamic and fluidity calls for a need to reimagine new metaphors to describe multilingual density. One way of describing them is to borrow from Illich and

Sander's description of vernacular grammars in the late fifteenth century, "lingua or tongue was less like one drawer in a bureau than one color in a spectrum. The comprehensibility of speech was comparable to the intensity of a color" (1989: 62–3).

Bosire argues that the

> hybrid languages of Africa are contact outcomes that have evolved at a time when African communities are coming to terms with the colonial and postcolonial situation that included rapid urbanization and a bringing together of different ethnic communities and cultures with a concomitant exposure to different ways of being. (2006: 192)

At the same time, "young people are caught up in this transition; they are children of two worlds and want a way to express this duality, this new 'ethnicity'." Out of this mix emerge new language varieties, such as "Sheng," a Swahili/English hybrid, which provides urban youth with "a way to break away from the old fraternities that put particular ethnic communities in particular neighborhoods/estates and give them a global urban ethnicity, the urbanite: sophisticated, street smart, new generation, tough" (ibid.). Higgins' (2009) work on English as a local and multivocal language in East Africa destabilizes some of the dominant conceptualizations of English as a distinct code, as a global language, as an entity bounded by particular domains of use. Instead, she suggests, we need to grasp the implications of the hybridity and linguistic bricolage in which English so often participates.

The next step, therefore, is to move towards an understanding of the relationships among language resources as used by certain communities (the linguistic resources users draw on), local language practices (the use of these language resources in specific contexts), and language users' relationship to language varieties (the social, economic, and cultural positioning of the speakers). From this point of view, therefore, we can start to move away from both mono- and multilingual orientations to language, and take on board recent understandings of translingual practices (Jacquemet 2005; Pennycook 2010) across communities other than those defined along national, ethnic, geographic, or cultural criteria. The interest here is in "the communicative practices of transnational groups that interact using different languages and communicative codes simultaneously present in a range of communicative channels, both local and distant" (Jacquemet 2005: 265). These transidiomatic practices, Jacquemet explains, "are the results of the co-presence of multilingual talk (exercised by de/reterritorialized speakers) and electronic media, in contexts heavily structured by social indexicalities and semiotic codes." For Jacquemet, such practices are dependent on "transnational environments," the mediation of "deterritorialized technologies," and interaction "with both present and distant people" (ibid.).

Such language use can also be usefully be described in terms of *metrolingualism* (Otsuji and Pennycook 2010), a product typically of modern and mainly urban interaction. Drawing on the notion of metroethnicity that seeks ethnic reconstitution by challenging ethnic and language orthodoxities through the possibilities of a new ethnic *cool* (Maher 2005), metrolingualism describes the ways in which people of different and mixed backgrounds use, play with and negotiate identities through language; it does not assume connections between language, culture, ethnicity, nationality, or geography, but rather seeks to explore how such relations are produced, resisted, defied, or rearranged. Although Jørgensen (2008) and Møller (2008) have posed similar questions about language reifications and proposed the notion of *polylingualism* in place of multilingualism, the notion of metrolingualism, like the idea of a multilingua

207

franca, has the advantage of avoiding the pluralization strategies of parallel terminology (multilingualism, plurilingualism, polylingualism) and instead posits mixed language as the singular norm where the notion of language in time and space (metro), rather than countability, becomes the language modifier.

The rise of new forms of urban multiple language use has a long history. These new *urbi-* or *metro-lingualisms* pose challenges to the study of multiple language and render it necessary to construct new metaphors to capture the unfolding social, political, and linguistic complexity. They draw on and use a wide range of local and non-local languages, and create new and fragmented semiotic systems; they are constantly in flux; they are predominantly oral; they are street languages, and as such are often linked to popular culture, crime, and urban unrest. To speak these languages, it is necessary to draw on multilingual resources, and yet these urban languages are also multilanguages in themselves, diverse, shifting, constantly evolving, and unpredictable in their usage. They may vary according to who is using them to whom, while at the same time each speaker may retain a form of multilingualism peculiar to them: a form of idiolectal multilingualism. The variability in the use of and facility in the use of multilingualism as play compels us to reintroduce the idea of individual creativity within multilingualism.

Conclusions and new research directions
Recent research has started to question whether these old categorizations of language—varieties, codeswitching, bilingualism, mother tongue, multilingualism, and borrowing—as well as the identities that are assumed along lines of language, location, ethnicity, culture really work any more. Developed in contexts very different to those in which language analysis is now being carried out (urban, grassroots, popular culture), many of these concepts simply do

not seem to address the forms of hybrid urbilingualism that are common across the world. Indeed, there are strong reasons to question the very notion of language as a discrete entity that is describable in terms of core and variation. On the one hand, then, there are the changing realities of urban life, with enhanced mobility, shifting populations, social upheaval, health and climate crises, and increased access to diverse media, particularly forms of popular culture. On the other hand, is the growing concern that we need to rethink the ways in which language has been conceptualized.

The assumption that monolingualism and multilingualism are two important pillars which might be used to frame sociolinguistic analysis, and that studies of multilingualism are attempting to move beyond the blinkered monolingualism that has constricted a lot of thought about language use, takes us a certain way but then stops short. For many people—whether the Quecha in Latin America (Mannheim 1991) or different people across Africa and Asia—the critical issue is not whether one is monolingual or multilingual but that one uses language. This is why the ultimate move here may not only be from monolingualism to multilingualism but also back to monolingualism, where the latter is understood in very different ways from the monological, one-variety concept that linguistics has been trying to escape. This is the monolingualism of humanity, which can be better captured not by pluri- poly- or multilingualism but by non-pluralized ideas such as urbilingualism, metrolingualism, or a multilingua franca.

Treating languages as socially and historically constructed provides space and latitude for social and political change, and takes cognizance of individuals' social and adaptive strategies and their resistance to some of the constructed languages. If Indigenous languages are socially constructed through a complex interplay of philosophy and politics, they are more akin to other artificial constructs such as customary law, which is a form of codified traditional law rather than any naturally occurring tradition. Joseph's (2006) reminder that languages are "political from top to bottom" is useful here as it draws attention yet again to the point that both the invention of languages and their disinvention are steeped in relations of power and politics.

In conclusion, we now return to the questions we posed at the beginning of the chapter. If languages are not "primordial," under what conditions did they emerge, and what are the implications of the processes of invention that brought them into being? Although research discussed above has started to document the histories of language invention, particularly in colonial contexts (Errington 2008), there is clearly a great deal more work that could be done here. In order to understand the metadiscursive regimes used in the construction of "languages," we need both a critical history of linguistics in its many contexts, as well as a great deal more work in linguistic anthropology in order to understand the ways in which languages are locally used and understood, and the effects of particular metadiscursive regimes on the workings of local languages. And finally, if we can do away with our language enumerations that sit so often at the heart of multilingualism, a great deal of productive research could start to open up the real complexities of grassroots metro- or urbilingualism.

Further reading

Errington, J. (2008) *Linguistics in a Colonial World: A Story of Language, Meaning and Power*. Oxford: Blackwell. (*Linguistics in a Colonial World* gives a significant account of the role of linguists within colonialism, showing how the political and epistemological orientations of empire worked together to produce particular ways of thinking about language(s).)

Heller, M. (2007) *Bilingualism: A Social Approach*.

210

Basingstoke: Palgrave Macmillan.
(Monica Heller's collection opens with an illuminating chapter in which she does a powerful critique of bilingualism, proposing a strong social approach. Her critique is similar to the one laid out in this book on issues about the limitations of constructs such as codes and boundedness as bases for the analysis of language. In addition to her introduction, there are a number of other chapters dealing with a wide range of topics from minority language movements to language rights and bilingualism in the mass media.)

Khubchandani, L. (2004) *Balance of the Current Sociolinguistic Research: New Trends and New Paradigms*, Linguapax Congress, Linguistic Diversity, Sustainability and Peace, Congress Report (19–23), Barcelona, April 2002,
www.linguapax.org/congres/plenaries/khubchandani.html

(Khubchandani provides an excellent example of postcolonial Indian interpretation of multilingualism.)

Ranger, T. (1983) "The invention of tradition in colonial Africa", in E. Hobsbawm and T. Ranger (eds) *The Invention of Tradition*, Cambridge: Cambridge University Press.

(Ranger's work on the invention of tradition in Africa is an early key text for thinking about invention. Although he subsequently had concerns that it downplays the agency and significance of local traditions, preferring instead Andersen's (1983) *Imagined Communities*, invention is preferable because the construct of invention neatly encapsulates the constructed nature of major African social formations. The social formation takes place over a long period of time, and indeed at times there is controversy about which features are relevant and how they should be represented, and interpreted.)

Williams, G. (1992) *Sociolinguistics: A Sociological Critique*. London and New York: Routledge.

(Williams provides a particularly incisive critique of some of the central concepts in sociolinguistics of multilingualism, corpus and state planning, and the limitations of language planning as an instrument of social change.)

Bibliography
Alim, S, Ibrahim, A. and Pennycook, A. (eds) (2009) *Global Linguistic Flows: Hip Hop Cultures, Youth Identities and the Politics of Language*, New York: Routledge.

Bauman, R. and Briggs, C. (2003) *Voices of Modernity Language Ideologies and the Politics of Inequality.* Cambridge: Cambridge University Press.

Becker, A. L. (1995) *Beyond Translation: Essays in Modern Philology,* Ann Arbor: The University of Michigan Press.

Blommaert, J. (2005) *Discourse*, Cambridge: Cambridge University Press.

Blommaert, J. (2008) 'Artefactual ideologies and the textual production of African languages', *Language and Communication*, 28(4) pp. 291–307.

Bosire, M. (2006) 'Hybrid languages: the case of Sheng', in O. F. Arasanyin and M. A. Pemberton (eds) *Selected Proceedings of the 36th Annual Conference on African Linguistics*, Somerville, MA: Cascadilla Proceedings Project.

Branson, J and Miller, D. (2007) 'Beyond "language": linguistic imperialism, sign languages and linguistic anthropology', in S. Makoni and A. Pennycook (eds) *Disinventing and Reconstituting Languages*, Clevedon: Multilingual Matters.

Bybee, J. and Hopper, P. (2001) 'Introduction to frequency and the emergence of linguistic structure', in J. Bybee and P. Hopper (eds) *Frequency and the Emergence of Linguistic Structure*, Amsterdam: John Benjamins.

Canagarajah, S. (2007) "The ecology of global English" *International Multilingual Research Journal* 1(2) pp.89–100.

Clifford, J. and Marcus, G. (1986) *Writing Culture: The Poetics of Ethnography*, Berkeley: University of California Press.

Crowley, T. (1999) "Linguistic diversity in the Pacific" *Journal of Sociolinguistics* 3(1) pp.81–103.

Dasgupta, P. (1997) "Foreword", in *Revisualizing Boundaries: A Plurilingual Ethos*, New Delhi; Thousand Oaks; London: Sage.

Davidson, D. (1986) "A nice derangement of epitaphs", in E. Lepore (ed.) *Truth and Interpretation Perspectives on the Philosophy of Donald Davidson*, Oxford: Blackwell.

Errington, J. (2001) "Colonial linguistics", *Annual Review of Anthropology* 30 pp.19–39.

Errington, J. (2008) *Linguistics in a Colonial World: A Story of Language, Meaning and Power*, Oxford: Blackwell.

Fabian, J. (1986) *Language and Colonial Power*, Cambridge: Cambridge University Press.

Fardon, G. and Furniss, R. (1984) *African Languages, Development and the State*, London: Routledge.

Grace, G. (n.d.) available online at http://www2.hawaii.edu~grace

Harpham, G. (2002) *Language Alone: The Critical Fetish of Modernity*, London: Routledge.

Harris, R. (1980) *The Language Makers*, Ithaca, NY: Cornell University Press.

Harris, R. (1981) *The Language Myth in Western Culture*, London: Duckworth.

Harris, R. (1990) "On redefining linguistics" in H. Davis and T. Taylor (eds) *Redefining Linguistics*, London: Routledge.

Harris, R. (1998) *Introduction to Integrational Linguistics*,

213

Oxford: Pergamon.

Harris, R. (2009) "Implicit and explicit language teaching", in M. Toolan (ed.) *Language Teaching, Integrational Linguistic Approaches*, London: Routledge.

Harris, R. and Taylor, T. (1997) (eds) *Landmarks in Linguistic Thought, vol. 1. The Western Tradition from Socrates to Saussure*, 2nd edn, London: Routledge.

Haugen, E. (1972) *The Ecology of Language*. Palo Alto: Stanford University Press.

Heller, M. (2007) "Bilingualism as ideology and practice" in M. Heller (ed.) *Bilingualism: A Social Approach*, London: Macmillan.

Heller, M. and Duchêne, A. (2007) "Discourses of endangerment: Sociolinguistics, globalization and social order", in A. Duchêne and M Heller (eds) *Discourses of Endangerment: Ideology and Interest in the Defense of Languages*, London: Continuum.

Heryanto, A. (1990) "The making of language: developmentalism in Indonesia" *Prisma* 50 pp. 40–53.

Heryanto, A. (2007) "Then there were languages: Bahasa Indonesia was one among many", in S. Makoni and A. Pennycook (eds) *Disinventing and Reconstituting Languages,* Clevedon: Multilingual Matters.

Higgins, C. (2009) *English as a Local Language: Postcolonial Identities and Multilingual Practices*, Clevedon: Multilingual Matters.

Hopper, P. (1998) "Emergent grammar", in M. Tomasello (ed.) *The New Psychology of Language*, Mahwah, NJ: Lawrence Erlbaum.

Illich, I. and Sander, B. (1989) *ABC: The Alphabetization of the Popular Mind*, London: Penguin.

Irvine, J. (1989) "When talk isn't cheap: language and political economy" *American Ethnologist* 16 pp. 248-67.

Irvine, J. (2009) "Subjected words: African linguistics and

the colonial encounter" *Language and Communication* 28(4) pp.291–408.

Jacquemet, M. (2005) "Transidiomatic practices: Language and power in the age of globalization" *Language and Communication* 25 pp. 257–77.

Jeater, D. (2007) *Language and Sciences: The Invention of the 'Native Mind' in Southern Rhodesia*, Portsmouth, USA: Heinemann/Greenwood.

Jenkins, J. (2006) "Current perspectives on teaching world Englishes and English as a lingua franca" *TESOL Quarterly* 40(1) pp. 157–81.

Johnstone, B. (1996) *The Linguistic Individual: Self-expression in Language and Linguistics,* New York and Oxford: Oxford University Press.

Jørgensen, J. N. (2008) "Polylingual languaging around and among children and adolescents" *International Journal of Multilingualism* 5(3) pp. 161–76.

Joseph, J. (2006) *Language and Politics*, Edinburgh: Edinburgh University Press.

Khubchandani, L. M. (1983) "Demographic Imperatives in Language Planning"
www.linguapax.org/congres/plenaries/Khubchandani.html

Khubchandani, L.M. (1997) "Bilingual Education for Indigenous groups in India" in J. Cummins and D. Corson (eds) *Encylopaedia of Language and Education*, vol. 5. Bilingual Education (pp.67–76) Dordrecht, Netherlands: Kluwer.

Khubchandani, L.M. (2003) "Defining mother tongue education in plurilingual contexts" *Language Policy* 2 pp. 239–54.

Kress, G. (2003) *Literacy in the New Media*, London: Routledge.

Kress, G. and van Leeuwen, T. (2001) *Reading Images the Grammar of Visual Design*, London: Routledge.

Kroskrity (2000) "Regimenting languages: Language ideo-

215

logical perspectives", in P. V. Kroskrity (ed.) *Regimes of Language: Ideologies, Politics and Identities*, Santa Fe, NM: School of American Research Press.

Le Page, R. and Tabouret-Keller, A. (1985) *Acts of Identity*, Cambridge: Cambridge University Press.

Love, N. (2009) "Science, language and linguistic culture" *Language and Communication* 29 pp. 26–46.

Maher, J. (2005) "Metroethnicity, language, and the principle of cool", *International Journal of the Sociology of Language* 175/176 pp. 83–102.

Makoni, S. (1998) "African languages as European scripts the shaping of communal memory", in S. Nuttall and C. Cotzee (eds) *Negotiating the Past: The Making of Memory in South Africa*, Oxford: Oxford University Press.

Makoni, S. and Makoni, B. (2009) "English and education in Anglophone Africa: Historical and current realities", in M. Shepard Wong and S. Canagarajah (eds) *Christian and Critical English Language Education Educators in Dialogue: Pedagogical and Ethical Dilemmas,* New York and London: Routledge.

Makoni, S. and Makoni, B. (2010) "Multilingual discourses on wheels and public English in Africa: A case for 'vague linguistique'", in J. Maybin and J. Swann (eds) *The Routledge Companion to English Language Studies*, Abingdon, Oxford: Routledge.

Makoni, S., Brutt-Griffler, J. and Mashiri, P. (2007) "The use of "indigenous" and urban vernaculars in Zimbabwe", *Language in Society* 36 pp.25–49.

Makoni, S., Makoni, B. and Rosenberg, A. (2010) "Wordy worlds of music: Implications for language in education" *Language, Identity, and Education* 9 (1) pp. 1–10.

Makoni, S. and Pennycook, A. (2007) (eds) *Disinventing*

and Reconstituting Languages, Clevedon: Multilingual Matters.

Mannheim, B. (1991) *The Language of the Inka Since the European Invasion*, Austin: University of Texas.

May, S. (2005) "Moving the language debates forward" *Journal of Sociolinguistics* 9(3) pp. 319–47.

Møller, J. S. (2008) "Polylingual performance among Turkish-Danes in late-modern Copenhagen" *International Journal of Multilingualism* 5(3) pp. 217–36.

Mudimbe, V. (1988) *The Invention of Africa: Gnosis, Philosophy, and the Order of Knowledge*, Bloomington: Indiana University Press.

Mufwene, S. (2001) *The Ecology of Language Evolution*, Cambridge: Cambridge University Press.

Mühlhäusler, P. (2000) "Language planning and language ecology" *Current Issues in Language Planning* 1(3) pp. 306–67.

Nakata, M. (2007) *Disciplining the Savages, Savaging the Disciplines*, Canberra: Aboriginal Studies Press.

Nero, S. (2006) "Language, identity and education of Caribbean English speakers" *World Englishes* 25(3/4) pp. 501–11.

Otsuji, E. and Pennycook, A. (2010) "Metrolingualism: Fixity, fluidity and language in flux" *International Journal of Multilingualism* 7 (3) pp. 240–54.

Pennycook, A. (2007a) *Global Englishes and Transcultural Flows*, London and New York: Routledge.

Pennycook, A. (2007b) "The myth of English as an international language" in S. Makoni and A. Pennycook (eds) *Disinventing and Reconstituting Languages,* Clevedon: Multilingual Matters.

Pennycook, A. (2010) *Language as a Local Practice*, London: Routledge.

Rajagopolan, K. (2007) "Revisiting the nativity scene"

Studies in Language 31(1) pp. 193–205.

Ranger, T. (1983) "The invention of tradition in colonial Africa" in E. Hobsbawm and T. Ranger (eds) *The Invention of Tradition*, Cambridge: Cambridge University Press.

Schiefflien, B. (1990) *The Give and Take of Everyday Life: Language Socialization of the Kaluli Children*, New York and Cambridge: Cambridge University Press.

Seidlhofer, B. (2001) "Closing a conceptual gap: The case for a description of English as a lingua franca" *International Review of Applied Linguistics* 11(2) pp. 133–58.

Spear, T. (2003) "Neo-traditionalism and the limits of invention in British Colonial Africa" *Journal of African History* 44 pp. 3–27.

Toolan, M. (2009) (ed.) *Language Teaching and Integrational Linguistics*, London: Routledge.

van der Tuuk, N. H. (1971) *A Grammar of Toba Batak*, The Hague: Martinus Hijhoff.

Voor De Trope, available online at www2.hawaii.edu/langue.html

Whorf, B. (1988) *Language, Thought, and Reality: Selected Writings of Benjamin Lee Whorf*, John Carroll (ed.), Cambridge, MA: MIT Press.

Woolard, K. (2004) "Is the past a foreign country?: Time, language origins, and the nation in early modern Spain", *Journal of Linguistic Anthropology* 14(1) pp. 57–80.

Yngve, V. (1996) *From Grammar to Science. New Foundations for General Linguistics*, Philadelphia: John Benjamins.

Yngve, V. and Wasik, Z. (eds) (2004) *Hard-Science Linguistics*, New York: Continuum.

IX

African Languages as European Scripts
The Shaping of Communal Memory

In this chapter I explore the impact of the invention and use of standardized African languages on the form and substance of African communal memory. I look at this particularly in the context of the current entrenchment of language rights in South Africa's new constitution, and the kinds of 'past' to which such policy implicitly makes an appeal.

'Invention' is a notion that has won widespread recognition, especially through the work of Terence Ranger (1989), but which is currently under stress. Arguing from a social constructivist perspective, Ranger and others are now adamant that 'invention' does not forcefully enough capture the involvement of Africans in their own history. In spite of this, I want to argue that 'invention' remains a robust concept, foregrounding, as it does, the artificiality of ethnicity, and the assumptions of primordialism upon which it is based. As such, it remains a useful way of discussing some of the vagaries of current South African discourses of multilingualism, the linguistic equivalent of the 'rainbow nation'.

In South Africa, missionaries played an active role in the invention of African languages. They drew the linguistic boundaries, determining what was to be regarded as constituting a specific language. The linguistic processes they set in motion had clear political dimensions and implied particular forms of social relations between Africans and Europeans and among Africans themselves. Isabel Hofmeyr

(1993: 48) argues that Africans actively took advantage of the presence of missionaries to articulate their dissatisfaction with existing political systems:

> Both among commoners and within the royal caste itself, then, there existed cause for dissatisfaction against the ruling lineage. The dissatisfaction was expressed by entering into a loose association with missionaries. For commoners, the mission and its schools which used a lot of Sesotho remained a source of attraction.

Hofmeyr does not, in my view, examine adequately what was happening to Africans in the process of entering into an alliance wth the missionaries, however. She does not emphasize strongly enough how the discourse missionaries were creating limited what could be said 'about', 'to', and discussed 'with' Africans—the extent to which the construction of African languages was designed not ony to restrict the universe of discourse entered into with Africans, but their participation in that discourse as well (Jeater 1994: 2).

The major objective of missionaries was to comprehend African cosmology in their own terms, and only those terms that could facilitate that process were included in the vernacular language. They were passing judgement about the society they were operating in (Cameron 1995: 33-47). Jeater (1994: 4) shows how in translation exercises, Africans who preferred to find alternative sources of cash were regarded as dishonest and lazy because they were not making themselves availabe for exploitation as colonial labour. The inventions were structured in a way that encouraged Africans to internalize European epistemology about themselves, creating a new view about their current affairs and superimposing new values on their past. The new values distanced the African convert elite from the conceptual world view of the vernacular population, and by implication distanced africans from their own past.

The construction of African languages reflected, in many cases, evangelical rivalry more than existing linguistic reality (Harries 1995: 154). For example, the emergence of a single standard for Zulu and Xhosa was prevented by the competing interests of different missionaries (Herbert 1992). The recent distinction between Zulu and siSwati was motivated first and foremost by political considerations reflecting the inadequacy of a linguistic definition of language (Le Page and Tabouret-Keller 1985; Pennycook 1994: 167). This involved splitting African speech forms into separate languages. Previously African speech forms had constituted a continuum "stretching across Africa from Atlantic to the Indian Ocean" (Le Page and Tabouret-Keller 1982: 161-93). The idea of African languages as constituting an array of separate boxes or, as Fardon and Furniss (1993: 3) call it, "Boundaries discourse", was based on the belief that different languages constitute mutually exclusive categories.

The discourse of African languages as separate categories, then, had its genesis in concepts in colonial thinking. An ideology of "linguistic fixity", as Paul Gilroy (1987) has termed it, was useful for social classification. Moreover, literacy and language education are as much tools for social control as means of social emancipation. Current constitutional provisions about language can be seen as a retrospective legitimization of a particular view about the past. Emerging discourses about multilingualism derive their strength and vitality through a deliberate refusal to recollect that in the past multilingualism has always been used to facilitate exploitation of Africans. Memory is as much about what people would like to recall as it is about what they would like to unremember (I prefer the term unremember because it underscores that forgetting is as much an active process as remembering). Discourses about the promotion of African

221

languages are likely to be received with skepticism unless standardized written forms can be recast through a process of an active and egalitarian reinvention.

Current discourses about multilingualism anxious to reverse the inequalities between languages as part of the apartheid legacy do not engage with the differences within each linguistic label operating under the guise of an African language. Proponents of multlingualism thus become ideological captives of the system they are seeking to challenge. Brink, in chapter 2 of this volume, comments that if we are to transcend the legacy of the past, language itself has to be reimagined:

> The past cannot be corrected by bringing to it the procedures and mechanisms and mind-sets that originally produced our very perception of that past. After all, it is not the past as such that has produced the present or poses the conditions for the future... but the way we think about it. Or, even more pertinently, the way in which we deal with it in language. (Brink, 1998)

This is as true in the more metaphorical sense in which Brink uses it as it is in a more literal, linguistic, sense.

All languages are fictions. Pennycook (1994: 28) illustrates the fictionality of English when he says that "English is fragmented, struggled over, resisted, rejected, diverse, broken, centrifugal and even incommensurable with itself". If English is a fiction, then African languages are even more highly fictionalized. Xhosa, for example, has many spoken varieties. Speakers of Hlubi and Bhaca from the Eastern Cape may experience problems when writing standard Xhosa, which is closer to a variety spoken by the Ngquka, derived from Rharhade. The situation is not peculiar to Xhosa. There is such great diversity within the box labelled 'Northern Sotho' that no dialect has successfully served as a standard. Non-standardized Zulu differs so much from the standardized version of Zulu that Zulu students in urban areas feel alienated from the very language that has been attributed to them as their mother tongue.

The labelling process has led to a construction of idealized languages which has begun to create problems for language teaching. Some teachers compare the teaching of standard Zulu to urbanized Zulu speakers with teaching a foreign language (Herbert 1992: 4). In some situations Zulu language teachers find themselves having to resort to the use of Iscamtho (an urban anti-language) to explain aspects of Zulu (Ntshangase 1995: 291). Recently published research suggests that the mixed African pan-ethnic varieties are now being used in the classroom not only as a last resort by teachers; pupils themselves frequently use these varieties as the unmarked norm for interaction within the classroom (Calteaux 1996). If a Zulu teacher has to resort to another language in order to explain aspects of Zulu, it means the students do not have the necessary expertise in the language attributed to them as their 'mother tongue'. Perhaps the three-way distinction that Rampton (1990: 98) proposes betwen 'affiliation', 'inheritance', and 'expertise' may be significant. The term 'language expertise' refers to the question of how proficient one is in a language; 'language affiliation' refers to the attachment or identification a person feels for a language, whether or not that person nominally belongs to the socal group customarily associated with that language; 'language inheritance' refers to the ways in which individuals can be born into a language tradition that is prominent within the family and/or community setting, whether or not they claim expertise in or affiliation to that language. Language teachers need to ask, with reference to each language nominally said to exist in a particular learner's linguistic repertoire, whether the learner's relationship with his or her language is based on expertise, on inheritance, on affiliation, or on a combination of all three.

The triad of concepts Rampton has introduced is of great assistance in explaining the phenomenon Ntshangase describes. The students Ntshangase has in mind may be affiliated to Zulu ethnically, and possibly have inherited some Zulu, but do not have demonstrable expertise in it. Their expertise may lie in another language which because of the constitution's orientation towards language history is not recognized because it has not acquired historical longevity and does not possess the weight of tradition in order to acquire constitutional legitimacy.

A major problem with the strategy is the artificiality of mother tongue. Young children living in urban townships may find themselves living next door to Nguni speakers, across the road from Sesotho, whilst their parents derive variously from Xhosa or other language groups. (Street 1993: 34)

Widespread use of pan-ethnic varieties reflects ways in which individual speakers can construct their own individual pasts. Language may be used to reveal certain identities, and to mask others. For example, the use of Pretoria Sotho by people who have migrated to urban areas enables them to conceal or distance themselves from their rural pasts (Malimbe 1990: 13). The use of pan-ethnic forms such as Pretoria Sotho also enables Africans to hide their ethnic origins. Language creates the space to forge a new past.

Language debates in African languages between language purists and those adopting a *laissez faire* attitude towards pan-ethnic varieties are potentially acrimonious. Usually, the purists are on the offensive, describing pan-ethnic forms as corrupt, bastardized, and impure linguistic behaviour (Zungu 1995: 108). Concern about the health of

224

languages, or apprehension that the health of a particular language is declining are, however, not at all peculiar to African languages. The use of split infinitives in English has frequently been cited by some users of Engish as signifying the declining health of English. Linguists for the most part agree, however, that languages do not fall sick. (Calteaux (1996: 50-1) points out that non-standardized varieties are increasingly beginning to replace standardized varieties in formal settings. She cites exciting evidence of the use of these varieties in domains previously restricted to standard-ized languages. For example, there is an increasing use of these varieties in traditional ceremonies such as marriages, celebrations of birth, and funerals. The ceremonies are per-ceived as a marker of the society's link with its past in the present. The use of emerging varieties is often construed as constituting a threat to that continuation, or creating a dis-jucture with that past. It does not matter whether that threat is real or imagined. What is important is that language is seen as symptomatic of that threat. Language in such con-texts is regarded not only as a form but as constituting the actual substance of that ritual, which in itself is representa-tive of a community's past (Connerton 1989: 41-72).

Conclusion
In this chapter, I have examined the effects of the invention of African languages on the values Africans have attached to their new past. I have also argued that concern about the re-standardization of African languages is much more than a linguistic debate. It reflects a concern on the part of the pur-ists about the possible establishment of a disjuncture be-tween their past and present: an expression of fear that they no longer control the future evolution of their practices.

My main argument is that the process of reinvention should involve introducing pan-ethnic speech forms into or-dinary institutional discourse as a replacement of an often archaic discourse traumatically out of step with ordinary usage. It is only through the process of egalitarian reinvention that African languages can be made more malleable. Societies, like individuals, may reinvent their past, by assuming new ways of speaking, distancing themselves from one past and creating a new one.

References

Brink, André (1998). "Stories of history: reimagining the past in post-apartheid narrative" In S. Nuttall and C. Cotzee (eds) *Negotiating the Past: The Making of Memory in South Africa*, Oxford: Oxford University Press, pp. 29-42.

Calteaux, K. (1996). *Standard and Non-Standard African Language Varieties in the Urban Areas of South Africa.* Pretoria: Human Sciences Research Council Publishers. Viewed 24 June 2020 at: https://files.eric.ed.gov/fulltext/ED402752.pdf

Connerton, P. *How Societies Remember*. Cambridge, Cambridge University Press, 1989.

Fardon, R. and Furniss, G. (eds.) (1994) *African Languages, Development and the State*, London and New York: Routledge.

Gilroy, P. (1987) *There Ain't No Black in the Union Jack: The Cultural Politics of Race and Nation*, Chicago, IL: University of Chicago Press.

Harries, P. (1995) "Discovering languages: the historical origins of standard Tsonga in Southern Africa," in R. Mesthrie (ed.) *Language and Social History: Studies in South African Sociolinguistics*, Cape Town and Johannesburg: David Philips, pp. 154-72.

Herbert, R.K. (1992) "Introduction: Language in a divided society" In R.K Herbert (ed) *Language and Society in Africa: The Theory and Practice of Sociolinguis-*

tics (pp. 11-19) Johannesburg: Witwatersrand University Press.

Hofmeyer, I. (1994) *We spend our years as a tale that is told: oral historical narrative in a South African chiefdom.* Johannesburg, South Africa: Witswatersrand University Press.

Jeater, D. (1994) "'The way you tell them': ideology and development policy," paper delivered at Paradigms Lost, Paradigms Regained, University of Witwatersrand.

Le Page, R. and A. Tabouret-Keller (1982). "Models and stereotypes of language and ethnicity" *Journal of Multilingual and Multicultural Development* 3 pp. 161-192.

LePage, R. and Tabouret-Keller, A. (1985) *Acts of Identity*, Cambridge: Cambridge University Press.

Malimabe, R.M. (1990) *The Influence of non-Standard Varieties on The Standard Setswana of High School Pupils.* Masters Degree Thesis, Rand Afrikaans University.

Ntshangase, Dumisani K. (1995) "Indaba yami i-straight: language and language practices in Soweto" in R. Mesthrie (ed.) *Language in South Africa, Studies in South African Sociolinguistics*, pp. 291-297. Cape Town & Johannesburg: David Philip Publishers.

Pennycook, A. (1994) *The Cultural Politics of English as an International Language*, London: Longman.

Rampton, M.B.H. (1990) "Displacing the 'Native Speaker': Expertise, Affiliation, and Inheritance" *ELT Journal* 44(2), pp. 97-101.

Ranger, Terence O. (1989). "Missionaries, migrants and the Manyika: the invention of ethnicity in Zimbabwe" In Vail, Leroy (ed.), *The Creation of Tribalism in Southern Africa,* pp.118-150. London: James Currey.

Street, Brian V. (1993). "The new literacy studies, guest

227

editorial" *Journal of Research in Reading* 16(2) pp. 81-97.

Zungu, P.J. (1995). *Language variation in Zulu: A case study of contemporary codes and registers in the greater Durban area.* D.Litt et Phil. Thesis. Durban: University of Durban Westville.

X

From Misinvention To Disinvention Of Language: Multilingualism And The South African Constitution

The aim of this chapter is to explore the political significance of the analytical categories used in discussions about
language in the South African Constitution. That Constitution has been heralded as intellectually progressive and politically enlightened because of the significance it attaches to
human rights and its acknowledgment of multilingualism in
the African context. In giving official status to nine African
languages, South Africa has charted a course in opposition
to that of other African countries, for example Malawi and
Namibia, whose constitutions stipulate English as the official language. In fact, the Malawian Constitution goes even
further by stipulating proficiency in English as a prerequisite
for public office. I will argue, however, that the South African Constitution, by recognizing nine African languages as
neatly divided, "bounded units" (Cook 2002), or "hermetically sealed units" (Makoni 1998a; Nuttall and Cotzee 1998),
is socially alienating and cognitively disadvantaging to the
very people it is intended to serve. Furthermore, I will argue
that the South African Constitutional language policy creates
a self-serving amnesia by encouraging Africans to "unremember" the historical and material contexts in which the
socalled African "languages" were invented, or "cobbled
together" as Brutt-Griffler (2002) prefers to put it.

The final version of the South African Constitution,
which forms the basis of the analysis in this chapter, was approved in 1996. The Founding Provisions are: the Sove-
reignty of South Africa, the Supremacy of the Constitution,

Citizenship, National Anthem, and Languages. The language provisions are as follows:

1 The official languages of the Republic are Sepedi, Sesotho, Setswana, siSwati, Tshivenda, Xitsonga, Afrikaans, English, isiNdebele, isiXhosa, and isiZulu.

2 Recognizing the historically diminished use and status of the indigenous languages of our people, the state must take practical and positive measures to elevate the status and advance the use of these languages.

3(a) The national government and provincial governments may use any particular official languages for the purposes of government taking into account usage, practicality, expense, regional circumstances and the balance of the needs and preferences of the population as a whole or in the province concerned; but the national government and each provincial government must use at least two official languages.

3(b) Municipalities must take into account the language usage and preferences of their residents.

4 The national government and provincial governments, by legislative and other measures, must regulate and monitor their use of official languages. Without detracting from provisions of subsection (2), all official languages must enjoy parity of esteem and must be treated equitably.

(Chapter One, Founding Provisions, The Constitution of The Republic of South Africa 1996: 4)

The language provisions continue:

230

5 A Pan South African Language Board established by national legislation must—
(a) promote and create conditions for the development and use of—
  (i) all official languages;
  (ii) the Khoi, Nama, and San languages;
  (iii) sign language;
(b) promote and ensure respect for—
    (i) all languages commonly used by communities in South Africa, including German, Greek, Gujarati, Hindi, Portuguese, Tamil, Telegu, and Urdu;
    (ii) Arabic, Hebrew, Sanskrit, and other languages used for religious purposes in South Africa.

(Chapter One, Founding Provisions, The Constitution of the Republic of South Africa 1996: 4-5)

The Bill of Rights in the final version of the Constitution protects the rights of individuals to "use the language of their choice." Sections (30) and (31) state that individuals have the right "to receive education in the official languages or language of their choice where that is practicable." Section (35) provides for the right of an accused person to be tried in a language that he/she understands or, if that is not practicable, to have the proceedings interpreted. The Founding Provisions make it imperative for the State to "take practical and positive measures to elevate the status and advance the use" of the "indigenous" languages. The Provisions also make it mandatory for the State to "ensure respect for all languages commonly used by communities in South Africa" —e.g. Hindi, Gujarati, Portuguese, Tamil, Telegu, Urdu, other languages used for "religious purposes"—the list of languages is indeterminate!

The South African Constitution, then, on which the country's national language policy is founded, recognizes eleven separate languages as official, nine of them constructed as "indigenous." What makes these languages separate and indigenous is far from clear. When did they become separate and indigenous, and for whom, and under what circumstances? These are crucial questions which are not addressed even in radical sociolinguistics (e.g. Phillipson 1992; Makoni and Kamwangamalu 2000) where the existence of separate indigenous languages is taken as self-evident, unproblematic, and an uncontested sociolinguistic fact. Increasingly one finds this matter addressed only in endnotes to academic work on the sociolinguistics of South Africa (Hornberger 2002).

The development of the indigenous languages to prepare them for their new Constitutional role is placed in the hands of various sectors of government, the key one being the Pan South African Language Board (PANSALB). The architects of the Constitution were fully aware that "the new Constitutional provisions relating to language are messy, inelegant and contradictory," as Albie Sachs, a South African judge who played a key role in the construction of the South African Constitution, so aptly put it. The extent of the inelegance, contradiction and messiness, however, has not been explored, nor even recognized by most sociolinguists.

To begin with, we should note that the discourse that constructs African languages as separate categories has its genesis in colonial thinking, namely in an ideology of "linguistic fixity" that disregards the sociohistorical contexts in which they were invented (Ranger 1985; Chimhundu 1992; Harries 1995; Makoni 1998b). The construct of "invention" or the related notions of "narration" and "imagination" (Anderson 1983; Bhabha 1990) have been productively de-

232

ployed in research dealing with cultural formations of ethnicity, national identity, and traditional legal systems. The upshot of arguments about "invention," "narration," and "imagination" has been to convincingly demonstrate that ethnicity and cultural institutions, such as traditional legal systems, are a product of colonial ideology and did not exist unproblematically out there in African space. Linguists dealing with African sociolinguistic issues have been slow to exploit the advantage of the insights generated from "invention" and related concepts. If traditional systems and ethnicity were part of colonial ideology, it is logical to ask to what extent other cultural formations, such as so-called "African languages," are part of the same colonial ideology. In this chapter, I seek to examine the analytical usefulness of the construct of invention as it applies to African languages. The question is of interest because it shows how languages are constituted historically and thus allows for the possibility of languages being deconstituted. The issue is also of current interest because it reflects the extent to which some of the contemporary problems with implementability of language policies in Africa are situated in the conceptualizations and ways of thinking about African languages.

Different languages were invented out of what was one language through a process marred by "faulty transcriptions and mishearings," mediated through partial competence in African languages, and motivated by an overly sharp separation between language structure and language use (Roy-Campbell 2000) reinforced by the use of dif-ferent orthographic systems. Initiatives for rendering African speech ("languages") in written form resulted in "an exaggerated multiethnic, multi-lingual, and multi-tribal picture of African colonies [that] has been painted through misinterpretation and inadequate study on the part of the early missionaries and manipulation for administrative convenience on the part of colonial governments" (Chimhundu 1992: 88).

For example, the speech of the Sotho and Tswana, whose languages are productively conceptualized as a continuum, were defined as separate languages. The Xhosa and Zulu peoples, whose languages are closely related, were defined as speaking different languages because of the rivalry between the different missionaries working with these two groups. Setswana, Sesotho, and Sepedi, three of the languages officially recognized within the South African Constitution, are very similar grammatically, morphologically, and lexically. The differences between these three languages are mainly in the area of phonology. These related speech forms were codified as separate languages because of missionary politics.

In some cases even the names given to some of the African speech forms were invented by Europeans. The most telling example is the name "Shona," a language spoken in Southern Africa, mainly in Zimbabwe. (However, because of massive migration from the north, it is also spoken in parts of South Africa as well, for example by the Tswana people.) Prior to European colonialism, the Shona peoples did not have a collective term to refer to themselves. In 1931, the name "Shona" was used for the purpose of facilitating administrative classification. The recommendation did not come from Shona language users themselves, but from a committee of missionaries who subsequently commissioned a language expert, Clement Doke, Professor of Linguistics at the University of Witwatersrand in Johannesburg, South Africa, to design an orthographic system for Shona—in spite of his lack of knowledge about the language.

It has been widely felt that the name Shona is inaccurate and unworthy, that it is not the true name of any of the peoples whom we propose to group under the term "Shona-speaking people," and further, it lies under strong suspicion of being a name given in con-

tempt by enemies of the tribes. It is pretty certainly a foreign name, and as such is very likely to be uncomplimentary like the name "kaffir."
(Southern Rhodesia 1929: 25)

After Shona was decreed into existence, a standard grammar was subsequently constructed under Clement Doke's direction and a vocabulary was created "of as many and as representative words as possible which shall include words from the major dialects." The vocabulary was largely drawn from missionary converts who were working as "laboratory assistants." The famous laboratory assistants were David Mandisodza, Joseph Chamunorwa, and Paul Malanga, converts to the American Methodist Church (Southern Rhodesia 1929). In this context, there was no pretense of linguistics operating under the banner of objective science. Rather, this was linguistics clearly being utilized to serve the interests and politics of missionaries and colonial administrators (Roy-Campbell 2000; Brutt-Griffler 2002). It is not only linguistics that has served colonialism well; other disciplines, such as anthropology, have also had their history marred by their role in the colonial enterprise.

"To give a proper name to languages requires a certain kind of consciousness of language, an assumption that languages can be standardized entities and that they can have names" (Mannheim 1991: 8). It is a linguistic consciousness that seems to be an outcome of formal Western education, a consciousness which is not necessarily a part of the social awareness of most peoples with limited or no formal education. Such peoples refer to what they speak as "human language." A language without a name would thus not be an oddity, it would have been the norm. The problem is akin to the virtual impossibility of discussing ethnicity other than in terms or labels that are "tribal."

Literacy and language education are as much tools of social control as forms of social emancipation. Discourses about multilingualism designed to reverse the inequalities of the apartheid legacy in which only Afrikaans and English were regarded as official do not take into account the linguistic differences within each of the languages labeled an "African language." In African language communities, there are significant linguistic differences between the official "standard" version of the language and the version that is actually used and spoken—as is the case with most languages. What is peculiarly African, however, is that the difference between the "standard" and the language used in practice "constitutes a gulf rather than continuity, and there is little movement across the divide. A reified standard may be honored, but it is rarely valued, and language must be valued to prosper" (Ridge *et al.* 2001: 10).

The essence of the argument is this: because African languages were not constructed and standardized taking into account the communicative practices of the users, there is a very sharp disjuncture between language praxis and standard forms of the languages. Notions of a "standard," particularly in written form, originated in the grammatical descriptions of the nineteenth century. In the case of African languages, however, the magnitude of the disjuncture is so great that there are potentially adverse effects for mother tongue education. Standard African languages are rarely used as primary languages in the homes and playgrounds in African communities, particularly in urban areas. A majority of students enter primary school speaking non-standardized versions of the official African languages and urban argots which draw heavily and freely on English, Afrikaans, and "non-official" African languages. The extent to which they draw on Afrikaans and English, however, varies depending on the social status and gender of the speaker. Women's speech draws more heavily on English as a marker of femininity, social

236

class, and urbanity while male speech relies more heavily on Afrikaans, which is a marker of male urbanity (Cook 2002).

The African languages listed in the South African Constitution and those frequently cited in the literature on African sociolinguistics reinforce the boundaries which were arbitrarily drawn by missionaries and subsequently awarded academic credibility through grammatical descriptions of Zulu, Xhosa, Tswana, and other "indigenous" South African languages. The framers of the South African Constitution have, unwittingly, perpetrated the misclassification of old and given it renewed credibility. The legacy of misclassification will be felt well into the twenty-first century unless serious sociolinguistic and political efforts are made to contain the mistakes of history.

Misclassification overlooks the great diversity within each of the distinct language labels, as can be easily illustrated through the case of one of the languages officially recognized in the South African Constitution: Xhosa. As with many other languages, Xhosa has several spoken varieties. It is said to be made up of such varieties as Ngqika, Thembu, Hlubi, Bhaca, Bomvana, Mpondo, Mpondomise, and others (Satyo 2000). Speakers of Hlubi and Bhaca from the Eastern Cape may experience problems with the standard Xhosa represented in textbooks. The written representation of African speech forms has historically run parallel to, but rarely intersected with, the daily language practices of most speakers of those languages. In fact, there seems to be a deliberate effort on the part of some speakers, particularly the youth, to distance themselves from the standard (Satyo 2001), which is rarely anybody's mother tongue.

There is such great diversity within some of the African language "boxes" that no dialect has successfully served as a standard. This should not be construed as an argument against the role of standard languages. Rather, it is an argument against the processes which formed the basis of the standardization of these languages in the first place. The selection of a specific dialect to serve as the basis of the standard language, the conventional procedure in most communities (Pennycook 1994), has been unsuccessful in the case of most African languages. The problem is so acute that it undermines any serious effort toward mother tongue education. For example, non-standard Zulu is so radically different from what is characterized as "Zulu" in urban settings that speakers who sociolinguistically feel affiliated with Zulu ethnically, or are administratively classified as "Zulu," may feel alienated, and their linguistic creativity may be stifled by the language assigned to them as their "mother tongue." The situation is not peculiar to Zulu. Cook (2002) provides evidence which suggests that most students from Tswana-speaking homes usually require remedial instruction in the form of the language assigned to them. This state of affairs results from the fact that the "mother tongue" assigned to students for educational purposes may not correspond with sociolinguistic reality—it may not be the language in which the learners are most proficient. The speakers are multilingual and multidialectal, proficient in non-standard versions of their languages and urban argots, but not in the reified and historically dated standard African language. For example, the standard Setswana taught in schools, which forms the written basis of most language teaching materials, has remained largely unchanged since 1937.

The notion of "mother tongue" may mean very different things when used for institutional purposes than when used in the real world. It is a relative concept depending on the discursive context and on whether one is talking institutionally or from the perspective of the language users. Because of the disjuncture between speaker and institutional constructions of mother tongue, mother tongue education may fail to realize its desired goals because the speakers are acquired by their mother tongues instead of the opposite! As a result of misclassification, mother tongue education may cognitively disadvantage the very people it is expected to benefit, as students are deprived of the necessary educational support they would have received had the full implications that they were learning in a non-home code been taken into account.

In language research, the discrepancy between classification of mother tongue based on speaker criteria and classification based on institutional criteria has not been the central concern of debates about the native speaker (Davies 1999). It is necessary to ask hard questions about underlying conceptions of mother tongue, particularly in social domains such as education. Shifting images of mother tongue should not be political icons in whose direction we have to reverently and invariably genuflect.

In the South African Constitution, languages created in historically dubious circumstances by missionaries and their African linguistic apprentices are accorded the status of uncontested judicial facts and become permanent sociolinguistic fixtures of the way the African landscape is imagined. The image is that of a landscape composed of many language boxes and linguistic "things," separate and distinct. This image runs counter to the lived and living experiences of most ordinary users of African speech forms. According to Satyo (2001), the language used by Xhosa youth in urban centers in South Africa is strongly influenced by Kwaito, a type of music popular with urban youth, somewhat akin to Hip Hop in the US. The speech of urban Xhosa youth is a form of language which reflects compelling evidence of innovative strategies for harmonizing resources from different languages as these youth build a pan-ethnic, urban identity. These pan-ethnic African speech forms sharply contrast with standardized African languages in terms of the images which the forms seek to convey. The speech transcends physical locality and is used to evoke a sense of urban space;

thus the speech forms are even used in rural areas by speakers emphasizing and foregrounding an urban identity, as aptly captured in the title of Cook's recent chapter, "Urban language in a rural setting" (2002). Cook demonstrates empirically how people who wish to project an urban identity, or who emulate styles associated with urban life, do so through language forms associated with urbanity. It is speech which is thought of not as "a language," but as linguistic forms with a "range of expressive inventories that not only enable people to communicate with each other, but allow people to communicate something about themselves to the world" (Cook 2002: 110).

The pan-ethnic, urban, hybridized linguistic forms contain lexical items which are an "embodiment" of linguistic information drawn from different languages. These pan-ethnic varieties are excellent examples of "lexical pastiche" which try to capture the nuances of social relationships by exploiting the social, historical, and political associations of words (Myers-Scotton 1993; Childs 1997; Satyo 2001). For example:

1   *Tsotsitaal* is a combination of *utsotsi*, Xhosa for "criminal," as in most other Bantu languages, and *taal* from Afrikaans, referring to a language. Thus, *tsotsitaal* literally refers to "speaking the language of criminals."

2   *Imkasi* means "Black township"; the word is a recycled form of the Afrikaans word *lokasie*, with a Xhosa prefix.

3   *Abantwana ijive* refers to treating girls like children (unlike boys who are taken seriously), from Xhosa *abantwana*, which means "children," and *ijive*, meaning lacking in seriousness, probably from the English word *jive*, itself thought to be derived from West African Wolof, *jev*, entering English

through the speech of American slaves. The implication of *abantwana ijive* is that all one can do with girls is engage in trivial matters.

Such linguistic forms and the processes that generate these forms reflect language harmonization developing organically from the grassroots, with neither respect for nor allegiance to typological distinctions characteristic of most linguistically inclined discourses about African speech. But the phenomenon is not peculiar to Southern Africa; linguists have drawn attention to its existence in other parts of Africa, for example in Central Africa. Goyvaerts (1996) presents language data from this region reflecting words comprised of constituents from four different languages: Swahili, Lingala, English, and French—e.g. *Mi iouink ki ndozala* (I am on my way to the market); *mi*, from Swahili *mimi*, *gouink*, from English *go/going*, *ki*, from French *qui*, and *ndozala*, from Lingala *zando*, market.

The version of multilingualism implicit in the South African Constitution is one best described as plural monolingualism: a variant and an extension of monolingualism. Instead of South Africans being encouraged to be multilingual, the policy could actually end up making each citizen merely competent in his/her own language. That is, since all the country's languages are officially recognized, all one need do is become competent in the standard version of his/her own language. The South African language policy should have specified only two or three African languages as official languages, a decision which would have been relatively easy to arrive at through a reconceptualization of "language." However, to propose official status for nine so-called "indigenous" African languages is to reaffirm the separateness of Black South African ethnic groups through language. It is a false separation, linguistically and ethnically, whereby the present South African government is, para-

241

doxically, proposing a policy which the apartheid South African government could not successfully implement. After the destruction of mixed areas, the most well-known being Sophiatown in Johannesburg and District Six in Cape Town, the apartheid government went to extraordinary—but ultimately unsuccessful—lengths to keep each language group to itself.

> The concentration of these languages in industrialized areas led to an inevitable mixing of people who spoke different Bantu languages in churches, work places, social gatherings, and other situations. The folly of trying to keep the same people separate was exposed as a shameful fiasco. In industrialized areas there was nothing to be gained for the Africans in creating tribal laagers [exclusive spaces]. Apartheid succeeded only in separating blacks from whites, because an overwhelming majority of whites wanted that separation. The honesty of the Afrikaner provided a convenient scapegoat for what the English-speaking [citizen] tacitly approved of and supported. (Maake 1994: 113)

The problem of the implementability of the South African national language policy (its "inelegance, contradiction and messiness") is a direct consequence of the very nature of the languages it seeks to promote. The policy itself is, in effect, based on an inaccurate analysis of the prevailing sociolinguistic condition. Contrary to views of local and international scholars alike (e.g. Desai 1994; Smitherman 2000), who welcome the national language policy, I contend that what should be welcomed is the very problem posed by implementation because this forces us to consider the sociolinguistic realities which any language policy needs to take into account. I would suggest that a productive way out of this

242

political, linguistic, and intellectual impasse is to institute a program to *disinvent* African languages, hence reconceptualizing the notions of language and ethnicity on which the South African language policy is founded. Notions about language and ethnicity in the South African Constitution are founded on "boxed" notions of language and ethnicity ultimately traceable to eighteenth-century German Romanticist ideas which treated territory, constructions of race, and conceptualizations of language as identical and indivisible. According to German Romanticism, language and identity/ethnicity were indistinguishable, with language considered to be the most powerful index of social identity. According to the indivisibility of language, race, and territory, you would, for instance, be said to speak Zulu if you were Zulu ethnically. That is, because you were affiliated with Zulu or inherited Zulu ethnically, you were, as a result, considered to be a speaker of Zulu. The possibility of someone who feels affiliated with Zulu ethnically, but who does not speak Zulu, is a contradiction within the framework of language, ethnicity, and race embodied in German Romanticist thought.

The disinvention proposal calls attention to the importance of reflecting on our tools of analysis and on the significant realization that linguists and nonlinguists may be using terms differently. For example, one possible way of conceptualizing African speech forms is to think of them as constituting a continuum "stretching across Africa from the Atlantic to the Indian Ocean" (LePage and Tabouret-Keller 1985). The notion of a language continuum does not deny that there are differences among language forms at the extreme ends of the continuum, for example Yoruba on the West Coast and Xhosa in the South. However, a conceptualization of African speech forms as comprising a continuum suggests that the notion of "African lingua franca" may be best envisaged not as a single language but as a multilayered and partially connected chain, that offers a choice of varieties and registers in the speakers' immediate environment, and a steadily diminishing set of options to be employed in more distant interactions, albeit a set that is always liable to be reconnected more densely to a new environment by rapid secondary learning, or by the development of new languages. (Fardon and Furniss 1994: 4)

The perspective of imagining African languages as "multilayered and interconnected chains" is radically different from that which forms the basis of early missionary thought, and it is a perspective that can be supported empirically. For example, the relationship between Zulu and Xhosa is one not only of mutual intelligibility but also of interconnectedness. Words which are regarded as nonstandard and are thus excluded from standard Xhosa appear in hlonipha and isikhwetha. Hlonipha and isikhwetha are special types of registers associated, respectively, with married women and young men in Xhosa. Hlonipha is a language variety used by recently married women, and isikhwetha is the type of language variety typically used by young men during circumcision. Similarly, words which are stigmatized as part of standard Zulu are acceptable when they enter Xhosa lexical usage through the specialized varieties of hlonipha and isikhweta (Satyo 1998).

The missionaries created languages which were describable as mutually exclusive boxes as opposed to interconnected patterns. In fact, the very notion of languages as discrete units, or "boxes," is a product of European positivism reinforced by literacy and standardization (Romaine 1984). Discussions about African vernaculars are as much about specific ways of imagining the African sociolinguistic landscape as they are about description. In this regard, it is only now that the full implication of the work of missionaries is beginning to dawn on us.

In countries in which the vast majority of the people are not literate, in the Western sense of the term, consciousness of languages as discrete boxes is likely to be alien. The "misinvention" of African languages had clear political consequences and implied particular forms of social relations, not only between Africans and Europeans, but also among Africans themselves. Hofmeyer argues that Africans actively took advantage of the presence of missionaries to articulate their dissatisfaction with existing political systems:

> Both among commoners and within the royal caste itself ... there existed cause for dissatisfaction against the ruling lineage. The dissatisfaction was expressed by entering into a loose association with missionaries. For commoners, the mission and its schools which used a lot of Sesotho remained a source of attraction. (Hofmeyer 1993: 48)

The discourse which the missionaries created in the process of specifying and inventing African languages was designed to limit what could be said "about," "to," and "discussed with" Africans (Mühlhäusler 1996). The construction of African languages was designed to restrict not only the universe of discourse entered into by Europeans with Africans but also the participation of Africans in the colonial world. (The extent of this construction of African languages has been ably outlined by Jeater [1994].) The major objective of missionary linguistics was to comprehend African cosmology in the missionaries' own terms, and only terms that could facilitate that process were included in the vernacular language. The missionaries were passing judgment on the societies in which they were operating. For example, Jeater demonstrates that Africans who preferred to find alternative

245

sources of income, rather than work in the missionaries' translation endeavors, were defined as "lazy" and "dishonest" because they did not make themselves readily available for exploitation as cheap colonial labor.

The linguistic inventions of the missionary era were structured in such a way as to encourage Africans to internalize European epistemology about themselves, creating a new view about their current affairs and superimposing new values on their past. In this process, the educated African elite became alienated from their home communities and the languages of those communities—hence the danger of presuming that through vernacular use and the promotion of indigenous African languages a common sense of belonging can be created, democratic practices enhanced and imperialism counteracted. Indeed the opposite occurs: the promotion of African languages that were "cobbled together" and invented during the colonial era continues the separation of the people on the basis of language, facilitates the divide-and-rule tactics of old and serves contemporary neoimperialist interests. Thus the framers of the South African Constitution, by using linguistic labels from the past they are seeking to challenge, are, in fact, legitimating that past. It is therefore appropriate to sound a cautionary note.

> Times of rapid change place great pressure on language. The new must find expression and an articulated social presence must be negotiated for it. However, the commanders of the new social space are often heirs both, unwittingly, to the discourses which maintained the old, and to those which prepared the way for their political success. The discourses which maintained the old embody the values of an order which has not yet gone and which may yet stage a comeback. (Ridge 2001: 16)

It is not only that the current language policy of the South African Constitution reinforces the attitudes and practices of the missionary past. More significantly, in the context of this chapter, it reflects a present-day sociolinguistic orthodoxy. Consider the case of code-switching. Most sociolinguistic research on codeswitching is premised on the assumption that speakers code-switch naturally from the different languages which they control. So, for example, a speaker who mixes English, Afrikaans, and African languages is assumed to have the ability to use English, Afrikaans, and African languages in their "unmixed" forms as separate codes. It is a logical inference, but unfortunately it is inaccurate and cannot be supported by the evidence from the sociolinguistic situation of urban African settings. In these urban centers the "mixed" forms are themselves the linguistic norm, the starting point in the process of language socialization for most people, and at times the only version of language for everyday encounters. Most people only encounter the "unmixed" speech as part of the formal process of education. The uneducated speakers may never have encountered the languages in their "unmixed" state. Thus the speakers cannot be said to have the capacity to speak languages which they do not control, may never have controlled, and are unlikely to get exposed to unless they get formally educated! It is relatively easy to understand the conceptual mistake made by the analysts of code-switching. Because they themselves may control English, Afrikaans, and African languages as separate codes, they assume that the speakers using the "mixed" forms are combining these three languages. What the analysts are overlooking is that their sociolinguistic autobiographies are very different from those of the people they are analyzing.

Because the sociolinguistic evidence suggests that mixtures resulting from the interconnected nature of language are indeed a defining part of the sociolinguistic situa-

247

tion, it is therefore possible that we are placing emphasis on and studying the wrong phenomenon. The area which needs urgent analysis is one in which attempts at linguistic "un-mixing" or "uncoupling" take place. The metaphors we need to create are those which can capture the faltering nature of linguistic "uncoupling," particularly in mother tongue education, which is generally premised upon assumptions about discrete codes. "Uncoupling" refers to a process whereby a speaker expunges words by manipulating phonological rules that are supposedly not part of the language the speaker is using. For example:

1 Standard Swati: Indvodza iye edolobheni ekuseni.
   (The man has gone to town).
2 Standard Xhosa: Indoda iye edolobheni kusasa.
   (The man has gone to town).
3 Standard Zulu: Indoda iye edolobheni ekuseni.
   (The man has gone to town).

All three sentences mean "the man has gone to town." A child ethnically classified as Swati who produces the utterance *Indoda iye edolobheni kusasa* will be regarded as speaking incorrect siSwati, i.e. not speaking "pure" siSwati (as standard African languages are increasingly being referred to, even in educational circles). She is pronouncing *indoda* as in Standard Xhosa and Zulu instead of *indvodza*. Similarly, a Zulu child who says: *Indoda iye edolobheni kusasa* will be said to be speaking incorrect Zulu because she says *kusasa* instead of *ekuseni*. The child's Zulu would thus be classified as incorrect even though it is correct Standard Xhosa!

The metaphor that most accurately applies to the African situation is not self-enclosed partitions, but "frontiers." The main strength of the "frontier" metaphor is that it resists notions of barriers and works on the basis of interconnectedness, unlike the underlying construct forming the basis of

248

notions about language in the South African Constitution. Conceiving of language as interconnected patterns enables me to talk about the number of languages a speaker controls. It is more prudent to talk about language repertoires or workable portfolios (Fardon and Furniss 1994). Language as "frontier" is more sensitive to the dynamics of social interaction. Frequency of interaction could lead to speakers becoming more like one another in their repertoire, in the repertoires they draw upon, and in the social meanings they attach to each selection from their repertoire.

Conceptions of language as interconnected patterns and scrambled systems seek to break, to rupture, the present from the overwhelming hold of the past. However, these conceptions are not legitimated by the South African Constitution, itself *par excellence* a residue of the past in contemporary form. The traces of the past in that Constitution are not unusual because all constitutions retain traces of their history in the way they are formulated. The language provision formulated in the South African Constitution is written in what Ridge calls "apocalyptic discourse." Such discourse "is deeply encoded and captures the end of history. This is a discourse that reflects a shift away from clear directions formulated with an awareness of context to exalted ideals as if beyond the claims of history—a shift away from actual to apocalyptic discourse" (Ridge 2000: 47).

The Constitutional discourse describing the Pan South African Language Board (PANSALB) is an excellent example of "apocalyptic discourse." The triumphalist tone used in relation to PANSALB is in sharp conflict with the discourse temperament in other sections of the chapter delineating Founding Provisions of the Constitution. PANSALB is placed in a difficult position in which it is given responsibilities it cannot reasonably be expected to meet. It is expected to "ensure respect for all languages commonly used by communities in South Africa"—an open-ended list

which cites eight languages over the fifteen already specified, and as if that were not enough, all languages used for
religious purposes—three are mentioned. PANSALB is
charged, at the highest level, with a task which is difficult, if
not impossible, to achieve.

The other responsibilities placed upon PANSALB
make very little sense in the real world. For example, Rich-
terweld Nama is the only existing Khoi language. There are
fewer than ten people who are speakers of San language.
There are about 70,000 speakers of Italian and less than 800
speakers of Telegu. However, it is the latter that is mentioned in the Constitution. An apocalyptic discourse, which sets
forth a perfect, ideal condition without suggesting any practical ways in which the historical processes can be realized,
is a paradox. What is required is an articulation with the real
world, not an apocalyptic vision, not proposals based on
historical accident or concepts inapplicable to the African
situation, but locally specific solutions. Such locally specific
solutions may be constructed, I suggest, through the notion
of *disinvention*.

Disinvention does not mean a return to arcane forms
of African language speak. It is a serious effort to capture
current language practices, which are generally pan-ethnic in
nature—hence, which cut across conceptualizations about
language/society/ethnicity affiliation implicit in the South
African Constitution. Disinvention is a prerequisite to capturing the role and forms of African languages as interconnected patterns and moves away from notions of languages
as boxes or discrete items. This can be realized through
detailed descriptions of current language practices. These
descriptions would be useful not only for disinventing
African speech forms, hence constraining the legacy of
nineteenth-century positivism, but also for facilitating the
new roles created for African language speech forms by the
Constitution.

The advantages of disinvention would not be limited to the Constitutional arena, but would extend to education as well. Most learners of African languages, mother tongue and second languages alike, find themselves confronted with a sharp divide between the official language, as embodied in current written texts, and the speech used in the everyday drama of life, moment by moment, situation by situation. One of the serious drawbacks apparent in any serious engagement with local speech communities is the limited amount of material for fostering literacy in the so-called African languages. A shift away from African languages as discrete boxes to interconnected hybridized forms would make it possible to produce a set of materials based on the same orthographic system. An orthographic commons would serve not only South Africa but also Southern Africa.

The disinvention project foregrounds the importance of retaining distinctions between standardized "indigenous" languages, non-standardized languages, and urban argots. The distinction can be made along a number of lines. The first one is historical. "Indigenous" languages were to some extent the creation and invention of missionaries using and interpreting data from their African apprentices. Non-standard and urban hybrids are more contemporary linguistic forms, the result, in part, of mass movements. "Indigenous" languages are currently standardized while local languages are not.

It is through the use of non-standardized and urban argots that some of the creativity and dramas of everyday life in the African sociolinguistic landscape are articulated. The non-standard speech forms also vary by gender and reflect and re-create the social histories and biographies of their users. Illustrative examples are provided in conversations recorded and analyzed by Cook (2002: 110-12). The excerpt from Transcript 1 is taken from a conversation between several working-class men in their thirties who are

251

socializing and flirting with the women. The excerpt from Transcript 2 captures a conversational moment between young women. The conversational excerpts reflect a fair amount of "mixing" in both conventional and unconventional ways.

Excerpt from Transcript 1

Speaker #1 Hei Popompo! Abuti Popompo, abuti Popompo! Ga waa apara bine ... bruku. (Hey Popompo! Brother Popompo, brother Popompo! You're not wearing underwear).

Speaker #3 Eish! Ga ke itsoore kajeno koo bereka yang waitse? (Hey! I don't know how I'll manage today, you know?)

Speaker #2 Wena o betere o ... otjela mo naming mare o ntsoore o patagantse. (You're fine ... you're living well but you keep saying you're struggling.)

Speaker #4 Aye ga gona sepe. (No, there's nothing like that)

Speaker #1 Ko ... go na le nama mos. (But there is meat.)

Speaker #3 Hei. (Hey.)

Speaker #5 Motjitji, go na le nama? (Motjitji, is there meat?)

Speaker #1 A?e, teng nama, monna. (The meat's there, man)

Speaker #2 Bo bo bo bo Cleophus. (Cleophus and ...)

Speaker #3 Ke tswa ko teng. (I just came from there.)

Speaker #2 Ko Cleophus? (From Cleophus's place?)

Speaker #3 Ee. (Yes.)

Speaker #1 Noo, o maaka, wena manga. (No, you're lying, you're lying.)

Speaker #2 Ko'ore goo fa wa shashara, waa ba Dolphina. (Because if you're lying ... Dolphina.)

The non-standard Setswana of the men draws heavily on Afrikaans and African languages (e.g. Zulu). Interestingly, Afrikaans is often regarded as the language of "the oppressor." Yet an analysis of the language of urban male youth,

252

such as those involved in the conversational interaction above, shows that Afrikaans, the language of "the oppressor," is subtly exploited as a marker of urbanity.

Excerpt from Transcript 2

Wendy E? e, le sa bua ka batho bao tu,batho ba ba sa existeng. E? e a re bueng ka batho. (No, don't talk about those people, people who don't exist. No, let's talk about real people.)

Masengo Nna, waiste ke eng? Ka re bathing ke mo rata gore ... (Me, you know what? I say, you guys, I really like him ...)

Wendy Ka re ga se go soGelwa lebatho ga re tswa contesting phakela, iyo. (I'm saying I was provoked by people when we came from the contest in the morning, yo!)

Dineo E? esa e bua eo.Waitsore keeng tsala ya me? Ke nako e eke buang ka yona, ga ke jouke bathing. O ko s'petlele. Ga se go robeng fela looto. (No, don't say that. You know what it is, my friend? It's that time, I'm talking about. I'm not kidding. He's in the hospital. He broke his leg.)

Wendy Ka re ka soGelwa tsheng'wa ke batho, ba mpolel'la gore, bampole'la gore ka a ba spitlela mare ke tawa. Thlabane suo fer, ke hirile fo Phokeng mare ka ba spitela. (I'm saying I'm being provoked and laughed at by people, they told me, they told ... I ignore them, but I came from Thlabane so far, I'm renting in Phokeng, but I reject them.)

Dineo Ba re nn'a ke pila. Leshambola le le tshwanang le nna e be ba tloo re nna ke pila, huu, waitse ba mborile waitse. (They said I'm not beautiful. Looking like I look, how can they say I'm not beautiful, when, you know they bore me.)

In the women's conversational excerpt, the salient aspects of the mixing are English words such as *joke, contest, exist.* If one looks at the entire conversation, it can be seen that some words occur quite frequently, such as the modification of *bore* to *mborile.* The Afrikaans speech forms can be grouped into two categories: conventional borrowings, such as *s'petlele* (hospital), and more stylized codeswitching, such as *suo ver (*so far). As in the excerpt from Transcript 1, words drawn from other African languages (*pila, leshammbola*) appear as well, but are not used as frequently.

Differences between standard and non-standard language systems are also evident at a syntactic level with an increased use of non-standard syntactic features even in the written standard. Consider the noun class system in Xhosa. According to descriptions of Xhosa, concordial agreement (between a noun and its assigned prefix) is the core of Xhosa. Descriptions of Xhosa dating to the earliest grammar by Casalis (1841) present the rule of concordial agreement as categorical, but in language practice the rule is variable. The difference between the noun-prefix agreement system in actual use and the idealized descriptions of standard/standardized Xhosa can be illustrated by the sentences below from the writing of educated Xhosa users (cited in Satyo 1998). (The s in parentheses after each noun indicates the noun class to which the noun belongs.)

1 Ulwimi (11) lithi lincede (5) ke nomtu ukuba azi ukuba yena ngowasiphi na isiwe—You can identify a person's nationality by the language he/she speaks.

2 Ungumtu ngokuba ekwazi ukutheba ulwimi (11) lakubo ... (5) livelise (5) nempucko yomntu okanye abantu abo batheba elo (5) lwimi (11)—He/she is human because he/she speaks a language ... his/her language will also reflect the culture of those people.

3 Ulwimi (11) lwesixhosa jikele labluke (5) kwaphela kwiilwimi ezininzi—Generally Xhosa differs markedly from other languages.

4 Abantu banolwimi (11) labo—People have their own languages.

Conclusion

The question of the specification of separate languages has always been an arbitrary procedure. In any event, disinvention is not an argument against such specification. It is an argument for mapping the landscape differently. The crucial issue here is which group decides on the arbitrary selection. In Southern Africa, at least, it was an outsider group—missionaries and colonial institutions—which decided with reference to their own convenience and without any consultation with the speakers of the languages being specified. In this respect, Zulu, Xhosa, Shona, and other Southern African "languages" are analogous to the artificial borders imposed by colonial powers in disregard of ethnic and sociocultural identities. The major objective of disinvention is to undo history, or at the very *least*, to contain it by disinventing languages so that when they are reconstructed they correspond more closely to actual linguistic boundaries. Ultimately, the *disinvention* project seeks not to do away with the concept of separate languages, but to recognize that languages are socially constructed and so can be socially deconstructed and reconstituted.

By reconstituting language, the disinvention project will be confronting the increasingly powerful movement toward language "purity" in South Africa in which standard African languages are equated with moral purity. Speakers of urban argots and non-standard African languages are regarded as morally irresponsible and corrupt. These speakers are morally suspect because they demonstrate that the so-called "impure" languages are indeed the norm of ordinary use.

South African media are likely to prove to be one of the most powerful agents through which disinvention takes place. Radio, television, popular magazines, and other forms of media are reconstituting and disinventing African languages. *Laduma*, a comic book on love, life, and sex, combines a wide range of languages, including Zulu, Xhosa, and English, to effectively communicate its message (Baleta 1996). Programs on South African television draw heavily on the panethnic urban hybrid used in the real-life experiences of speakers, as is evident in popular programs such as *Simunye Grooves* (*simunye*, Swati for "We are one"), *Gabon Motho*, *Suburban Bliss*, *Going Up*, *Generations*, and *Egoli* (gold). In a very real sense, the media are demonstrating the powerful role of urban hybrids and argots as linguae francae. When officially sanctioned as media of instruction in teaching/learning, these linguae francae may resolve the educational problems which standard African languages are now causing in South African schools. Not only does this urban, hybridized speech reflect the sociolinguistic practices of students; local teachers are also expert in this lingua franca.

The past and its legacy in South Africa, as in other societies in transition, cannot be changed by using the same modes of thought which produced it. Change requires new thought and new ways, linguistically, of conceptualizing the problem. As Brink puts it:

> The past cannot be corrected by bringing to it the procedures and mechanisms and mind-sets that originally produced our very perception of it. After all, it is not the past as such that has produced the present or poses the conditions for the future ... but the way we think about it. Or even more pertinently,

the way in which we deal with it in language. (Brink 1998: 23)

References

Anderson, B. (1983) *Imagined Communities: Reflections on the Origin and Spread of Nationalism*, London: Verso.

Baleta, A. (1996) "At last—sex education project that reaches teens," *Cape Argus*, 30, November.

Bhabha, H.K. (ed.) (1990) *Nation and Narration*, London and New York: Routledge.

Brutt-Griffler, J. (2002) *World English: A Study of Its Development*, Clevedon: Multilingual Matters.

Casalis, E. (1841) *Études sur la langue SeChuana*, Paris: Imprimerie Royale.

Childs, G.T. (1997) "The status of Isicamatho, an Nguni-based urban variety of Soweto," in A. Spears and D. Winford (eds) *The Structure and Status of Pidgins and Creoles*, Amsterdam and Philadelphia, PA: John Benjamins, pp. 341-70.

Chimhundu, H. (1992) "Early missionaries and the ethno-linguistic factor during the invention of tribalism in Zimbabwe," *Journal of African History*, 33 p. 255-64.

Cook, S. (2002) "Urban language in a rural setting, the case of Phokeng, South Africa," in G. Gmelch and W. Zenner (eds) *Urban Life: Readings in the Anthropology of the City*, Prospect Heights, IL: Waveland Press, pp. 106-13.

Davies, A. (1999) *An Introduction to Applied Linguistics: From Practice to Theory*, Edinburgh: Edinburgh University Press.

Desai, Z. (1994) "Praat or speak but don't theta: on language rights in South Africa," *Language and Education*, 8 (1 and 2) pp. 21-37.

Fardon, R. and Furniss, G. (eds.) (1994) *African Languages, Development and the State*, London and New York: Routledge.

Gilroy, P. (1987) *There Ain't No Black in the Union Jack: The Cultural Politics of Race and Nation*, Chicago, IL: University of Chicago Press.

Goyvaerts, D. (1996) "Kibalele: form and function of a secret language in Bukuvu (Zaire)" *Journal of Pragmatics*, 25 pp. 125-43.

Harries, P. (1995) "Discovering languages: the historical origins of standard Tsonga in Southern Africa," in R. Mesthrie (ed.) *Language and Social History: Studies in South African Sociolinguistics*, Cape Town and Johannesburg: David Philips, pp. 154-72.

Hofmeyer, I. (1994) *We spend our years as a tale that is told: oral historical narrative in a South African chiefdom*. Johannesburg, South Africa: Witswatersrand University Press.

Hornberger, N. (2002) "Multilingual language policies and the continua of biliteracy: an ecological approach," *Language Policy*, 1 (1) pp. 27-51.

Jeater, D. (1994) "'The way you tell them': ideology and development policy," paper delivered at Paradigms Lost, Paradigms Regained, University of Witwatersrand.

LePage, R. and Tabouret-Keller, A. (1985) *Acts of Identity*, Cambridge: Cambridge University Press.

Maake, N. (1994) "Dismantling the Tower of Babel: in search of a new language policy for a post-apartheid South Africa," in R. Fardon and G. Furniss (eds) *African Languages, Development and the State*, London and New York: Routledge, pp. 111-22.

Makoni, S. (1998a) "In the beginning was the missionaries' word: the European Invention of African Languages," in K. Prah (ed.) *Between Distinction*

258

and Extinction, Cape Town: Centre for Advanced
Studies of African Society.
Makoni, S. (1998b) "African languages as European scripts:
The shaping of communal memory," in S. Nuttall
and C. Cotzee (eds) *Negotiating the Past: The
Making of Memory in South Africa*, Cape Town:
Oxford University Press, pp.242-8.
Makoni, S. and Kamwangamalu, N. (eds) (2000) *Language
and Institutions in Africa*, Cape Town: Centre for
Advanced Studies of African Society.
Mannheim, B. (1991) *The Language of the Inka since the
European Invasion*, Austin, TX: University of Texas
Press.
Mühlhäusler, P. (1996) *Linguistic Ecology: Language
Change and Linguistic Imperialism in the Pacific
Region*, London and New York: Routledge.
Myers-Scotton (1993) *Dueling Languages: Grammatical
Structures in Codeswitching*, Oxford: Clarendon
Press.
Nuttal, S. and Cotzee, C. (eds) (1998) *Negotiating the Past:
The Making of Memory in South Africa*, Cape Town:
Oxford University Press.
Pennycook, A. (1994) *The Cultural Politics of English as an
International Language*, London: Longman.
Phillipson, R. (1992) *Linguistic Imperialism*, Oxford:
Oxford University Press.
Prah, K. (ed.) (1998) *Between Distinction and Extinction:
The Harmonization of African Languages*,
Johannesburg: Witwatersrand University Press.
Ranger, T. (1985) *The Invention of Tribalism in Zimbabwe*,
Gweru: Mambo Press.
Ridge, S.G. (2000) "Language policy and democratic
practice" in S. Makoni and N. Kamwangamalu (eds)
Language and Institutions in Africa, Cape Town:

Centre for Advanced Studies of African Society, pp.45-65.

Ridge, S.G. (2001) "Discourse constraints on language policy in South Africa," in E. Ridge, S.G. Ridge, and S. Makoni (eds) *Freedom and Discipline: Essays in Applied Linguistics from Southern Africa.* New Delhi: Bahri Publishers, pp.15-30.

Ridge, E., Ridge, S.G., and Makoni, S. (eds) (2001) *Freedom and Discipline: Essays in AppliedLinguistics from Southern Africa*, New Delhi: Bahri Publishers.

Romaine, S. (1984) *The Language of Children and Adolescents: The Acquisition of Communicative Competence*, Oxford: Blackwell.

Roy-Campbell, Zaline Makini (2000) "The language of schooling: deconstructing myths about African languages," in S. Makoni and N. Kamwangamalu (eds) *Language and Institutions in Africa*, Cape Town: Center for Advanced Studies of African Society, pp. 111-31.

Satyo, S. (1998) "Soft harmonization and cross-fertilizing vocabularies: the case of Nguni languages," in K. Prah (ed.) *Between Distinction and Extinction: the Harmonization and Standardization of African Languages*, Johannesburg: Witwatersrand University Press, pp.213-29.

Satyo, S. (2000) "Foreword" in S. Makoni and N. Kamwangamalu (eds) *Language and Institutions in Africa*, Cape Town: Centre for Advanced Studies of African Society.

Satyo, S. (2001) "Kwaito-speak: a language variety created by the youth for the youth," in E. Ridge, S.G. Ridge, and S. Makoni (eds) *Freedom and Discipline: Essays in Applied Linguistics from Southern Africa*, New Delhi: Bahri Publishers, pp. 139-48.

Smitherman, G. (2000) "Language and democracy in the United States and South Africa," in S. Makoni and N. Kamwangamalu (eds) *Languages and Institutions in Africa*, Cape Town: Centre for Advanced Studies of African Society, pp.65-92.

Southern Rhodesia (1929) *Report of the Director of Native Development for the Year 1929*, Salisbury, Southern Rhodesia: Government Printing House.

XI

Plural Formations of Literacy and Occam's Razor Principle
A Commentary

The near absence of metalinguistic discourse has led me to argue that heterogeneity is constitutive of linguistic practice. Language mixing, linguistic overlap, and plural linguistic practices are all part of daily life and do not for the most part evoke any special metadiscourse, they simply are a reality, moreover speakers are always baffled by the importance researchers give to the topic. (Canut 2009:87)

Research into literacy in Africa is now a well-established field, which raises this question: Why another book on literacy? In this commentary, I seek to outline the productive lines of research that the contributors make. I am profoundly grateful for the opportunity to reflect on the field of literacy, especially in Africa, which is generally one of the most intriguing continents, perhaps due to its immense diversity.

In my reflection, I explore to what extent plural formations of literacy constitute a violation of Occam's razor principle by postulating more distinctions than warranted.

Scripts and histories
This volume makes substantial contributions to literacy in Africa as a field of study because of the breadth of its geographical coverage. It contains chapters on literacy in South

Africa, Mozambique, Uganda, Sudan, Eritrea, Morocco, Senegal (and Cameroon), Gambia and Nigeria, covering all regions (Southern, Central, Horn, North and West) of Africa, all major postcolonial language contexts (English, French, Portuguese), and both rural and (peri) urban contexts. In addition to its diverse geographical coverage, the authors adopt a sharp critical approach to the issues they are addressing in literacy. They demonstrate the limitations of Euro-American perspectives on literacy and scholarship in colonial and postcolonial Africa. Bondarev and Tijani (2014) for instance in their chapter on Tarjumo of Kanuri Islamic scholars demonstrate that distinctions between oral/written, reciting/reading and illiterate/literate in sociolinguistics and anthropology posit an analytical challenge even with the help of dynamic and continuum-like approaches due to the immanent entextualization and multilayered mediation of religious interpretation and instruction.

One of the governing principles of scholarship in this book is the utilization of historical approaches to literacy as evident in detailed documentation of the use of different versions of Arabic-based scripts (*Ajami*) in West Africa. The principles are neatly captured by Friederike Lüpke and Sokhna Bao-Diop (2014) when they write:

> Despite being (near to) invisible to educators, language planners and development activities, a pre-colonial literacy tradition continues to be practiced throughout those areas of Africa that are in the sphere of influence of Islam.

The widespread utilization of *Ajami* (Arabic-based orthographies for African languages) is a type of local language practice (Pennycook 2010). Local language practices are significant because it is conceivable that nonformally (Western) educated Africans in West Africa are more likely to be con-

264

sidered literate in their use of Arabic-related script than in either French or English Roman-based literacy practices. Writing about Senegal Lüpke and Bao-Diop (2014) echo several earlier commentators when they comment about the wide spread use of Ajami. Diagne (1978), for instance, stressed that approximately 95% of Muslim Senegalese are introduced to reading and writing based on Arabic characters and only 10% learn to read and write in French. In terms of language policy, the fact that students learn to read and write in French is therefore uneconomical. Whilst *Ajami* texts traditionally have held less prestige than Latin-based literacies, due to the rise of new technologies and the use of social media, *Ajami* is, in fact, spreading in many areas through print and electronic media.

The depth of Arabic-related literacy is apparent in the widespread use of literacy in mundane but socially important interpersonal and intrapersonal activities, such as grocery lists, private letters, compiling accounts, and religious and even profane literature! The fact that *Ajami* as a script was at times used in profane literature indicates the degree to which literacy practices were not only educational but also a form of leisure – a project of playfulness. Playfulness is a serious enterprise that takes place when a particular level of maturity has been reached, in this case in the use of literacy.

Further evidence of the long historical depth of literacy practices through the use of *Ajami* is cited in Dmitry Bondarev and Abba Tijani's (2014) chapter, who state that the ruling dynasties in the Lake Chad region between the 12th and 14th centuries were already engaged in Qur'anic education. Literacy in Islamic geographical regions preceded European colonial encounters.

The widespread usage of *Ajami,* in Berber, and Amazigh written forms challenges the commonly-held view that Africa was a purely oral continent and that writing was an outcome of colonial conquest. The prevailing ideological position that Africa was largely an oral continent is indicative of the weight of the colonial regime on some sections of popular societies. What was a product of colonialism was the introduction and reframing of African languages using Romanized alphabets, not literacy itself. By drawing readers' attention to a less well known Arabic-associated script, *Ajami*, the volume demonstrates the role of religion in African literacy. This should not be construed to mean that *Ajami* as a script is always associated with Islam. For example, there are languages that at one time were written in *Ajami* even when their users did not necessarily adhere to Islam.

Sudan is an important case in point. In the Sudan there was a period when Bantu-related languages were written in a Romanized alphabet; these were subsequently rewritten in *Ajami* only to be rewritten in a Romanized, Latin-based script again. The use of each script was motivated by clear ideological reasons, so the shift was not a technical issue only. For example, for Abdel Rahim Mugadam and Ashraf Abdelhay (2014), the use of Romanized and Arabic-related scripts is a way of framing Sudanese histories. They suggest that the use of a Latin script to write Arabic can be construed as a way of "dissociating" Southern Sudanese Arabic from Islam and an attempt to include Southern Sudanese Arabic within an imagined larger Christian community. Even though technically there is no relationship between Islam and *Ajami*, the relationship between Islam and *Ajami* and Arabic is ideologically plausible because Arabic was introduced together with Islam as a religion starting from the seventh century in Morocco.

Another example in which there was a sharp controversy about which script to use which does not fall within the ambit of the book is Somalia. There were sharp contro-

266

versies in Somalia whether to use a Latin-based script or *Ajami*. In 1972, Mohamed Siad Barre, the then President of Somalia intervened in the controversy and legislated that Somali should be written in a Latin based script. The controversies about which script to use also occurred in Morocco as Abderrahman El Aissati's chapter discusses. The controversies in Morocco concerned not only different scripts but also which version of a script to use.

Even though decrees have been passed by African parliaments and heads of state have intervened into the sensitive matter of scripts and spelling going so far as to even determine which characters to use in the script, the decrees have not had immediate local impact since most writers continue drawing upon different scripts and mixing spellings in a manner consistent with their knowledge and preference.

Changes and lenses

An important theme the book explores is the impact of modern technology on literacy practices. For example, one frequently occurring type of data is *textspeak*, e-mail messages, visual signs, etc. One of the objectives of the analysis is to explore the meanings of forms in textspeak. Fie Velghe's chapter based on ethnographic fieldwork in Cape Town, South Africa, shows a widespread utilization of mobile forms which has created new communicative environments, new channels, new linguistic and cultural forms' consequently producing, a form of "emergent normativity" as the description below demonstrates:

> The text is a transcription of one of the many text messages Lisa addressed to me. In this message it is immediately clear that Lisa feels quite comfortable with the textspeak or the repertoire she is writing in and that there are stable patterns in her use of abbre-

viations, homophones, and contractions etc. Within one and the same message, she's omitting apostrophes (three times she is using im instead of I'm), applying the same contractions (twice bt instead of but) and using homophones (twice2moro) in exactly the same way. (Velghe 2014: 69)

If Velghe's chapter is read concurrently with El Aissati's, the complexity of academic research into literacy becomes self-evident. When Velghe's uses the concept of "emergent normativity" and "supervernacular literacy" she is arguing that there are norms even in the use of nonstandard language varieties. The existence of norms is well articulated by El Aissati which is worth quoting at length:

Graphic notations of varieties coexisting next to the standard, which is more the norm that the exception, are usually a matter left to the individual writer and grassroots initiatives. Despite efforts by experts to code a nonstandard variety, variation in writing will subsist as a result of a lack of a central organization which would dictate the rights and wrongs of spelling, of the simple absence of a regional standard variety, or because of identity factors. There are usually no serious sanctions awaiting the writer who does not abide by the laws of a non-standard orthography. This does not hold for the standard language. Users are expected to apply orthography rules as outlined by dictionaries and handbooks, and the practice of school and institutions. (El Aissati, 2014: 147)

One of the problems most of us are faced with as researchers is the prism through which we should view our data analysis. For example, even though in most cases we attempt to view the data we are dealing with as non-standard oral forms, we to a very large extent find ourselves having to unintentionally use written standard language as a norm, so when we are analyzing non-standard varieties we cannot help but view them through the prism of a standard (written) language creating an impression that standard written language is the norm and non-standard (spoken) varieties cannot therefore be analyzed on their own terms. Unfortunately, even if the use of a standard written language is justifiable its use as lens creates a new set of conceptual problems. The idea of using a standard language lens is founded on the basis of "mythical super code" (Harris 2009:38) which is contradictory to the emphasis on literacy as local practice advocated in the volume. The analysis of texts through a standard language lens is further complicated by the multiple meanings of what constitutes a standard. Distinctions between standard and non-standard may vary between contexts and indeed between language users. Analysts may have different understandings of what constitutes boundaries between standard and non-standard varieties. Harris (2009) writes: "In every field of human activity, postulating a plurality of standards makes nonsense of the 'standard' itself."

If writing is not a given category, as Pablé and Hutton (2015) remind us, it is not adequate to claim that there was writing in the twelfth and fourteenth centuries; instead, one must bear in mind that what we construe as writing in current scholarship may not have been understood as such in pre-colonial contexts. As scholars begin to write and critically engage with histories of African language scholarship in a manner congruent with critical histories of colonial linguistics, we must be wary of projecting contemporary distinctions between speech and writing to preceding epochs. Even in contemporary Africa, it is conceivable that what researchers construe as writing may, in fact, not be considered as such by the subaltern. At grassroots level, writers may

269

feel they have much more freedom to use and combine different scripts (i.e.diagraphia). But Sebba (2012) cautions us that even if digraphia exists in theory, the individual language user rarely has a free choice of which to use: "Where true digraphia does exist, however, the choice of one or other by an individual is almost certain to have social meaning."

From an analyst's perspective, some texts may be construed as a mixture of different scripts (script mixing), but from a layperson's perspective, the text may not be based on a combination of scripts. In such situations, the perspectives being adopted by the analyst may be significantly different from those of the layperson. For the layperson, there may be no strict or a firm distinction between the scripts. There are a number of contributions in the volume which must be applauded for the serious efforts they make to try and incorporate the layperson's perspectives. For example, chapters by Sarita Monjane Henriksen and George Openjuru exploit the relevance and conceptual utility of layperson's experiences of literacy. Openjuru (2014) explores the complex nature of the relationship between literacy and Ugandan rural livelihoods. Because of Openjuru's concern with exploring the relationship between literacy and livelihoods, he draws upon a wide range of literacy artifacts which includes shops signboards, plain writing on pieces of paper, brochures, documents, and argues for their inclusion in adult literacy education programs.

Reflections, interests and critical issues
In Openjuru's chapter it is apparent that in some rural areas in Uganda, some local people are suspicious of researchers who are keen to look at their financial records even for research purposes. In such cases Openjuru's informants may feel that people who are purporting to be researchers are in actual fact government officials. The fear that literacy may

end up working against the interests of its users is effectively captured in the following extract from Openjuru's chapter:

> It is difficult for me to give you my business records and information because I do not know what you will do with that information. You could be coming from the office of the revenue people or spying on us since we are not from this place. (Openjuru, 2014: 242)

Lüpke and Bao-Diop (2014) touch on an important issue that most of us have encountered but is worth restating here: the problem of gaining access to local communities and efforts to reduce the impact of our presence on the performance of the "subjects" – aform of the "observer's paradox". One way of addressing the problem is to adamantly insist that researchers are "language makers," as are the interviewees, eliminating the need to make artificial distinctions between researchers and interviewees. Yet Lüpke and Bao-Diop's problems run deeper than the "observer's paradox" in that there are not only linguistic but are also problems of trust as they aptly point out. In their research, members of the community in which they were seeking to research were suspicious of their motives. They regarded Lüpke and Bao-Diop as government officials or one of the many NGOs. Lüpke and Bao-Diop resolved the ethics of the problem through a dramatic change of methodology: "employing a male, Muslim guide and assistant who made contact in the absence of the first author ... through this intermediary, it was possible to gain the trust of a number of stakeholders of *Ajami* writing in Ngaoundéré, Marouna and Garouna."

I am strongly impressed by the extent to which the Lüpke and Bao-Diop wrote candidly about the problems with which they were confronted when trying to gain access to the communities. It is also illuminating how they try and appraise what the intermediary said to convince the communities to open up. Perhaps in future researching *with* the communities thus taking into account the communities' problems rather than imposing the researcher's agenda *on* them might be worth considering as one way of gaining access to the communities. It is natural for the communities to willingly take part if they feel there are advantages in doing so.

In her chapter Henriksen (2014) makes a compelling argument about the importance of bilingual teaching programs in which students are provided with opportunities to learn in both Portuguese and their mother tongue. She shows that, as many other scholars before her, that bilingual programs are clearly emotional and cognitively beneficial to most students in sociolinguistically complex societies such as Mozambique. She is right to attribute the continued use of Portuguese to colonial and postcolonial structures. Her ideological analysis points at the political and linguistic framework of Luzitanization (*lusitanização*), an ideology supported by Portugal during the colonial era but now dominated by Brazil (see Severo and Makoni, 2015). Luzitanization is supported by powerful institutions such as the Community of Portuguese Language Countries (CPLP) and the International Institute of the Portuguese language (IILP). Their main objective is the promotion, protection, enrichment and dissemination of Portuguese as a vehicle of culture, education and information to enhance access to scientific, and technological use in international forums. These transnational institutions seek to promote Portuguese, using common and specific strategies in each of the national contexts where they operate, considering the different sociolinguistic contexts of these countries. Irrespective of the strategies applied their objective is to promote a dominant monolingual Portuguese ideology as part of Luzitanization. This makes it extremely difficult for Mozambique to shift its language to move beyond a situation in which Portuguese is dominant.

Another issue that runs through most of the chapters is how contributors analytically move beyond idealistic notions about literacy to placing emphasis on literacy as local practices thus overcoming the powerful impulses which are prone to distinguish between knowledge of language and knowledge of the world, grammatical and dictionary knowledge, and form and meaning.

In a well-documented chapter on Eritrea, Yonas Mesfun Asfaha, Jeanne Kurvers and Sjaak Kroon (2014) discuss a catalogue of types of literacy teaching based on cultural literacy practices. Reading their paper from a critical sociolinguistic perspective, I struggled to understand their constructs of "letter-sound correspondences" and "whole language approach". When language is seen as an open-ended and socially grounded system, as I do, a whole approach to language in literacy teaching is difficult to sustain. This objectifies language and seems to presuppose a one-to-one relationship between speech and scripts and a view that written languages are spoken discourses on paper. However turning the critique on myself here – something critics ought to do more often – my reading here is not very charitable as it fails to situate these theoretical constructs in their own right, and their own terrain. 'Whole language' and 'phonics' need to be appreciated as abstractions of literacy pedagogies, not theories of language.

A critique of a critic enables me to partially understand the intellectual spaces which I have contributed to in part as a result of my work, while at the same time being increasingly aware of my work's limitations. The critique of a critic is analogous to trying to shift from seeing my own scholarship from inside outwards, to an outside inwards. Full awareness of being critical to oneself, although a worthy cause, is extremely difficult to accomplish because it requires blocking my vision of myself.

The term *literacy* with its variants (unexpectedly) occurs frequently in the book. The critical issue is whether from a novice reader's perspective it is intellectually prudent to create and celebrate "new" terms to such an extent that reading some of the chapters becomes extremely difficult. I am confident that the authors are able to make more sophisticated reading of their work than I can. Having expressed this confidence, I, however, take the liberty to express my disquiet at use of the numerous terms and the difficulties of drawing distinctions between some of them. Perhaps we are violating Occam's Razor principle by making more distinctions than is necessary to articulate our argument.

The excellent chapter by Charlyn Dyers and Fatima Slemming (2014) captures the dilemma I have. On the one hand, they astutely distinguish at a theoretical level between a wide range of literacy terms, multilingual linguistic resources at grassroots level, portability of multilingual resources, and multimodal literacies. All these terms and their variants may be used to describe the sociolinguistic contexts in which their research in Cape Town is situated. The critical issue for me is not that new terms should not be created, but that perhaps in terms of practice it might be extremely difficult to distinguish between multilingual linguistic resources, portable multiliteracy resources and other cognate terms, and this book, from my perspective, is as much about theoretical exposition of literacy as it is about literacy as practice.

When is a language (not) a language?
This question may be regarded as heresy, but a close reading of Bondarev and Tijani's chapter on Tarjumo compels me to pose this question when they claim that Tarjumo does not have speech functions or written literature. The observation is intriguing because many languages do not have a written

language, and speakers of those languages might not necessarily need one. If the proposition that not all languages have a written language is true, the absence of "written literature" cannot be a defining feature of Tarjumo. Furthermore, defining Tarjumo as having no speech functions is difficult to imagine because even Latin has speech functions. Tarjumo is also described as "texts lifted out of discourse" and re-embedded in a new context; detachability and decontextualization are not relevant for describing Tarjumo. I am, however, willing to concede that Tarjumo might be a language, albeit a unique one thus the importance of the potential existence of languages that might not be easily described if framed in structuralism terms.

In an attempt to overcome the structuralism mind-set regarding language, a growing body of literature accepts that language does not break down neatly into autonomous, clearly-defined languages; Kasper Juffermans summarizes the literature quite effectively in this volume. This observation, which is increasingly becoming a mantra of sociolinguistics, is not new at all, despite claims to the contrary. Noam Chomsky (2000) in *Knowledge of Language* and Donald Davidson (1986) in an aptly titled chapter "A nice derangement of epitaphs" were quite skeptical of the existence of languages. The mythical status of language is concealed by the fact that we have names for languages. Hausa, Arabic, Wolof, Berber, and Tarjumo are some language names that form the basis of linguistic description in this book.

Two main observations need to be made. First, in the sociolinguistic literature, each language is attributed a single name (e.g., English, Chinese, etc.). Rarely do languages cited in the literature have more than one name. Reviewers and editors often compel authors for the sake of clarity to them) to use a single name. Ethnologue keeps a list of alternative names, but also chooses one name among many other alter-

275

natives. (Obviously, the use of a single name overlooks situations in which many different names are used to refer to a single language, and many languages are named using a single name).

In a manner which is consistent with a sociolinguistic reality in which many different names are used to refer to the same language, El Aissati cites evidence that Berber can also be referred to as Amazigh. The idea of one language, one name is pervasive in Western monolingual-oriented linguistic metalanguage and makes it difficult to capture the sharp ideological positions that are possible in the use of multiple names for the "same" language, as the Berber/Amazigh example shows. These names are not interchangeable, however, as El Aissati reminds us. The use of the name Berber is an endorsement of official state ideologies, while Amazigh is part of the political apparatus associated with rebel movements.

Second, the controversy about whether languages have names or not is only significant insofar as it is assumed that there exists something called *a language*. Languages are not natural objects. Rather,

> A 'language'... is a metalinguistic extrapolation that has become attached to a particular language name, it does not matter whether the name is *English, French,* or whatever. It does not even matter whether it has an army or navy. But there has to be a name. No name; no language. That is the higher order metamyth... (Harris 2009: 41-42).

Opening conclusion
I refer to this section in a potentially contradictory manner by calling it an "opening conclusion" in order to draw attention to the fact that the arguments I am making in the conclusion actually open a new dialogue and not to finalize a

discussion. In the opening conclusion I will address two issues. First, I will draw attention to the idea of plural formation as a genre in sociolinguistics. Plural formations mask rather than resolve intellectual problems which are conjured by the idea of singularities. For example, the shift from literacy to literacies, or from monolingualism to multilingualism, does not adequately address intellectual problems which are ostensibly created by our conceptual understanding of literacy, monolingualism, multilingualism and other closely related terms. Secondly, I am proposing that, from my perspective, it is insignificant whether one is referring to either literacy or literacies, monolingualism or multilingualism, English or Englishes unless the ideological orientation and voice of the informants and the voice of the analysts are brought to the fore as well (Juffermans and Van Camp 2013). In a similar vein, Canut (2009: 93) reminds us that

> It is only when speakers move about or meet a stranger that they become conscious of their particular linguistic features and the processes of comparison and transformation are put in place leading to the overlap of different varieties which cannot be categorized.

Theorizing about language, languages and literacy is always mediated by a variety of socio-cultural, historical and intellectual factors.

Furthermore, what will be required is a high degree of double consciousness and reflexive awareness of the fluidity, density and complexity of our linguistic experience, yet also of the power of the reifications, constructs and fictions that shape our communicational world. Communication and the study of communication must wrestle with the apparent continuities that we experience within the ongoing stream of life, our sense of order and habit, and our search for and need for order, set against the sense of flux and contingency that we experience when we try to define the essences or entities that anchor us to the world and each other (Pablé and Hutton 2015). If we situate literacy as a type of communication and semiotic system, we find ourselves in a paradox because while on the one hand, we seek to advocate for a particular approach to literacy to serve our specific objectives, on the other hand, it is difficult, inspite of our intentions, for our actions, motives and consequences to be fully transparent even to ourselves because of the interplay between the multiple impact of biological, social and contextual processes.

In using the construct of 'supervernacular', indeterminacy becomes central to language. The meanings of inscriptions cannot be determined by formal analysis and enumeration of the functions. It is unlikely that any degree of analysis and any amount of notational ingenuity can bring to interpretation a greater degree of precision than that accessible to the users of the literacy practices. Even though the analysis of supervernaculars are likely to be indeterminate research, writing about supervernaculars cannot proceed unless there is some consensus about which interpretation is considered more plausible than others. Supervernaculars may be variable in the nature of the data which forms the basis of analysis, but the interpretation is inescapably normative. Furthermore, the critique that dynamic approaches to language are likely to be more effective than static models of analysis is contradictory because even though intellectually the analysis has to be dynamic, it is still based on static models. It is impossible to a postulate any analysis without fixing and converting the analysis static and fixed! Dynamic approaches require static frameworks to function.

It is plausible that writing is a key factor in supervernacular like in other sociolinguistic practices particularly

278

when carrying out data analysis. Whatever transcription is used in the rendering of supervernaculars it is inescapable that one form of writing or other has to be used. Writing has its affordances and limitations. My provisional view of supervernaculars is influenced by what I understand to be educated literacy and the role of language therein. I cannot help but frame supervernaculars through my lenses of educated literacy, and writing is integral to that frame.

Supervernaculars are attractive because they challenge ideologies of writing which have permeated literate societies. As Pablé and Hutton (2015: 36) comment: "Printing and the standardized typeface creates a visual stability which we project onto language as a whole; the print against the empty paper (or screen) background suggests that words and sentences can be separated from context, analyzed as free-standing autonomous objects, and moved around as counters in games of logic and abstract reasoning."

Supervernaculars challenge writing as a semiotic ideology which conjures the idea of visual stability, uniformity and homogeneity, conventionalizing the status of the written word. Also:

> the possibility of isolating and analyzing written forms against a blank, featureless background, combined with other features of writing such as the un-ambiguous identification of spaces between words, and the combinatorial nature of writing, i.e.the open-ended recurrence of a closed set of units which are deemed identical across their instances, have profoundly shaped the way linguists understand spoken language. When linguists talk about language, what they seem to be describing is an idealized version of writing. (Pablé and Hutton 2015: 36)

Unless we are able to carefully craft our arguments in support of literacies and other plural genres, I would argue for the merits of a return to an old fashioned literacy or monolingualism, but a different type of literacy and monolingualism, a literacy embedded in humanity, creative monolingualism and not a mechanical one (Makoni and Pennycook 2012). Literacies and other plural formations unless robustly constructed cannot effectively resolve sociolinguistic problems in part because it is not possible to resolve problems by situating our thinking in exactly the same framework which produced them in the first place. The third dimension of my concluding statement is my argument that the current interest in supervernaculars arises in part because of the subtle domination of scriptivism and writing as a semiotic system in the practice of philosophization in sociolinguistics.

The intellectual orientation which I am proposing is not new at all, it may however be novel only in so far as the emphasis it places on specific dimensions. I am comfortable with frameworks which regard literacy practices as an important marker of identity. By proposing that literacy is an important identity marker each individual can therefore not suspend their identity, literacy practices will therefore be a permanent marker. I am not proposing that literacy practices do not atrophy, but they do so under special circumstances and may be more robust than initially expected. The robustness of literacy practices is useful given the changes which may take place in some contexts.

Since literacy practices are an important individual identity marker, and individuals are situated in fluid and dense forms of the present, and given the unpredictability of the future, literacy practices have to be understood as shaping and shaped by the contexts they are embedded in. There are no two or more individuals with identical literacy practices because each person's personal history and experience of literacies is unique even if the individuals share the same context of situation. Each individual's literacy practices are unique not only relative to other people but even to themselves. By this I mean that the literacy practices which an individual exhibits at one point in time cannot be repeated in future, and are not a replication of past literacy practices. The argument of uniqueness and that each literacy practice cannot be easily repeated should, however, not be pressed too far. The reason is that each individual's historical usage, and his/her past, current and future literacy practices are interwoven even though each literacy practice is unique. Even though there are no two individuals with identical literacy practices, individuals who have comparable social and personal histories may have some literacy practices which potentially overlap, the fact that they overlap should not necessarily detract from the argument of uniqueness of literacy practices.

Literacy practices are intricately linked to an individual's identity, however, literacy practices may be conceptualized as open-ended, and ongoing processes. Development of an individual's literacy practices is rendered feasible because of the open space within every literacy practice.

References

Bondarev, Dmitry and Tijani, Abba (2014). "Performance of Multilayered Literacy: Tarjumo of the Kanuri Muslim Scholars" In Kasper Juffermans, Yonas Mesfun Asfaha and Ashraf Abdelhay (eds.), *African Literacies: Ideologies, Scripts, Education*, Newcastle upon Tyne: Cambridge Scholars Publishing, pp.118-146.

Canut, Cecile (2009). "Discourse, community, identity: Processes of linguistic homogenization in Bamako. In: *The Languages of Urban Africa*, ed. Fiona McLaughlin, pp. 86-102. London: Continuum.

Chomsky, Noam (2000). *Knowledge of Language: Its Nature, Origins and Use*. New York: Praeger.

Davidson, Donald (2002 [1986]). *Subjective, Intersubjective, Objective: Philosophical Essays of Donald Davidson*. Oxford: Oxford University Press.

Diagne, Pathe (1978). *Transcription and harmonization of African languages in Senegal. UNESCO meeting of experts on the transcription and harmonization of African Languages, held in Niamey, Niger, 17-21 July.*

Dyers, Charlyn and Fatima Slemming (2014). "Neither Helpless nor Hopeless: Portable Multiliteracies, Discourses and Agency in a 'Township of Migrants'" in Cape Town" In Kasper Juffermans, Yonas Mesfun Asfaha and Ashraf Abdelhay (eds.), *African Literacies: Ideologies, Scripts, Education*, Newcastle upon Tyne: Cambridge Scholars Publishing, pp.332-354.

El Aissati, Abderrahman (2014). "Script choice and power struggle in Morocco" In Kasper Juffermans, Yonas Mesfun Asfaha and Ashraf Abdelhay (eds.), *African Literacies: Ideologies, Scripts, Education*, Newcastle upon Tyne: Cambridge Scholars Publishing, pp. 147-177.

Harris, Roy (2009). "Implicit and explicit language teaching" In: *Language Teaching, Integrational Linguistic Approaches*, ed. Michael Toolan, 24-46. London: Routledge.

Henriksen, Sarita Monjane (2014). "Ideologies of Language and Bilingual Education in Mozambique" In Kasper Juffermans, Yonas Mesfun Asfaha and Ashraf Abdelhay (eds.), *African Literacies: Ideologies, Scripts, Education*, Newcastle upon Tyne: Cambridge Scholars Publishing, pp.271-304.

Juffermans, Kasper (2014). "Englishing, Imaging and Local Languaging in the Gambian Linguistic Landscape" In Kasper Juffermans, Yonas Mesfun Asfaha and Ashraf Abdelhay (eds.), *African Literacies: Ideologies, Scripts, Education*, Newcastle upon Tyne: Cambridge Scholars Publishing, pp. 206-236.

Juffermans, Kasper and Kirsten Van Camp (2013). "Engaging with voices: Ethnographic encounters with the Gambian language in education policy" *Anthropology and Education Quarterly* 44(2) pp. 142-160.

Lüpke, Friederike and Bao-Diop, Sokhna (2014). "Beneath the Surface? Contemporary Ajami Writing in West Africa, Exemplified through Wolofal" In Kasper Juffermans, Yonas Mesfun Asfaha and Ashraf Abdelhay (eds.), *African Literacies: Ideologies, Scripts, Education*, Newcastle upon Tyne: Cambridge Scholars Publishing, pp.88-117.

Makoni, Sinfree and Alastair Pennycook (2012). "Disinventing multilingualism: from monological multilingualism to multilingual francas" In: *The Routledge Handbook of Multilingualism*, eds. M. Martin-Jones, A. Blackledge and A. Creese, pp. 439-454. London: Routledge.

Mugadam, Abdel Rahim and Abdelhay, Ashraf (2014). "The Politics of Literacy in the Sudan: Vernacular Literacy Movements in the Nuba Mountains" In Kasper Juffermans, Yonas Mesfun Asfaha and Ashraf Abdelhay (eds.), *African Literacies: Ideologies, Scripts, Education*, Newcastle upon Tyne: Cambridge Scholars Publishing, pp.178-205.

Openjuru, George Ladaah (2014). "Rural Livelihoods Literacies and Numeracies and their Implications for Adult Literacy Pedagogy: The Case of Bweyale in Uganda" In Kasper Juffermans, Yonas Mesfun

Asfaha and Ashraf Abdelhay (eds.), *African Litera-cies: Ideologies, Scripts, Education*, Newcastle upon Tyne: Cambridge Scholars Publishing, pp. 237-270.

Pablé, Adrian and Christopher Hutton (2015). *Signs, Meaning and Experience: Integrationism and Semiotics*. Berlin: Mouton de Gruyter.

Pennycook, Alastair (2010). *Language as a Local Practice*. London: Routledge.

Sebba, Mark (2012). "Orthography as social action: scripts, spelling, identity and power" In: *Orthography as Social Action*, eds. Alexandra Jaffe, Jannis Androutsopoulos, Mark Sebba, Sally Johnson, pp.1-20. Berlin: Mouton de Gruyter.

Severo, Christine Gorski and Sinfree Makoni (2015). "Luzitanization and Bakhtinian perspectives on the role of Portuguese in Angola and East Timor" *Journal of Multilingual and Multicultural Development*, 36(2) pp.151-162.

Velghe, Fie (2014). "Lessons in textspeak from Sexy Chick: supervernacular literacy in South African instant and text messaging" In Kasper Juffermans, Yonas Mesfun Asfaha and Ashraf Abdelhay (eds.), *African Literacies: Ideologies, Scripts, Education*, Newcastle upon Tyne: Cambridge Scholars Publishing, pp. 63-87.

Yonas Mesfun Asfaha, Sjaak Kroon and Jeanne Kurvers (2014). "Building Early Reading on Syllables and Cultural Literacy Practices: Evidence from Eritrea" In Kasper Juffermans, Yonas Mesfun Asfaha and Ashraf Abdelhay (eds.), *African Literacies: Ideologies, Scripts, Education*, Newcastle upon Tyne: Cambridge Scholars Publishing, pp.305-331.

XII

'The Lord Is My Shock Absorber': A Sociohistorical Integrationist Approach To Mid-Twentieth-Century Literacy Practices In Ghana

Abstract

Taking a sociohistorical perspective, this chapter analyses the language practices of taxi inscriptions in Ghana during the mid-twentieth century. Through the lens of Integrationism, the chapter explores whether recent scholarship in sociolinguistics has advanced African linguistic scholarship beyond existing ideologies of named, countable African languages.

1. Objectives

I have three main objectives in this chapter. First, I develop a historical perspective of African sociolinguistics through an analysis of mid-twentieth-century inscriptions by taxi drivers in Ghana who possess little education. The analysis enables me to view the nature of mid-twentieth-century Ghanaian life at a specific historical juncture of Ghanaian history from the grassroots up. A theory of language is necessary for a study of mid-twentieth-century history because research into history in Africa presupposes a particular view of language. Debates and contestations of philosophies about language, particularly emerging new metaterms, therefore, not only are pertinent to sociolinguistics but also clearly have pedagogical implications for the teaching of and research into cognate disciplines, such as history in Africa.

Second, I evaluate whether substantial success has been achieved in challenging a code ideology, with a particular focus on African scholarship. I use the term *code ideology* to refer to ontologies about language encapsulated in constructs, such as code-switching, code-mixing, truncated codes, and other closely allied terms. The idea of a code ideology is apparent in the naming of languages, for example, Arabic, English, Twi, Ga, Swahili, and Shona. Notions about language founded on ideas about codes may have to be rethought if they are to be germane in dealing with complex communicative practices in precolonial and postmodern societies. Perhaps, one way of making further progress is to produce a new set of meta-terminology that more effectively describes the sociolinguistic practices of the precolonial, colonial, postcolonial, and postmodern worlds. Examples of relatively new metaterms used to address the aforementioned problems include *superdiversity*, *supervernaculars*, *languaging*, and *polylanguaging*.

Third, using Integrationism as a specific prism, I explore the extent to which some of the aforementioned terms have advanced African linguistic scholarship substantially beyond code ideologies of named, countable African languages. Even though Integrationism can serve as a critique of a code ideology, it is itself open to critique because it lacks a methodology and an empirical basis. Therefore, it cannot substantially enhance our understanding of how people in mid-twentieth century 'de facto manage to communicate' (Duncker 2011, p. 533). In order to address the empirical problem, I draw upon research methods in archaeology and history, such as (retro) contextualization (Duncker 2010), to formulate an empirical basis for an Integrationist enterprise, which clearly has implications for framing of language and, hence, ways of practising and researching history.

In the light of these objectives, the chapter is divided into the following sections:

1. A rationale for the selection of mid-twentieth-century taxi inscriptions as epistemological research sites.
2. A historical and linguistic biography of 'wheeled transport' in West Africa.
3. A summary of the key principles of Integrationism.
4. An Integrationistic perspective on metaterms such as *languaging, supervernaculars,* and *polylanguaging.*
5. Discussion of the use of 'poetic ethnography', (retro) contextualization, and recontextualization as methods of data collection and analysis.
6. An evaluation of Integrationism as a way of framing mid-twentieth-century taxi inscriptions and its educational implications for the teaching and research of history in Africa.

2. Rationale for the Selection of Mid-Twentieth-Century Taxi Inscriptions

The study is situated in mid-twentieth-century West African taxi inscriptions in order to develop a historical perspective of African sociolinguistics. Locating the study in the mid-twentieth century fills a gap in the development of ways of framing literacy practices in Africa. Inscriptions have been used as forms of decoration for a long time in Ghana, just as gold weights were used as a form of decoration in precolonial Ghana. In addition, inscriptions are found in many different places, such as beauty salons, and on many different items, including canoes, beer bottles, wheelbarrows, bicycles, umbrellas, and, recently, wax prints. The presence of inscriptions on many different artefacts reflects the degrees to which literacy practices have a long history and have always permeated different facets of African sociopolitics. An analysis of the inscriptions, therefore, provides a unique lens into African literacy practices and the role of theories of language therein.

3. A Biography and Linguistics of Taxis and Cars

Ghanaians, like many Africans and other people across the globe, have a strong affection for cars. In Ghana during the mid-twentieth century, cars were symbols of wealth and status, which is intriguing since 'wheeled transport' did not exist in the precolonial era (Law 1980). The culture of cars has created avenues for prominent scholarly research, including linguistic analysis of taxi inscriptions, 'automobilization' (Klaeger 2009 in Gewald) of religion, trade, and the mechanization of Africa. Biographies of 'wheeled transport' constitute a rich source of linguistic and cultural data. According to Kopytoff (1986 in van der Geest):

> The biography of cars in Africa would reveal a wealth of cultural data: the way it was acquired, how and from whom the money was assembled to pay for it, the relationship of the seller to the buyer, the uses to which it is regularly put, the identity of its most frequent passengers, and those who borrow it. The frequency of borrowing, the garages to which it is taken and the owner's relationship to the mechanic, the movement of the car from hand to hand over the years and in the end, when the car collapses, the final disposition of its remains.

4. Key Principles of Integrationism

4.1 Background

Integrationism, as an analytical framework, was introduced and developed over a number of decades by Harris (1981, 1987, 2009, 2010); however, no single analytical philosopher can be characterized as the sole originator of Integrationism. A number of philosophical orientations had substantial influence on Harris, including Gilbert Ryle (1990-1976) of the ordinary language movement, J. R. Firth (1890-1976), Malinowski (1884–1942), and Saussure's *Course in*

General Linguistics (1916). However, Integrationism claims neither that its philosophy is completely new nor that it provides definitive solutions to contemporary sociolinguistic issues in Africa. Nonetheless, it provides an important lens through which some of the emerging metaterms may be viewed, together with implications of such framing on the teaching of, and research into, history in Africa.

4.2 Semiotics

Integrationism is construed as a project in semiology, in which communication is central and language a 'variable extra' (Harris 2009, p. 44) that is framed as dense, fluid, and transient. Language in colonial and postcolonial contexts is a product of social, elite, and political intervention and a consequence of intervention into language contexts. From such a perspective, language is a 'distillation of the linguistic practices of the literary elite' (Love and Ansaldo 2010, p. 592). Hence, as Love and Ansaldo (2010, p. 593) rightly point out, 'Languages can be constructed in as many different ways as the constructors—including linguists'.

4.3 Repetition

Harris (1998, pp. 82-83) is emphatic on the point that 'repetition is not an option, not even for one of the original participants'. Each communicative event is unique in terms of both time and space. The uniqueness of each event should not, however, be pressed too far because prior events leave 'traces' of the past in the present; hence, the present is largely interlocked with the past. These sociolinguistic traces are useful as they can be utilized in the future; thus, each interaction does not necessarily begin de novo. A degree of repetition is necessary, if not inevitable, in a framing of language. The degree of acceptable repetition in Integrationism is radically different from orientations in which (all) potential languages can be generated from an invariant set of ling-

289

uistic rules. Integrationism as a philosophy is incompatible with code-ideology theoretical frameworks, which seek to reduce human communication and language to an analysis founded on a postulation of the ontological existence of rules as autonomous, nameable, and countable African linguistic entities.

4.4 Segregationism

Contrary to an Integrationist perspective, Segregationism alludes to the notion that linguistic and non-linguistic phenomena constitute two academically separate domains of inquiry, and that language may be autonomous, and segregated from other areas of social experience, geography, and history. Thus, the study of languages has autonomy within scholarship, and has its own methodology and programme(s) of research. It is supposedly independent of neighbouring cognate domains. Segregationism differs from Integrationism because the former seeks to distinguish languages from each other; language from non-language, context, and action; language use from language learning; and internal from external aspects of language (Makoni 2011a, b). Conversely, from an Integrationistic perspective, language and critical African sociolinguistics challenge the idea of language as 'well defined', discrete, and hermetically sealed units that are countable and nameable (Blommaert 2008; Makoni 2011a).

4.5 Creativity

Individuals are active sign makers, and they interpret the nature of signs in many, and, at times, contradictory ways. Nevertheless, language makers, sign makers, meaning makers, sign creation, and interpretation remain important aspects of the human experience. In fact, sign making entails producing signs and interpreting them as hearers or readers. Each individual's experience of signs is idiosyncratic at a specific moment of its production and creation. Each interactional event is also unique because 'the only way of understanding the heterogeneity characteristic of cities is to focus the analysis on the subjective trajectories of each speaker' (Canut 2009, p. 89).

Another powerful construct that plays a central role in Integrationism is the idea of a layperson, which captures the social–linguistic experiences of ordinary language users and does not depend exclusively on determinations made by professional linguists (Harris 2009). The notion of a layperson includes investigating why we understand language the way we do and what the consequences are of such a way of framing languages in our individual and social lives. Language experience is critically important in Harris' layperson perspectives. Because of the nature of language, it is impossible to analyse language without experiencing it. From Integrationist thinking, 'regularities are bound to the experiencer, and to contexts, and therefore vary from individual to individual, and from one context to another, one person sees the regularity, while another doesn't' (Pablé 2012). Furthermore, Integrationism is sceptical of bi-planar relations (form/meaning relations), fixed code, and the fallacy of telementation, in which language serves as a conduit through which messages are transmitted.

5. From Language to Languaging

In an attempt to overcome the structuralist mindset regarding language, a growing body of literature accepts that language does not break down neatly into autonomous, clearly defined units; this observation, which is increasingly becoming a mantra of sociolinguistics, is not new at all, despite claims to the contrary. Noam Chomsky (2000) in *Knowledge of Language* and Donald Davidson (1986) in an aptly titled chapter 'A Nice Derangement of Epitaphs' were quite sceptical of the existence of languages. The mythical status of language is concealed by the fact that we have names for languages. Language names, such as Hausa, Arabic, Wolof, Berber, and Tarjumo, form the basis of linguistic description in sociolinguistics in Africa.

Two main observations need to be made. First, in the sociolinguistic literature, each language is attributed a single name (e.g. English, Twi, Ga, and Fante). Rarely do languages cited in the literature have more than one name. Yet Berber, for instance, can also be referred to as Amazigh. The idea of one language, one name is pervasive in Western monolingual-oriented linguistic metalanguage and makes it difficult to capture the sharp ideological positions that are possible in the use of multiple names for the so-called same language, as the Berber/Amazigh example shows. These names are not interchangeable, however, as El Aissati (2014) reminds us. The use of the name *Berber* is an endorsement of official state ideologies, while *Amazigh* is part of the political apparatus associated with rebel movements.

Second, the controversy about whether languages have names is only significant insofar as it is assumed that something called *language* even exists. Languages are not natural objects. Rather, "a 'language' ... is a metalinguistic extrapolation that has become attached to a particular language name, it does not matter whether the name is English, French, or whatever. It does not even matter whether it has an army or navy. But there has to be a name. No name; no language. That is the higher order metamyth" (Harris 2009, p.41-42) Integrationists drew attention to a philosophical approach to handling the claim that language does not break down into neatly bound units when they suggested that first-order categories do not neatly break into second-order categories. *First order* refers to here-and-now activities, ongoing communicational activity, or contextually meaningful behaviour that is situated in real time and real space and unfolding in unplanned ways. *Second order* refers to metalinguistic categories that include names of languages, societies, communities, etc. Using these terms indicates that first-order categories cannot neatly break down into second-order categories. As such, communication does not neatly break down into languages, an idea that has radical implications for the nature of analysis since language does not present itself for study as a neatly disengaged range of homogeneous phenomena, patiently awaiting description by an impartial observer, as suggested by the misleading expression *linguistic data*. On the contrary, language offers a paradigm case of interference by investigation, which is construed to mean language is both a medium and object of analysis.

A relatively large number of scholars have addressed this issue using the notion of *languaging* (Swain 2006, 2009, 2010; Garcia 2007, 2009; Creese and Blackledge 2010; Jacquemert 2005; Maturana and Varela 1998; Becker 1994, 1995; Khubchandani 1997; Ramanathan 2009). Swain (2006), with a focus on second language acquisition, construed *languaging* as a tool to mediate cognition, an activity, a form of producing a visible and audible product. From this perspective, languaging is everything. Swain and Lantolf adopted a totalistic interpretation of languaging, leaving very little room for ways of framing alternatives. Languaging in Swain and Lantolf's orientation is too powerful, making it weak as an explanatory construct.

On the other hand, Maturana and Varela (1998), scholars from Chile, approached the idea of languaging from a philosophical position. They construed language as an *autopoeisi*, a self-organization, and self-production system in which human actions occur. The striking aspect of Maturana and Varela's view is that the term *languaging* indeed occurs for the first time in Spanish translation. The term *languaging* as defined by Maturana and Varela (1973) preceded many variations in Western sociolinguistics.

Ramanathan's (2009) framing is closely aligned with that of Mignolo (1996, 2000), and both are explicitly political. Ramanathan regarded languaging as a form of and a resistance to being silenced. From that approach, languaging is a rebellious act, a form of resistance at one point in a historical moment. However, Mignolo adopted a political position and a longer historical perspective. He construed languaging as a product of colonial or elite interruption of communication in precolonial or, as I would like to put it, outside elitedom. *Languaging* is, therefore, a process, a product of communication disruption. Languaging cannot exist outside communication, but the converse applies as well: Communication may occur without language because language is a 'variable extra'. Mignolo's framework has a sharp sense of history and can explain the complex relationship between macro, meso, and micro forces. This sense of temporal history and construction of time is clearly appropriate and might serve postcolonial linguistic scholarship.

6. An Integrationist Account of Supervernaculars

The notion of *supervernacular* is increasingly popular and may become 'the key concept for an emerging sociolinguistics framework'. Because the term is widely used, at least in African contexts, it merits close analysis. I see this chapter as part of efforts to make sense of the meanings of the meta-terms allied to supervernacular. *Supervernacular* is modelled after Vertovec's (2007) notion of *superdiversity*, which he defined as 'multiplication of diversity'. *Super* in *superdiversity* denotes *hyper*, while *super* in *supervernacular* may be construed to mean *trans*. The latter can be construed to refer to movements across regions and semiotic boundaries. In short, the *super* in *superdiversity* does not have the same meaning as the *super* in *supervernacular*. The *super* in *supervernacular* resonates with notions such as *polylanguaging* and its closely related term *polylinguistic*.

294

Although what *languaging* means in *polylanguaging* is unclear, if *supervernacular* is based on *superdiversity*, the differences in the meanings of *super* in *superdiversity* and *supervernacular* have to be addressed; otherwise, *supervernacular* might be misleading. This is not to say that *supervernacular* cannot be used to refer to both *hyper* and *trans*. I am, however, extremely uncomfortable with the notion of diversity when used to refer to 'mass movements' for three main reasons. First, the romantic notion of diversity in Vertovec, Blommaert, Rampton, and their associates is a version of a description of reality that can only be advocated by those who are part of the powerful elite, such as researchers. Second, those of us who have spent most of our professional lives outside our countries of origin find the celebration of diversity extremely uncomfortable. It is the powerful who celebrate the notion of diversity; those from other parts of the world feel the idea of diversity is a careful concealment of power differences. When we celebrate mass movements, we need to distinguish between those who are compelled by circumstances to travel and those who do so willingly. *Superdiversity* contains a powerful sense of social romanticism, creating an illusion of equality in a highly asymmetrical world. Third, I find it disconcerting, to say the least, to have an open celebration of diversity in societies marked by violent xenophobia, such as South Africa. Furthermore, diversity stresses the differences between individuals, languages, groups, etc. Whether we are diverse or not depends on the power of the social microscope being used. It is ironic that while sociolinguistics is celebrating diversity, super or not, other strands of research that also address issues surrounding migration, real or imagined, seem to be returning to a notion of assimilation running contrary to what supervernacular and superdiversity might mean:

Examining public discourse in France, public policy in Germany, and scholarly research in the United States, I find evidence of a modest 'return of assimilation' in recent years. Yet what has returned, I emphasize, is not the old, analytically discredited and politically disreputable 'assimilationist' understanding of assimilation, but a more analytically complex and normatively defensible understanding (Brubaker 2004, p. 5)

Mass movement of populations is not new to Africa, so if diversity is accentuated by migration, then prior to colonialism considerable migration occurred; however, it is framed as nomadism. The differences lies in the terminology: people moved—they simply did not need passports: "African history, like that of any other continent, reveals plenty of population movements linked to multiple factors such as nomadism, rural exodus, economic migrations and conflicts" (Canut 2009, p. 92).

Ultimately, it is worthwhile to stress that notions about diversity are extremely powerful when used as metaphors to describe species. The danger to guard against in this case is one in which we unintentionally biologize a social phenomenon. If a social phenomenon is biologized, then social intervention is likely to be construed negatively because it will interfere with a natural ecology.

7. Much Ado About Nothing
I strongly support Blommaert and Rampton's (2011, 2012) project of creating new metadiscursive terms as a strategic way of facilitating understanding and visualizing sociolinguistic patterns, which cannot be easily captured in the diversity made salient in postcolonial and postmodern Africa with new, relatively cheap technology. This includes cell phone sociolinguistic resources whose mobility is not constrained

by 'territorial fixedness, physical proximity, socio-cultural sharedness and common background' (Blommaert 2011, p. 3).

Blommaert and Rampton (2011) challenge us to frame *supervernaculars* in a wide range of ways. The term *supervernaculars* may be understood to refer to 'semiotic codes, chat codes, gaming codes, standard codes, mobile texting, minilanguages, or as a global medialect of condensed abbreviated English' (Mcintosch 2010, in Orman 2012a) and many others. From an Integrationist perspective, Blommaert and Rampton's proposition that a *supervernacular* can be construed from an Integrationist perspective entails a combination of Segregationist and Integrationist metaphors. By describing texting, e-mail messaging, and codes, *supervernaculars* are considered on the basis of a code ideology, reinforcing exactly the conventional ideology the notion of *supervernaculars* seeks to challenge. On the other hand, the idea of sociolinguistic resources affirms an Integrationist orientation. An example of the problematic nature of moving beyond code-based framing of language is elegantly captured in the following quotation: "A hybrid combination of linguistic forms ('multi-racial'/'multi-ethnic'... straightforwardly identifiable lexically, phonologically and grammatically/syntactical) elements of language" (Rampton 2011, p. 289).

On the one hand, the impulse to move beyond the notion of codes is strong. On the other hand, a powerful counterforce restates characteristics of codes—lexical, phonological, grammatical, and syntax elements. Perhaps the notion of a *supervernacular* may not be as radical as we are led to believe because it is based on conventional notions of language, a position reinforced when Blommaert (2011, p. 4) stated that '*supervernaculars* have all the attributes of a language'. This is based on what Harris refers to as Segregationist linguistics (Pablé and Hutton 2015; Makoni 2011a, b).

The search for invariant rules in supervernaculars reflects the extremely powerful nature of the ideologies of code-based views of language. These views lead to a search for invariant rules, efforts to establish fixed meanings, and efforts to consolidate form-meaning relationships. This quest seems counterintuitive in a framework that seeks to describe wide circulations of semiotics. The trans-movements and circulations of 'semiotic codes' should render it difficult, if not impossible, to predict the meanings that the discourse practices. The challenge in *supervernacular*-inspired research is how to introduce and sustain notions of indeterminacy and unpredictability consistent with the ideological impulse towards mass movements, while still distancing it from code-based views of language.

If *superdiversity* is taken seriously at an epistemological level, then a diversity or multiplicity of interpretations of signs must be accepted, if not encouraged. It is conceptually self-contradictory to argue for the importance of *superdiversity* in theory but fail in practice to take into account inconsistency and contradictory interpretations that are consistent with common functioning of anthropolinguistic communication. Communication involves vagueness, contradictory meanings, and inconsistency between form and meaning that demand frequent reinterpretation in the light of pragmatic cues that bring into focus and stabilize forms in context. I find the notion of a *supervernacular* extremely complicated not only because of the relationship it has with traditional notions of codes and orthodox ways of framing language but also because I am not certain how the notion of *vernacular* is comprehended in supervernaculars, a situation rendered extremely difficult because of the many different interpretations of the term *vernacular* in sociolinguistics.

The following are at least five different ways in which the idea of *vernacular* can be defined:

1. Primary
2. Native
3. Indigenous language variety
4. Non-standard language varieties
5. A continuum ranging from basilectal to colloquial varieties

Regardless of whether this list is exhaustive (which is un-likely), the critical issue for me is exploring the implications for sociolinguistics if *super* is added to *vernaculars* and if *vernaculars* are defined with more than one meaning. If *super* in *supervernacular* means *trans,* and vernaculars are understood as non-standard, then a *supervernacular* may be construed as a manifestation of non-standard language, either spoken or written language varieties. If *super* means *trans*, the term *supervernacular* might be equivalent to *transidiomatic expressions.* If *super* in *supervernacular* is understood in the way it is understood in *superdiversity* as 'hyper', then *supervernacular* may mean a hypervernacular whose intensity of variation may be characterized and sit-uated along multiple continua, analogous to the meaning of *vernacular.* The complexity of the term *supervernacular* is apparent in the many ways Blommaert (2011) defines *supervernaculars*, as demonstrated in the following cases:

(1) Supervernaculars "have all the features we commonly attribute to 'languages'"
(2) Supervernaculars only occur as dialects

In (1), *supervernaculars* are languages plus something else. I am not clear what constitutes (all) the features 'we common-ly attribute to language'. In addition, (1) does not clarify the issue for me because what I regard as attributes of language may be based on what I understand to be a theory of language and communication. From an Integrationist perspective, the following might be regarded as attributes of language: indeterminacy in the relationship between form and meaning, language as a myth, communication as central, and language as an extra variable (Makoni 2011a). The challenge for me is whether I can integrate the idea of a *supervernacu-lar* within Integrationism, and if so, how? (2) is difficult to read. If *supervernacular* can only occur as dialects, then this undermines the very essence of the rationale for creating a term such as *supervernacular* and its intellectual apparatus.

8. From Supervernaculars to Polylanguaging in Superdiversity

The complexity in having a grasp of *supervernaculars* is that in some cases, a subtle shift occurs from *supervernaculars* to *superdiversity*, and the idea of polylanguaging is introduced, as in 'Polylanguaging in Superdiversity' and 'Superdiversity on the Internet: A Case of China' (Varis and Wang 2011). It is critically important to observe that the shift here is from vernacular to superdiversity, conflating distinctions between diversity and vernaculars. The argument that *polylanguaging,* interchangeably also referred to as *polylinguistic,* can be situated in superdiversity begs the question: What is the postulated relationship between polylanguaging and supervernaculars? To address this issue, one must make sense of what *languaging* means in a wide range of terms. *Polylanguaging, translanguaging,* and others may be taken as equivalents. *Polylanguaging* does not resolve the issue because the term *languaging* is in itself ambiguous and has been used in many different and, at times, conflicting ways, as I argued previously.

I bring this section to a close by citing some of the categories in a paper by Rampton (2011) that may demand a sophisticated reading and whose distinction may be difficult to sustain, both in theory and practice:

1. From "multi-ethnic adolescent heteroglossia" to "contemporary urban vernaculars"
2. Møller finds that "polylingual languaging continues among young men in their mid-twenties"
3. The linguistic features ascribed to Turkish and Danish get more and more integrated over the years
4. Youth language
5. Heteroglossic speech stylization
6. 'Community English'
7. Multiracial vernacular
8. This de-ethnicized, racially mixed local language (operates as) a constraining, taken-for-granted medium subsisting through all interactions

9. Empirical Challenges in Integrationism
Because language is so deeply embedded in context, history, geography, language classrooms, and the absence of distinctions between language and non-language, an extreme position in Integrationism argues that there is no such thing as linguistic data. The idea that 'linguistic data' do not exist has been a source of controversy within Integrationism (see Duncker 2011), in which scholars argue for the importance of data and empirical analysis if Integrationism is to advance knowledge regarding how people experience language, both throughout history and in contemporary times.

The methodology proposed in eliciting and analysing empirical data capitalizes on the concept of *(retro) contextualization* drawn from history and archaeology. By (retro) contextualization, language is situated in the spatio-historical context within which it was initially produced. (Retro)

301

contextualization is always partial because reconstructing the original setting is extremely difficult, and it is also always difficult to determine and establish what the language meant in its original setting.

10. A Brief Statement on the History of Taxis in Ghana
Taxis first appeared in Ghana in 1945, and the passenger fare was two and one-half pennies (*tro-tro*). The importation of *tro-tro* taxis was discontinued in 1959, when a company called the Bedford Assembly began importing the *tro-tros* in a process referred to in the Ghanaian context as 'complete knock out (C.K.O)', which means the parts, seats, engines, roofs, etc., were imported separately and assembled by Ghanaians. In 1966, the importation C.K.O of the *tro-tros* was banned, and a new type of lorry—a 'passenger bus'—appeared on the scene. The assembly plant was named *Motoway (sic)* and was intended to replace the old truck. When the new buses were sold in another town, the person who got the contract called his bus *Soccer* since he used it to transport a soccer team. The 'old' buses were subsequently replaced by new passenger buses called *'V.C.10'* or 'RINGO STAR' (see *In No Time to Die: A Book of Poems, Depicting Slogans of Ghana's Mammy Lorries*).

11. Mode of Data Collection: 'Poetic Ethnography' and (Retro) Contextualization
The data I use were collected by two architects. Schreckenbach (Kyei and Schreckenbach 1975) interviewed the drivers to make sense of the inscriptions, while Kyei (Kyei and Schreckenbach 1975) photographed the inscriptions and, whenever necessary, drew illustrations as part of a general interest in the environment in Accra in Ghana. The innovative aspect of the research involves converting what the driver said into another genre, in this case poetry. The combination of inscriptions and poetry was called 'poetic ethno-

302

graphy' (van der Geest, http://www.sjaakvandergeest.sosci.uva.nl/pdf, accessed March 20, 2013). Data analysed in this chapter are largely drawn from Kyei and Schreckenbach's (1975) book *No Time to Die: A Book of Poems, Depicting Slogans of Ghana's Mammy Lorries.* Pages from the book are reproduced in the Appendix (Fig. 5.1).

One of the main advantages of 'poetic ethnography' is that, through an analysis of the poems, I am able to gain insight into the original meanings the taxi drivers intended to articulate in the inscriptions on the taxis. In poetic ethnography, the problem of gaining insights into the intended meanings of authors and painters is partially resolved because the poems are recorded. The poems, therefore, provide opportunities to situate the inscriptions within their original context, a form of (retro) contextualization. Van der Geest, (http://www.sjaakvandergeest.socsci.uva.nl/pdf/highlife, accessed March 20, 2013), unlike Kyei and Schreckenbach (1975), reports actual narratives by taxi drivers when commenting on the meanings of the inscriptions.

The inscription FEAR BEAUTIFUL WOMAN, written on a taxi, stimulated the following poem by Kyei. The original poem is on the left, while the version on the right includes translation of certain words:

Fear beautiful woman	The same way your eyes
The same way she	hot for her
attracted you	
The same way she attracts	Fear beautiful woman
other men.	The same way she
The same way she tricks	attracted you
you	The same way she attracts
For your kudi,	other men.
The same way she tricks	The same way she tricks
other men for their kudi	you
	For your money

303

The same way she tricks
other men for their money
The same way your eyes
hot for her,

The same way other
men's
Hot for her
The same way you lobby
stiff for her
The same way other men
chase am
So some time all you men
go clash over her.
And fight come
And blows pi-pe pi-pe pi-
pe
And blood spill botwoo!

And mean die.

Like I say fear beautiful
woman

The same way other
men's
Hot for her
The same way you lobby
stiff for her
The same way other men
court her
So some time all you men
go clash over her.
And fight come
And blows pi-pe pi-pe pi-
pe
And blood spill from you
both!
And mean die.
Like I say fear beautiful
woman

The inscriptions adopt a male-centred perspective, whereby
women generally are treated as deceitful and unfaithful and
cheat men, as illustrated in the following lines: 'Fear beautiful woman, the same way she attracted you the same way
she attracts other men.' Women are portrayed as adept at
cheating and deceiving men. The discourse can be read as a
dialogue with other men based on the personal histories of
the driver. The narrative is male-centred because rarely in
the inscriptions are women given an opportunity to articulate
their own position in self-defence.

The following poem was stimulated by the inscription 'Still HOME HARD':

HOME HARD   Thus struggle I struggle.

304

I go on empty stomach
HOME HARD
Thus struggle I struggle.I
go on empty stomach
sometimes
At times, too.
My wife and children and
I we chop only kenkey[1]
and shito
And tatare for a whole
week, like that
Then we grow lanka-lanka
Like bamboo stick,
Chief, home hard.[2]

When gradually inside
good,
I return home
With money for every
busuni
Then they glad
Thanking me say:
Oh Koo, you've done well
Oh, Koo, hold us like that
But in actual fact,
It is the same abusuafo

Who follow me
everywhere?
With their forking juju
Chief, hmm.
I say home hard.
sometimes
At times, too.
My wife and children and
I we eat only maize and
hot sauce
And struggle for a whole
week, like that
Then we grow thin
Like bamboo stick,
Chief, life at home is
difficult
When gradually inside
good,
I return home
With money for
everybody
Then they glad
Thanking me say:
Oh Koo, you've done
well.
Oh, Koo, hold us like that
But in actual fact,
It is the same people
Who follow me
everywhere?
With their forking
witchcraft
Chief, hmmm.
I say life at home is
difficult

---

[1] Fermented maize meal. See
www.bing.com/search?q
(accessed March 20, 2013)
[2] *Chief* is a term used with
endearment and does not
always refer to an individual
with traditional
authority.

In the poem based on the inscription 'Still HOME HARD' the driver is expressing his frustration with the burden of discharging responsibilities for his family. He construes it as so difficult that he refers to it as 'struggle, struggle'. The repetition of the word *struggle* is for rhetorical effect and highlights the responsibilities he has to discharge. Similarly, the repetition of *lanka* is also a way of capturing the intensity of the challenge with which he is confronted. The poem shares with the previous one the narrative of the hypocrisy of women. The hypocrisy is evident in that the people who welcome him when he gets back home are the same people who bewitch him: 'It is the same people/ Who follow me everywhere?/And spoil my work/with their forking juju'. The driver seems to be in dialogue with others because of the continuous reference to 'Chief, hmm./ I say home hard'.

The third example is of a further poem which responds to the taxi inscription NO BUSINESS NO WIFE (not reproduced in the Appendix). The poem is an explication of the inscription:

Marriage be	Marriage be
No monkey business	seious business
I hard proper	It is difficult
You may supply	You may supply
Buy shoes, dresses,	Buy shoes, dresses,
Hand-bags, cloth, wig	Handbags, cloth, wig
Every time, supply supply	Every time, supply supply
Wife's bogus things	Wife's bogus things
Pickni too	young children, too
Ibi business go bring am	It's your responsibility to bring them

Unlike Kyei and Schreckenbach (1975), van der Geest collected actual narratives by taxi drivers (http://www. sjaakvandergeest.socsci.uva.nl/pdf, accessed March 20, 2013). The narratives offer insights into what the inscriptions may have meant in what was thought to be the original settings in which the inscriptions were found, a form of (retro) contextualization. For example, the inscription 'I shall return' found on a taxi originated from the experience of a politician, according to the taxi driver: 'A prominent politician has a number of tro-tros in Accra. When Rawlings came to power in 1979, the man went into exile. Later, his vehicles had the following inscription: "I shall return"'.

A taxi driver who had the inscription 'The Lord is my shepherd' explained its history: 'Some time ago, my uncle in the US came home and bought a taxi for one of my cousins who had been suffering from grinding poverty. "The Lord is my shepherd" meaning that the Lord guides him, he will not lose hope no matter the difficulty'.

11.1 Interpretation of Inscriptions
Some of the meanings of the taxi inscriptions were vague and enigmatic. In fact, some meanings were nearly impossible to determine unless one read the accompanying poem that captured the narratives of the driver. Asking the drivers the meanings of some of the inscriptions did not necessarily provide a comprehensive solution, indicating the limitations of (retro) contextualization. In fact, asking the drivers for the inscriptions' meanings was often the beginning of a complex attempt at interpretation. For example, in some cases, the same driver gave conflicting interpretations of the same inscriptions on his taxi. In other cases, the interpretations were challenged by other drivers who may have felt that the biographical narrative given by the first driver was not accurate. Conflicting interpretations of the same inscription suggest that no individual possessed an exclusive monopoly of the

307

meanings, a position effectively captured by Nicolai (2008, p. 321):

> The inconsistency and contradictory interpretations by some drivers is consistent with ordinary functioning of anthropolinguistic communication, but nevertheless shows that in practice, communication involves vagueness of meaning and formal variation which require constant reinterpretation in view of cues which bring into focus and stabilize forms in context.

The veracity of some of the drivers' biographical details was also contested by other drivers familiar with the driver and the circumstances surrounding the specific inscriptions. The issue from an Integrationist perspective is not so much whether the 'recollections' were true or false, because the biographical details provided by the driver(s) could not be verified independently. In such cases, the degree to which the driver was able to infuse the inscriptions with meaning was the crucial factor. The inscriptions made sense when they were contextualized. Contextualization must encompass both immediate situations and the speaker's knowledge, regardless of whether the knowledge is correct.

11.2 Interpretation of the Inscriptions/Creative Incomprehensibility

The importance of the driver's creative imagination for making sense of the inscriptions reflects the powerful impulse to establish meaning, even if the inscriptions are meaningless. Given the centrality of how the driver's imagination and creative construal of the inscriptions made it feasible to understand the meanings of some of the inscriptions, establishing the biographical details that formed the basis of the contextualization entailed determining the nature of the relationships among the taxi owner, taxi driver, and passengers. As a result, I make two propositions. First, there is 'no sponsorless language'. By 'no sponsorless language', Pablé (2012) means that everyone is responsible for what they say, regardless of where it is said and the objectives it finally serves. The notion of sponsored language adds a very powerful issue about responsibilities, even though it may be too idealistic and perhaps impossible to hold everyone responsible for what they say and its effects. Nevertheless, the proposition is still defensible.

Second, as Harris (Haas 2011) also argues, a layperson's expertise is as valid as that of professional linguists. I am aware that I am vulnerable to the charge of inconsistency by saying one thing and doing the exact opposite, a charge that most Integrationists face (Pablé and Hutton 2015). For example, saying, on the one hand, that a layperson's expertise is as valid as that of professional linguists, while, on the other hand, articulating a professional linguist's position.

12. Form and Meaning, Bi-Planar Relations

The relationship between form and meaning in some African contexts is extremely variable, perhaps more so in oral history than in other communicative practices. The indeterminacy captures well the arbitrariness of the form/meaning relationship. Van der Geest (1996) illustrated this arbitrariness when, during his research on ageing, he asked eight elderly persons to explain the meaning of the same proverb. Because of the frequency with which the elderly use proverbs, one would assume they would have a shared understanding of a proverb's meaning. However, the 12 meanings elicited from these 8 people reflect the arbitrariness of the relationship between form and meaning, at least in African contexts, and even in formulaic constructions that the elderly use widely in local communities.

These varying interpretations raise two important issues: First is the importance of reflecting upon what one is saying, and the effects of the discourses. The issue is not whether one interpretation is closer to the 'original meaning' because it is extremely hard to determine with any degree of certainty the original meaning of a proverb or stretch of discourse. In Integrationism, human beings are actively engaged in communication; they create and recreate meanings. Second, speaker perspectives are likely to be different from those of the researcher. The researchers in van der Geest's (http://www.sjaakvandergeest.soc.uva.nl/pdf) study and the interviewer in the taxi project may have different positions from those of the informants because, as researchers, they are exposed to many more inscriptions and have been part of more discussions about inscriptions than each individual elderly informant or taxi driver. As a result, the interpretations, perspectives, and contextualizations made by the interviewers in both the proverb study and the taxi study may be different from those of the informants. In such cases, multiple points of view exist—those of the taxi drivers, the elderly, and the researchers—and all of which are equally valid.

13. Intertextuality, Discourse Mobility, and 'Automobilization' of Language

Some of the taxi inscriptions are amalgams taken from proverbs, religious verses, names of popular people or admired places (*Uncle Sam, Chicago boy*), and statements or admonitions. In some cases, the drivers combined verses from the Bible and terms associated with cars, a creative juxtaposition that produces a humorous metaphor, such as 'The Lord is my shock absorber'. The 'automobilization' of religion refers to the ways in which verses from the Bible or religious statements, such as '*Rock of Ages*', '*I thank God*', '*Many are called*', '*Help me oh God*', and '*In God we trust*', are written

310

and integrated with illustrations on taxis. Automobilization gave rise to language mobility because the taxis 'shuttled' between different regions (e.g. urban and rural areas). The 'automobilization' of religion and the mobility of language (i.e. the 'mixing' of communicative practices) creates opportunities to experience 'bits and pieces' of language from different parts of the country.

5.14 Integrating Taxi Inscriptions with the (Age) State of the Taxi

In addition, the meaning of a single inscription may change with time. For example, the meaning of 'LUFTHANSA' written on a new taxi will be radically different when the taxi is old. When the taxi is new, 'LUFTHANSA' can be construed as a prestigious, fast, world-class air carrier. But 'LUFTHANSA' may be ironic when found on the same taxi when it is old and dysfunctional. Similarly, the inscription 'OLYMPICS' may refer to speed and elegance when the taxi is new but becomes extremely ironic on the same taxi when it is old, moves slowly, and is dysfunctional.

In other cases, inscriptions have to be read as part of an ongoing dialogue. The dialogue in this case is the one (re)constructed between the inscriptions at the front and those at the back of the taxi. An interpretation of taxis in particular must begin from the assumption that the inscriptions are meant to be meaningful. This search for meaning makes it necessary to read the inscriptions at the front and those at the back together to construe them as meaningful. For example:

Who de (is) free? (Front of the taxi)
Only Jesus. (Back of the taxi)

From an Integrationist perspective, meanings cannot be simply 'read off' structures (a position that echoes a Segregationist perspective or code-driven interpretations). The

311

interpretations have to take into account other fragments of discourse that either precede them or are juxtaposed with them. In Integrationism, no texts stand in isolation because the semiotic practices carry with them social and historical associations. The critical issue here, whether the texts are read jointly or against the status of the taxi, is not a feature of the inscriptions but a result of the ways in which individuals read the inscriptions, because it is individuals who attribute meanings to the texts.

15. Inscriptions and Metadiscourses

Most drivers explained that the meanings of the inscriptions on their taxis reflected their fears of being bewitched by close family members who might be jealous of their perceived success. It is striking that the drivers did not define themselves in terms of their ethnicity or the language they believed they spoke, making it important to note that constructs frequently deployed in some African sociolinguistics are not present in the discourses of laypeople framing languages and history as local practices.

I can, therefore, argue that some of the powerful constructs in African sociolinguistics (e.g. heteroglossia) may share some features with Integrationism insofar as both construct human beings as agents that are actively creating meaning and treat meaning as contextual and time-bound. Integrationism, and to some extent heteroglossia, stresses the social and historical embeddedness of human communication. Context and time boundedness within Integrationism refer to both the communication and the analysis by the researcher or layperson. The analyst, therefore, cannot escape context.

16. Conclusion

In this chapter, I outlined the main features of Integrationism, using it as a prism through which some of the major metaterms such as *languaging* and *supervernacular* can be viewed. I have argued that even though Integrationism might be a productive mode of analysis and may complement some of the current metaterms that are gradually being used in Africa, it still needs to confront some of its empirical challenges if it is to capture communicative practices in different domains. I have proposed that research methods, such as (retro) contextualization, widely used in history and archaeology, might serve as a basis for an empirical project of Integrationism. My primary objective has been to move discussions about perspectives on language in Africa beyond sociolinguistics into other cognate disciplines, such as history, because the practice and writing of history is founded on an assumption of a particular view of language, hence the relevance of current controversies of language beyond sociolinguistics in Africa.

Appendix

HOME HARD

This struggle I struggle.
I go on empty stomach sometimes.
At times, too,
My wife and children and I,
We chop only kenkey and shito
    and talare for
    a whole week, like that.
Then we grow lanka-lanka
    like bamboo stick.
Chief, home hard.

When gradually inside good,
I return home
    with money for
    every busuani.
Then they glad
    thanking me say:
Oh, Koo, you've done well.
Oh, Koo, hold us like that!
But in actual fact,
It is the same abusuafo
Who follow me everywhere
    and spoil my work
    with their forking ju-ju.
Chief, hmmm,
I say, home hard.

BLACKMAN PALAVER

Every place Blackman dey,
    ibi trouble trouble trouble
    sonn-n-n-n-n-n-n-n-n-n-n-n-n!
He get for hin ear.
South Africa the same,
America the same,
England the same,
Every place too
    small small dey.
Ah-ah!
Wey thing at all
Blackman do?
This Blackman thing
    I dey talk so,
Boo, ihard oo!
    ihard proper!
But what man
    go do self?
This earth here God give,
He give for Blackman too.
So I say me Blackman
I no go mind
    for anybody at all,
I go live for this earth
    live live live aa-a-a-a-a-a!
Till I go die self.
Ibi God Hinself plan
    put me for here,
True.
For this Blackman palaver thing,
I no mind at all,
True.
Me I say
    the people wuu do so,
All need heart talk,
    heart change proper;
True!

Fig. 5.1 Taxi inscriptions and poems

314

THEY ACT AS IF LOVERS

They act as if lovers,
Some people I know.
Heaven knows that
Deep in the bottom of their hearts,
There is only malice
        and hate
        and cursing
        and death
They wish upon my head;
But the moment
They see my monkyimonka face,
They put cloth on the ground
        for me to walk on
Praise me
Pamper me
Fondle me
And even carry me shoulder high.
And act
As if
Lovers — which is all lie-lie.
They act as if lovers,
Some people I know.

FEAR BEAUTIFUL WOMAN

Fear beautiful woman.
The same way she attracted you,
The same way she attracts other men.
The same way she tricks you
        for your kudi,
The same way she tricks other men
        for their kudi.
The same way your eyes hot for her,
The same way other men's eyes
        hot for her
The same way you lobby stiff
        for her,
The same way
        other men chase am.
So some time all you men
        go clash over her.
And fight come
        and blows pi-pe pi-pe pi-pe!
        and blood spill botwoo!
        And men die.
Like I say,
        fear beautiful woman.

NHYIRA NKA BOAFO

Nhyira nka boafo
Ɔno na ɔwɔ ahumɔbrɔ
        nteasee
        akokoduru
        Ɔdɔ
Ɔno na ɔnye pesemenkomenya.
Nhyira nka boafo
(Blessed Be The Helper;
He is the man of sympathy
        of understanding
        of selflessness
        of magnanimi y
        of courage
        of love
Blessed be the helper.)

Like you want alomo
        with tough baya s'elf,
Money talk.
You want go movie,
Money talk.
You want hire room,
Money talk.
You want become been-to,
Money talk.
You want buy singlet,
Money talk.
You want buy okro soup
        In passion week,
Money talk.
You want send
        your child to school,
Money talk.
You want buy sandals
        to comfort your A.D. One One feet small,
Money talk
You want go to Star Hotel,
Money talk.
You want wear kente,
Money talk.
Anybody want ride
        in my tro-tro self, too.
Money talk.
Oh, this world,
Everything be money money sonnn!
Money rules all.

Fig. 5.1 (continued)

315

A DAY WILL COME

A day will come
When this **tro-tro** truck you see
Will help install me
A V. I. P.

A day will come
When I, riff-raff
As I may look,
Will put on the finest clothes.

A day will come
When I, small man
As I look,
Will rise up
To tower above giants.

A day will come
When I, a nincompoop
As you think I am,
Will out-shine
Even the toughest lot.

A day will come
When I, the moa as I look
Will stretch up my wings
And fly beyond myself.

AUNTY NANA

Aunty Nana:
Obiara wɔ ne dɔfo.
Bia biara a wowɔ mu no,
Nnipa bi sere wo
    ebi kyiri wo
    ebi nsɔ dɔ wo.
Ewiase yi,
Sɛ wodu bun mu a,
Na wohu
Wɔn a ekyiri wo
Ne wɔn a wotaa wakyi.

(Aunty Nana:
We each have our loved ones
In whatever situation
You find yourself,
Some people laugh at you
Some hate you
While others simply love you.
In life
When you find yourself
In really deep waters,
That is the time
You truly discover
Those that hate you
And those that are with you.)

Fig. 5.1 (continued)

316

References

Becker, A. L. (1994). "Repetition and otherness: An essay" In *Repetition in Discourse: Interdisciplinary Perspectives*, ed. B. Johnstone, pp.162–175. Norwood, NJ: Ablex

Becker, A. L. (1995). *Beyond Translation: Essays Toward a Modern Philology*. Ann Arbor: University of Michigan Press.

Blommaert, J. (2008). "Artefactual ideologies and the textual production of African languages" *Language and Communication* 28(4) pp.291–307.

Blommaert, J., and B. Rampton (2011). "Language and superdiversity: Special issue" *Diversities* 13(2) pp.1–83.

Blommaert, J., and B. Rampton (2012). *Language and Superdiversity*. MMG Working Paper 12.

Brubaker, R. (2004). *Ethnicity Without Groups*. Harvard: Harvard University Press.

Canut, C. (2009). "Discourse, community, identity: Processes of linguistic homogenization in Bamako" In *The languages of Urban Africa*, ed. F. McLaughlin, pp.80–103. New York: Continuum.

Chomsky, N. (2000). *Knowledge of Language: Its Nature, Origins and Use*. New York: Praeger.

Creese, A., and Blackledge. A. J. (2010). "Translanguaging in the bilingual classroom: A pedagogy for learning and teaching" *Modern Language Journal* 94(1) pp. 103–115.

Davidson, D. (1986). *Subjective, Intersubjective, Objective*. Oxford: Oxford University Press.

Duncker, D. (2010). "What is it called? Conventionalization, glossing practices and linguistic (in)determinacy" *Language and Communication* 33(4) pp.400–449.

Duncker, D. (2011). "On the empirical challenge to integrational linguistic studies" *Language Sciences*

33(4) pp.533–543.

El Aissati, Abderrahman (2014). "Script choice and power struggle in Morocco" In Kasper Juffermans, Yonas Mesfun Asfaha and Ashraf Abdelhay (eds.), *African Literacies: Ideologies, Scripts, Education*, Newcastle upon Tyne: Cambridge Scholars Publishing, pp. 147-177.

Garcia, O. (2007). "Foreword" In *Disinventing and Reconstituting Languages*, eds. S. Makoni and A. Pennycook, pp.xi–xv. Clevedon: Multilingual Matters.

Garcia, O. (2009). *Bilingual Education in the 21st Century* (with contributions by Hugo Baetens). Malden: Wiley-Blackwell.

Haas, M. (2011). "The question is not whether integrationism can survive outside linguistics, but whether linguistics can survive outside integrationism: An interview with Roy Harris. *Language Sciences* 33 pp.498–501.

Harris, R. (1981). *The Language Myth*. London: Duckworth.

Harris, R. 1987. *The Language Machine*. London: Duckworth.

Harris, R. (1998). *Introduction to Integrational Linguistics*. Oxford: Pergamum.

Harris, R. (2009). "Implicit and explicit language teaching" In *Language teaching integrational approaches*, ed. M. Toolan, 24–47. London: Routledge.

Harris, R. (2010). *The Great Debate About Art*. Chicago: Prickly Paradigm.

Jacquemert, M. (2005). "Transidiomatic practices: language and power in the age of globalization" *Language and Communication* 25 pp.257–277.

Khubchandani, L. (1997). *Revisualizing boundaries: A plurilingual ethos*. New Delhi: Sage.

Klaeger, G. (2009). "Religion on the road: The spiritual

experience of road travel" In *The speed of change: Motor vehicles in Africa*, ed. J. Gewald, pp.212–231. Leiden: Brill.

Kopytoff, I. (1988). "The cultural biography of things: Commoditization as process" In *The Social Life of Things: Commodities in Cultural Perspectives*, ed. A. Appandurai, pp.64–91. Cambridge: Cambridge University Press.

Kyei, G., and H. Schreckenbach (1975). *No Time to Die: A Book of Poems, Depicting Slogans of Ghana's Mammy Lorries*. Chicago: Catholic Press.

Law, R. (1980). "Wheeled transport in pre-colonial West Africa" *Africa* 50(3) pp.249–262.

Love, N., and U. Ansaldo (2010). "The native speaker and the mother tongue" *Language Sciences* 32(6) pp.589–593. doi:10.1016/j.langsci.2010.09.003.

Makoni, S. (2011a). "Sociolinguistics, colonial and postcolonial: An Integrationist perspective" *Language Sciences* 33(4) pp.680–688. doi:10.1016/j.langsci.2011.04.020.

Makoni, S. (2011b). "Language and human rights discourses lessons from the African experience" *Journal of Multicultural Discourses* 7(1) pp.1–20.

Maturana, H. and F. Varela (1973). *De Maquinas y Seres Vivos: La organización de lo vivo*. Santiago: Editorial Universitaria. [A Spanish translation of a manuscript originally written in English that later was to be reproduced in the volume *Autopoiesis and Cognition: the Realization of the Living*. Reidel, Dordrech, 1980]

Maturana, H., and F. Varela. 1998. *The Tree of Knowledge: The Biological Roots of Human Understanding*. Boston: Shambahla.

Mcintosh, J. (2010). "Mobile phones and Mipoho's prophecy: the power and dangers of flying language"

American Ethnologist 37(2) pp.337–353.

Mignolo, W. (1996). "Linguistic maps, literary geographies, and cultural landscapes: Languages, languaging and (trans)nationalism" *Modern Language Quarterly* 57(2) pp.181–196.

Mignolo, W. (2000). *Local Histories/Global Designs.* Princeton: Princeton University Press.

Nicolai, R. (2008). "How languages change and how they adapt: Some challenges for the future" *Journal of Language Contact* 2(3) pp.111–328.

Pablé, Adrian (2012) "Logophilia, logophobia and the terra mota of persona linguistic experience" *Language and Communication* 32 pp.257–264.

Pablé, Adrian and Christopher Hutton (2015). *Signs, Meaning, and Experience: Integrational Approaches to Linguistics and Semiotics.* Berlin: De Gruyter.

Ramanathan, V. (2009). "Silencing and languaging and the assembling of the Indian nation-state: British public citizens, the epistolary form and historiography" *Journal of Language, Identity and Education* 8 pp.203–219.

Rampton, B. (2011). "Multi-ethnic adolescent heteroglossia to contemporary urban vernaculars" *Journal of Language and Communication* 31(4) pp. 276–296.

Swain, M. (2006). "Languaging, agency and collaboration in advanced language proficiency" In *Advanced Language Learning: The Contribution of Halliday and Vygotsky,* ed. H. Brynes, pp.95–108. London: Continuum.

Swain, M. (2009). "Languaging: University students learn the grammatical concept of voice in French. *Modern Language Quarterly* 93 (1): 5–29.

Swain, M. (2010). "Self-scaffolding mediated by languaging: Microgenetic analysis of high and low performers" *International Journal of Applied Linguistics* 20(10) pp.23–49.

van der Geest, S. (1996). The elder and his elbow: Twelve interpretations of an Akan proverb. *Research in African Literatures* 27(3) pp.110–118.

Varis, P, and X. Wang (2011). "Superdiversity on the Internet: A case from China" *Diversities* 13(2) pp.71–83.

Vertovec, S. (2007). "Introduction: New directions in the anthropology of migration and multiculturalism" *Ethnic and Racial Studies* 29(6) pp.961–978.

Lightning Source UK Ltd.
Milton Keynes UK
UKHW021326270123
416064UK00014B/976